VOICES of EAST ASIA

Voices of East Asia provides significant yet accessible readings in translation chosen to stimulate interest in the long and rich cultural history of East Asia, the countries of China, Japan, and Korea. The readings range from ancient to modern, elite to popular, and include poetry, stories, essays, and drama. Each section begins with a broad but brief overview of that country's political and cultural history. Each reading is preceded by a concise explanation of its literary and cultural context. As expertise in East Asian studies has exploded in the West in recent decades, a novice could be overwhelmed by all the materials available now. In this volume, however, the reader will find a manageable set of texts that may be read on their own, as part of a world literature course, or as supplementary readings for an East Asian history class. As economic and political news from East Asia sweeps across the world, this anthology aims to provide a taste of the enduring traditions upon which contemporary East Asia is built, a glimpse into the hopes and fears, love and sorrow in the hearts of the people behind the headlines.

This anthology will be welcomed by students and scholars of Asian history, culture, society, and literature.

Margaret Childs is Associate Professor in the Department of East Asian Languages and Cultures at the University of Kansas, USA.

Nancy Hope is Associate Director of the Kansas Consortium for Teaching about Asia and the Associate Director for Special Projects of the Confucius Institute both at the University of Kansas, USA.

Also Available from Routledge

Voices of South Asia
Essential Readings from Antiquity to the Present

Edited by Patrick Peebles

Voices of Southeast Asia
Essential Readings from Antiquity to the Present

Edited by George E. Dutton

Voices of East Asia
Essential Readings from Antiquity to the Present

Edited by Margaret Helen Childs and Nancy Francesca Hope

VOICES of EAST ASIA

EAST ASIA

Essential Readings from Antiquity to the Present

Edited by
Margaret Helen Childs and
Nancy Francesca Hope

Routledge
Taylor & Francis Group

NEW YORK AND LONDON

First published 2015
by Routledge
711 Third Avenue, New York, NY 10017

and by Routledge
2 Park Square, Milton Park, Abingdon, Oxon, OX14 4RN

Routledge is an imprint of the Taylor & Francis Group, an informa business

© 2015 Taylor & Francis

Library of Congress Cataloging-in-Publication Data

Voices of East Asia : readings and images from China, Japan, and Korea / edited by Margaret Childs and Nancy Hope.
    pages cm
Includes bibliographical references.
    1. East Asian literature—Translations into English.   2. Chinese literature—Translations into English.   3. Japanese literature—Translations into English.
4. Korean literature—Translations into English.   I. Childs, Margaret Helen, editor.   II. Hope, Nancy, editor.
    PL494.V65 2015
    895—dc23
    2014038024

ISBN: 978-0-7656-3833-5 (hbk)
ISBN: 978-0-7656-3834-2 (pbk)
ISBN: 978-1-315-71925-2 (ebk)

Typeset in Times
by ApexCovantage, LLC

Printed and bound in Great Britain by
TJ International Ltd, Padstow, Cornwall

Contents

Preface

The goal of this anthology is to provide a wide audience with significant yet accessible readings in translation chosen to stimulate interest in the long and rich cultural history of East Asia, the countries of China, Japan, and Korea. The readings range from ancient to modern, elite to popular, and include poetry, stories, essays, and drama. Each section begins with a broad but brief overview of that country's political and cultural history. Each reading is preceded by a concise explanation of its literary and cultural context. As expertise in East Asian studies has exploded in the West in recent decades, a novice could be overwhelmed by all the materials available now. In this volume, however, the reader will find a manageable set of texts that may be read on their own, as part of a world literature course, or as supplementary readings for an East Asian history class. As economic and political news from East Asia sweeps across the world, this anthology aims to provide a taste of the enduring traditions upon which contemporary East Asia is built, a glimpse into the hopes and fears, love and sorrow in the hearts of the people behind the headlines.

Over the years various systems have been used to express East Asian scripts in the Roman alphabet. This book uses pinyin, the official system devised by the People's Republic of China, in introductory material, but retains the system found in source texts, usually Wade-Giles, in some of the premodern readings. The complexity of the Chinese sound system and the differing romanization systems necessitated our inclusion of a pronunciation guide. Romanization of Japanese and Korean has been more consistent through the years and their sound systems are simpler than Chinese. A simple rule for Japanese is that most syllables consist of a consonant and vowel and the vowels are pronounced as in Italian (i.e., "a" as in "pasta," "i" as in "pizza," "u" and "o" as in "duo," and "e" as in "egg"). Korean has its own alphabet, called *hangul*, containing fourteen consonants and ten vowels. This book uses McCune-Reischauer romanization, which is the most widely used Korean language romanization system.

Names are presented in the traditional East Asian order: family name first, then given name. In ancient times in Japan, the convention was to express names using a possessive: thus, Taira no Tadanori means Tadanori of the Taira clan. In the case of modern writers who publish in English, names tend to be written in Western style, but Nakazawa Keiji's autobiography is an exception. Many writers took pen names and came to be known by those names: Ihara Saikaku is commonly referred to as Saikaku; Natsume Sōseki as Sōseki.

Such a wide-ranging anthology occasioned consultation with a wide range of colleagues. We would like first to thank Steve Drummond for giving us this opportunity. For crucial help in choosing the selections, translating them, and writing the introductory material, we would especially like to thank Vickie Doll, Elaine Gerbert, Megan Greene, Michiko Ito, Ji-Yeon Lee, Keith McMahon, Laurel R. Rodd, Maya Stiller, Crispin Williams, and Kyoim Yun. The flaws remain our sole responsibility.

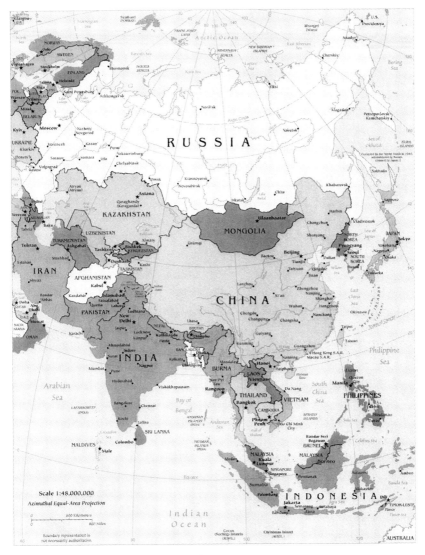

Map of Asia. (CIA, The World Factbook)

East Asian Timeline		
China	**Japan**	**Korea**
ca. 5000-2100 BCE: Neolithic	ca. 4000-300 BCE: Jomon Period	ca. 4000-300 BCE: Neolithic, Bronze Age and Iron Age
ca. 2100-1600 BCE: Xia Dynasty		
ca. 1600-1050 BCE: Shang Dynasty	ca. 300 BCE-300 CE: Yayoi Period	ca. 300-108 BCE: Old Choson
ca. 1046-256 BCE: Zhou Dynasty		
221-206 BCE: Qin Dynasty		
206 BCE-220 CE: Han Dynasty		108 BCE-313 CE: Chinese colonies
220-589 CE: Six Dynasties Period	300-538: Kofun Period	ca. 50 BCE-668 CE: Three Kingdoms Period
589-618: Sui Dynasty	538-710: Asuka Period	Koguryo 37 BCE-668 CE Paekche 18 BCE-660 CE Silla 57 BCE-935 CE
618-906: Tang Dynasty		
	710-794: Nara Period	668-936: Unified Silla
907-960: Five Dynasties Period	794-1185: Heian Period	
960-1279: Song Dynasty		918-1392: Koryo Dynasty
1279-1368: Yuan (Mongol) Dynasty	1185-1333: Kamakura Period	
1368-1644: Ming Dynasty	1336-1573: Muromachi Period	
	1568-1600: Momoyama Period	1392-1910: Choson (Yi) Dynasty
	1600-1868: Edo Period	
1644-1911: Qing (Manchu) Dynasty	1868-1912: Meiji Period	
	1912-1926: Taishō Period	1910-1945: Japanese colonial rule
1912-1949: Republic Period	1926-1989: Showa Period	
1949-present: People's Republic of China	1989-present: Heisei Period	1948-present: Republic of Korea and Democratic People's Republic of Korea

Chinese Pronunciation and Writing Chart

Because Chinese is written using Chinese characters, several systems have been created to write Chinese using the alphabet. In 1979, pinyin (literally "spelled out sound") became the official system in the People's Republic of China. While most Chinese words are now written in English following pinyin, older spellings using the Wade-Giles system can still be found and so are noted below. (Alternative spellings of Chinese place names and proper names in either pinyin or Wade-Giles have been provided in this textbook as needed.)

Pinyin	Wade-Giles	English equivalent
q	ch'	Ch as in "check" so Qing Dynasty or Ch'ing Dynasty is pronounced as "ching"
zh	ch	J as in "judge" so Zhou Dynasty or Chou Dynasty is pronounced as "joe"
c	ts' and tz'	Ts as in "sits" so cai or ts'ai (meaning vegetable) is pronounced as "ts-eye"
z	ts and tz	Dz as in "woods" so zu or tsu (meaning family or tribe) is pronounced as "dz-oo"
x	hs	Sh as in "she" so xi or hsi (meaning west) is pronounced as "she"

All other sounds can be pronounced as written in English, but the Pinyin and Wade-Giles systems have some other differences when writing Chinese using the alphabet.

Initials (consonants at the beginning of a word)

b	p	Bei (meaning north) in pinyin = pei in Wade-Giles
d	t	Daoism = Taoism
g	k	Guo (meaning country or state) = kuo
r	j	Ren (meaning humaneness) = jen

Finals (vowels at the end of a word)

e	eh	lie (meaning energetic) = lieh
ian	ien	Tian (meaning heaven) = t'ien
ong	ung	Song Dynasty in pinyin = Sung Dynasty in Wade-Giles
uo	o	Shuo (meaning great) = sho

VOICES of EAST ASIA

Part I

China

According to legend, Chinese history begins with two rulers who invented writing, fishing, trapping, agriculture, and commerce. After them came the Yellow Emperor, who created a centralized state. Then there were the most famous early rulers, the three Sage Kings, Yao, Shun, and Yu, whose virtue ensured peace and prosperity In their domains. Yu is credited with building a vast system of dikes and canals that reduced floods and founding the Xia dynasty (ca. 2100–ca. 1600 BCE). The cruelty and corruption of the last of the Xia rulers inspired revolt and the founding of the Shang (or Yin) dynasty (ca. 1600–ca. 1050 BCE). Archeological evidence confirms the existence of the Shang dynasty during the latter half of the second millennium, and legend becomes verifiable history in the ninth century BCE. The most important legacy of Shang times is the Chinese writing system, which evolved into the system of pictographic, ideographic, and phonetic characters in use today. This in turn gave rise to the emphasis on line and brushwork so characteristic of Chinese art. The Shang dynasty was, in turn, overthrown when King Wu of Zhou rebelled against another despotic emperor. Credit for consolidating the Zhou regime (1046–256 BCE) is given to King Wu's brother, the Duke of Zhou, who is revered as a wise and loyal regent and adviser.

This pattern of the rise of dynasties founded by bold and virtuous men and their fall due to corruption and decadence came to be called the dynastic cycle. The Zhou kings contributed to this political theory by creating the idea of the "Mandate of

Heaven," which means that Heaven controls the right to rule and bestows it based on virtue and benevolence.

The central power of the Zhou dynasty dwindled until it became just one of several smaller states that competed for territory and legitimacy from about 770–221 BCE. Amid that warfare, many philosophers debated human nature, the proper goals of government and society, and the best ways to achieve those goals. One of the "Hundred Schools of Thought" of those centuries was that of Confucius (551–479 BCE), who argued that social order was best achieved by ethical behavior and leadership by example. Other important schools were Legalism, which proposed maintaining order by strictly imposing harsh punishments, and Daoism, which encouraged individuals to seek harmony both internally and externally through a mystical appreciation of the impersonal and perfectly balanced forces of nature.

Late in the third century, the armies of Qin (221–206 BCE) united China through mass slaughter, but the first Qin emperor created the basis for an enduring Chinese empire by centralizing authority and by standardizing weights, measures, roads, and the writing system. He was so fervent an adherent of Legalism that he ordered the burning of Confucian libraries. He also ordered the building of the Great Wall and the Terracotta Army.

A peasant rebel founded the Han dynasty (206 BCE–220 CE), and eventually wise policies and political stability led to prosperity and cultural progress that shaped Chinese civilization for the next two millennia. Confucian books were re-created from memory or recovered from hiding places. Five ancient texts were labeled "Confucian" and canonized as the Five Classics: (1) the *Book of Songs*; (2) the *Book of Documents*, speeches and anecdotes of ancient rulers; (3) the *Book of Rites*, lists of rituals for daily life and life's milestones such as marriage and death; (4) the *Book of Changes*, a diviner's handbook; and (5) the *Spring and Autumn Annals*, a record of events from 722 to 481 BCE at the court of the state of Lu, home of both the Duke of Zhou and Confucius.

A university was founded in 124 BCE with the Five Classics as the primary curricula, and examinations were used to select government officials. Thus education became a means to success, and benevolent government became a common ideal. Also, international trade flourished—much of it along what would come to be known as the Silk Road—and the teachings of Buddhism were welcomed. As Chinese science and technology blossomed, clocks, paper, porcelain, and the water-powered mill were invented.

The fighting that ended the Han dynasty inspired *Romance of the Three Kingdoms*,[1] written in the fourteenth century. This very long and extremely complex story of loyalty and treachery, military exploits, and Confucian values is considered one of the four greatest Chinese novels.

The Sui dynasty (589–618 CE) reunited China several centuries later, but its ruler was weakened by military failures. Tang rulers (618–906), on the other hand, succeeded through a combination of diplomacy and military brilliance in expanding China to its largest extent to that date. During the Tang dynasty, culture again flourished. Extensive international trade turned the capital Chang'an into a cosmopolitan city of almost 2 million residents. State support for Buddhism is reflected in the historical events that inspired another of the great novels, *Journey to the West*, which is based on the story of the actual monk Xuanzang (602–664), who left China for India to gather Buddhist scripture and was given a hero's welcome when he returned in 645. His translations of scripture from Sanskrit to Chinese were a strong stimulus for the development of Buddhism in China. There was potential for conflict between Buddhist teachings that encourage a focus on one's spiritual state of mind and Confucian principles that require people to prioritize their familial and social obligations, but the idea that one could simultaneously embrace Buddhist ideas privately and Confucian ethics in public life resolved the problem. Daoism also continued to provide guidelines for life for those who were not in public service.

The poetry of Li Bai (701–762) and Du Fu (712–770) represent a pinnacle of Tang cultural achievement. Li Bai is noted for his technical skill and mastery of the literary tradition. His favorite themes are universal: friendship and the sense of freedom that wine could provide. Du Fu is considered a technically superior poet who is especially beloved for his poems describing the turmoil of a rebellion that broke out in his time and for expressing compassion for the suffering of common people, such as conscripted soldiers. Both Li Bai and Du Fu were popular in Japan and often quoted in Japanese literature.

The Tang dynasty was weakened when Emperor Xuanzong (713–756) fell madly in love with the concubine Yang Guifei and neglected his duties. When rebellion ensued, the emperor's guards blamed Yang Guifei and strangled her. A popular poem by Po Ju-I expressing the emperor's grief, "Song of Everlasting Sorrow," helped inspire the Japanese masterpiece *The Tale of Genji*. The rebellion was quashed, but the Tang dynasty was permanently weakened.

Once again China was fragmented until a brilliant general reunified the nation. During the Song Dynasty (960–1279), the bureaucracy was revitalized by reforms to the examination system. The capital at Bianjing (now Kaifeng) was a city of more than 400,000 people living both inside and outside the city gates, as recorded in a handscroll by Zhang Zeduan (1085–1145). Commerce and the arts flourished together, especially landscape painting and pottery. Movable type was invented. The Song dynasty philosopher Zhu Xi (1130–1200) reaffirmed the importance of education, self-cultivation, and the mutual responsibilities of human relationships. He said the essence of Confucian philosophy could be found in Four Books: *Great Learning* and *Doctrine of the Mean* (from the *Book of Rites*), *Analects*, and *Mencius*. Various interpretations of these texts evolved over the centuries as scholars continually wrote new commentaries, but the basic values presented in these texts provided a stable cultural ideology for the next 800 years. In contrast to this noble legacy, foot-binding began among the aristocracy during the Song dynasty and eventually spread to all levels of Chinese society. This painful practice, which required girls to cripple themselves for the sake of having tiny feet, did not die out until the early twentieth century.

The Mongol empire absorbed China in 1279, but since the Mongols kept themselves separate and ruled through Chinese institutions, their Yuan Dynasty (1279–1368) had little lasting direct influence on Chinese culture. However, since the route to success via the civil service examinations became blocked, scholars turned their energies to calligraphy, painting, and more accessible forms of literature such as drama (e.g., *The West Chamber*). Although these forms were not as highly respected as poetry and therefore usually written anonymously, they proved highly popular. The Mongols invaded Japan in 1274 and again in 1281, but were repelled with the help of a timely typhoon. This is the origin of the Japanese expression *kamikaze*, "divine wind," a term later used by suicide pilots during World War II. It was also China under Mongol rule that Marco Polo visited and described when he returned in 1295 to Venice from Peking after a seventeen-year trip.

The Mongol dynasty was weakened by infighting and popular unrest caused by famine and flooding. Multiple rebellions broke out, and one commoner, an orphan who had been a Buddhist monk, emerged to lead the rebels to victory and found the Ming dynasty (1368–1644). The ethnically Chinese rulers of the Ming Dynasty emphasized stability and relied heavily on the Confucian tradition they believed had produced glory in the ancient past. Ming dynasty painters like Xie Jin (1369–1415) also drew upon established motifs and conventions, especially in landscape painting. Ming emperors became more autocratic and circumvented traditional governing structures by relying more and more on the eunuchs who maintained their harems and helped rulers communicate with officialdom, but change came in other areas. Increasing literacy created a market for popular novels and Confucian scholars responded: three of the great books still known and loved today took recognizable form during the Ming dynasty: *Water Margin, Romance of the Three Kingdoms,* and *Journey to the West.* Also of note is the arrival in China of Jesuit missionaries and the consequent deepening awareness in Europe of Chinese civilization.

The Manchus had developed a powerful state north of China just when Ming China was in the hands of weak and corrupt leaders. Taking advantage of the turmoil caused by rebellion in China, Manchu forces occupied Beijing in 1644 and soon conquered the rest of China. The conservative and inward-looking orientation of the Ming rulers persisted in the Qing dynasty. Like the Mongols, they kept themselves apart from the Chinese and employed Chinese to staff the bureaucracy. They were successful in expanding the borders of the Chinese empire, but not in controlling corruption. When Europeans traders arrived in the late eighteenth century, the Qing emperors were incapable of effective action. In the aftermath of the Opium War (1839–1842), Great Britain forced China to import opium. Then the Christian-inspired Taiping Rebellion (1850–1864) against the ruling Manchu-led Qing dynasty cost the lives of 20 million Chinese and was suppressed only with the help of French and British forces. Without the resources to resist, China agreed to more and more economic concessions to Western countries. In 1900, inspired by anti-foreign and anti-Christian violence carried out by members of secret societies, the Qing government declared war on the West but was quickly defeated.

In 1911 rebellion broke out again, and the Manchu government fell. A founder of the Nationalist People's Party, Sun Yat-sen (1866–1925), a medical doctor who had spent time in Hawaii and converted to Christianity, became the first president of the Republic of China. In need of military support, the presidency was offered to Yuan Shihkai (1859–1916), commander of an army in northern China. The ambitious Yuan quickly betrayed the cause, but Sun was able to maintain the republic in southern China. When World War I ended in April 1919, the Chinese were angered by the terms of the Treaty of Versailles: Japan had taken territory under German control in Shandong province and was allowed to retain it. On May 4, 1919, a student demonstration marked the beginning of a widespread anti-imperialist and Chinese nationalist movement. This is the context in which Lu Xun (1881–1936) wrote stories scathingly critical of traditional Chinese culture.

When Sun Yat-sen died in 1925, Chiang Kai-shek, then commandant of a military academy, stepped up and defeated rival elements in northern China in 1926, but then suddenly attacked the Communists who had been organizing in Shanghai since 1921. This won him recognition from Western nations, but consolidating the republic and modernizing Chinese social and economic institutions remained daunting challenges. In 1931, Japan occupied Manchuria, but Chiang focused on rooting out Communists. Late in 1934, the Communists were surrounded, but they broke through and marched 6,000 miles, fighting off attacks, illness, freezing cold, and starvation as they went. Just one in five made it to refuge in far northwest China a year later. The Communists and Nationalists called a truce when Japan attacked China in 1937, but resumed their civil war after the end of World War II. The People's Republic of China was declared on October 1, 1949. The Nationalists retreated to Taiwan on December 10.

Mao Zedong (1893–1976), who became the leader of the Chinese Communists during the Long March, led a disciplined Red Army to victory over the Nationalists and then autocratically ruled China as chairman of the Communist Party until his death. Of peasant origin himself, he respected and trusted Chinese peasants and they revered him. Mao began the work of transforming Chinese society by executing opponents of Communism, organizing peasants into collectives, and industrializing. This was effective in raising the standard of living of the masses and Mao became confident enough to allow political criticism in 1957; surprised by the vociferous complaints, however, he punished the outspoken and restored censorship. In 1958, hoping for dramatic economic progress, the Communists formed massive communes and decentralized industrialization under a policy called the Great Leap Forward. Instead of progress, however, China suffered a great famine that cost 30 million lives between 1959 and 1962. Communes started to be disbanded as Mao faced serious political challenges. In 1966, Mao launched the Great Proletarian Cultural Revolution by exhorting students to reassert the principles of the Communist revolution by attacking capitalists and traditional culture. In response, groups of students rampaged through the country, destroying temples, libraries, and museums, invading private homes to destroy family altars and heirlooms, and harassing or murdering people for little more than being well-educated. Education was disrupted and manual labor demanded of everyone. On the other hand, science and technology advanced, gender equality was promoted, health care became more widely available and free, and standards of living rose.

When Mao died in January 1976, more practical leaders came to power. The first of these was Deng Xiaoping (1904–1997), who allowed open markets, encouraged productivity, and opened China to foreign investment. His attitude that results were more

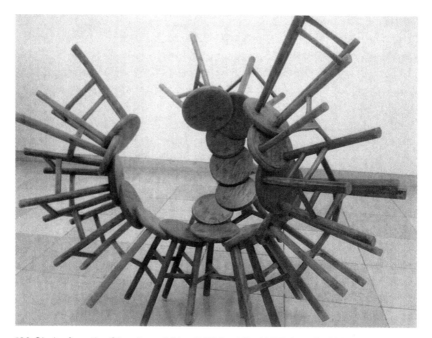

"20 Chairs from the Qing dynasty" by Ai Weiwei (b. 1957), installed 2009. *(Wikimedia Commons, "An Installation of Chairs by Chinese Artist Ai Weiwei")*

important than strategy (captured in his comment "it does not matter if a cat is black or white as long as it catches mice") caused him political trouble while Mao was in power, but proved wise in the long run. Deng laid the groundwork for strong economic growth that has culminated in China's current status as the world's second-largest economy.

While there is still censorship and political repression in China, there is significant latitude for cultural expression, and the arts are flourishing once again. The works of Mo Yan, a Nobel Prize winner in 2012, contain a considerable degree of social criticism as do the sculptures and installations of noted artist Ai Weiwei (b. 1957).

Note

1. Luo Guanzhong and Moss Roberts, *Three Kingdoms: A Historical Novel* (Beijing: Foreign Languages Press, 1999).

1

Book of Songs

We can hear both high and low social classes expressing a range of emotions, from joy to lamentation, in the 305 songs of the *Book of Songs*. The collection, which is known as one of the five Confucian classics, dates from the sixth century BCE as a whole, but some songs are much older. Besides songs of courtship, there are songs about farming, hunting, feasting, performing sacrifices, honoring rulers, and waging war. Most are relatively short, and most employ rhyme, repetition, and metaphor. Perhaps because their meaning was ambiguous, a tradition of reading them as political allegory developed, and many came to be interpreted as moral judgments on specific historical figures. Such identification is reflected in the titles given to them by translator James Legge.

For many centuries it was thought that Confucius had personally compiled the *Book of Songs*. Even though he explicitly valued songs for their capacity to provide moral guidance, he probably did not do this. Rather, many songs were collected by rulers to measure the temper of the times and determine how well they were doing. Since songs were considered to be spontaneous expressions of human feeling, it was thought that quiet and joyful pieces reflected a well-ordered society, while expressions of resentment and anger were found during times of disorder. The reverse also was thought true. Since people expressed feelings in song, song then influenced human conduct. "The Great Preface" to the *Book of Songs* thus notes that people express their feelings in words, stronger feelings in "sighs and exclamations," still stronger feelings in song, and their strongest feelings in dance. It also asserts that poetry is useful to "move Heaven and Earth and to excite spiritual Beings to action" and to teach proper relationships within families and society at large.[1]

Originally sung or chanted, the songs are now often referred to as poems or odes. Though the music that accompanied them has been lost, it was once a crucial part of their performance since music was understood to have valuable properties. Music was thought to inspire self-discipline since the listener had to conform to the rhythm of the piece, to create a sense of unity between the performers and the audience, and to bring joy, making the "moral learning" provided by songs pleasurable too.[2]

Questions

1. Compare and contrast the images of women presented in poems 1, 2, and 4. To what extent do you find the Western conventional stereotype of a Chinese woman as oppressed and submissive?
2. What kinds of attitudes toward the state and its leaders can be found in poems 3, 5, and 6?
3. What is the implicit contract between ancestors and descendants found in poems 7 and 8, which describe sacrifices?

Book of Songs

Book of Songs based on James Legge, *The Chinese Classics with a Translation, Critical and Exegetical Notes, Prolegomena, and Copious Indexes*, vol. 4, *The She King* (Hong Kong: Lane, Crawford, 1871), pp. 1–4, 23–24, 26, 38–40, 167–168, 171–172, 586, 631–633.
Poems 1–6 are from the "Airs of the States" section, which contains 160 poems. Poems 7–8 are from the "Hymns," which were performed at ritual sacrifices or other official events.

1. Part I, Book 1, Ode 1: Celebrating the virtue of the bride of King Wan, and welcoming her to his palace

Kwan-kwan[3] call the ospreys,
On the islet in the river,

The modest, retiring, virtuous, young lady:
For our prince she is a good mate.

Here long, there short, is the duckweed,
To the left, to the right, swaying in the current,
The modest, retiring, virtuous, young lady:
Waking and sleeping, he sought her.

He sought her and found her not,
And waking and sleeping he thought about her.
Long he thought, oh, long and anxiously:
On his side, on his back, he turned, and turned again.

Here long, there short, is the duckweed,
On the left, on the right, we gather it.
The modest, retiring, virtuous, young lady:
With lutes, small and large, let us give her friendly welcome.

Here long, there short, is the duckweed,
On the left, on the right, we chose and present it.
The modest, retiring, virtuous, young lady:
With bells and drums let us show our delight in her.

2. *Part I, Book 2, Ode 3: The wife of a Great Officer bewails*
   his absence on duty, and longs for the joy of his presence.

Yaou-yaou sing the crickets,
And the grasshoppers spring about.
When I cannot see my lord,
My sorrowful heart is agitated.
Let me have seen him,
Let me have met him,
And my heart will then be stilled.

I ascended that hill in the south,
And gathered the turtle-foot ferns.
When I cannot see my lord,
My sorrowful heart is very sad.
Let me have seen him,

Let me have met him,
And my heart will then be pleased.

I ascended that hill in the south,
And gathered the thorn-ferns.
When I cannot see my lord,
My sorrowful heart is wounded with grief.
Let me have seen him,
Let me have met him,
And my heart will then be at peace.

3. *Part I, Book 2, Ode 5: The love of the people for the memory of the Duke of Shao makes them love the trees beneath which he had rested. The Duke of Shao was the brother of King Wu, founder of the Zhou dynasty (1046–221 BCE).*

This shade-giving sweet pear-tree;
Neither prune it nor chop it down.
Under it the chief of Shao lodged.

This shade-giving sweet pear-tree;
Neither prune it nor break a twig of it.
Under it the chief of Shao rested.

This shade-giving sweet pear-tree;
Neither prune it nor uproot it.
Under it the chief of Shao halted.

4. *Part I, Book 3, Ode 1: An officer of worth bewails the neglect and contempt with which he was treated. (Another interpretation reads this as the lament of a woman pressured by her brothers to marry against her will.)*

It floats about, that boat of cypress wood;
It floats about, bobbing in the current.
I am troubled and sleepless,
As if I had a painful wound.
It is not because I have no wine,
And not because I cannot amuse myself.

My mind is not a mirror;
I cannot simply follow another's lead.
I have brothers who should help me,
But I cannot depend on them.
When I turned to them for support
They were only angry with me.

My heart is not a stone;
It cannot be rolled about.
My heart is not a mat;
It cannot be rolled up.
My deportment has been dignified and good,
No one can condemn my behavior.

My anxious heart is troubled;
I am demeaned by others.
I am very distressed,
I have been insulted many times.
Silently, I mull over my situation.
In frustration I beat my breast.

There are the sun and the moon,
They seem to have shrunk and grown dim.
My sorrow cleaves to my heart,
Like an unwashed dress.
Silently I mull over my situation,
But I cannot spread wings and fly away.

5. *Part I, Book 9, Ode 4: A young soldier consoles himself
   with thoughts of home.*

I ascend the tree-clad hill,
And look in the direction of my father's house.
My father is saying, 'Alas! my son, drafted into service,
Morning and night he can never rest.
May he be careful,
That he may come back, and not remain there!'

I ascend that bare hill,
And look in the direction of my mother's house.

My mother is saying, 'Alas! my child, drafted into service,
Morning and night he has no sleep.
May he be careful,
That he may come back and not leave his body there!'

I ascend that ridge,
And look in the direction of my elder brother's house.
My brother is saying, 'Alas! my younger brother, drafted
    into service,
Morning and night on duty with his comrades.
May he be careful,
That he may come back and not die!'

6. *Part I, Book 9, Ode 7: Against the oppression and extortion of the government of Wei.*

Large rats! Large rats!
Do not eat our millet.
Three years have we had to put up with you,
And you have shown us no consideration at all.
We will leave you,
And go to that happy land.[4]
Happy land! Happy land!
There shall we find our place.

Large rats! Large rats!
Do not eat our wheat.
Three years have we had to put up with you,
And you have shown us no kindness at all.
We will leave you,
And go to that happy State.
Happy State! Happy State!
There shall we have what we are due.

Large rats! Large rats!
Do not eat our rice!
Three years have we had to put up with you,
And you have shown no appreciation at all.
We will leave you,
And go to those happy borders,

Happy borders! Happy borders!
There shall we have something other than sad songs to sing.

7. *Part IV ii, Book 1, Ode 4: An ode of thanksgiving.*

Abundant is the year, with much millet and much rice;
And we have our high granaries,
With myriads, and hundreds of thousands, and millions of
    measures of grain.
We have made wine and sweet liquors,
To present to our ancestors, male and female,
To conduct all the rites respectfully,
And summon blessings of every kind on us all.

8. *Part IV, Book 3, Ode 1: For a sacrifice to Tang, the founder of the Shang dynasty, supposedly enthroned in 1766 BCE.*

How admirable! How complete!
Here are arrayed our tambourines and drums.
They resound harmoniously and loudly,
To delight our meritorious ancestor.
The descendant of Tang invites him with this music,
That he may soothe us with the realization of our hopes.
Deep is the sound of the tambourines and drums;
Shrilly sound the flutes;
All harmonious and blending together,
With the notes of the sonorous chimes.
Oh! Majestic is the descendant of Tang;
Very admirable is his music.
The large gongs and drums fill the ear;
The various dances are grandly performed.
We have admirable visitors,
Who are pleased and delighted.
From of old, before our time,
Former men set us the example;
How to be mild and humble from morning to night,
And to be reverent in discharging the obligations.
May he accept our sacrifices in summer and autumn,
Thus offered by the descendant of Tang.

Notes

1. James Legge, *The Chinese Classics with a Translation, Critical and Exegetical Notes, Prolegomena, and Copious Indexes*, vol. 4, *The She King* (Hong Kong: Lane, Crawford, 1871), p. 34.

2. Michael Nylan, *The Five "Confucian" Classics* (New Haven, CT: Yale University Press, 2001), pp. 99–100.

3. The sound of male and female birds calling to each other.

4. "That happy land" probably refers to a neighboring state enjoying benevolent government.

2

Book of Documents

The *Book of Documents* contains speeches, conversations, and terse accounts of deeds attributed to the rulers of ancient China, beginning with the legendary Emperor Yao and including rulers of the Zhou dynasty. They focus on the nature of exemplary rulership. The entry below is the very first item, which describes how Yao ceded his throne to Shun based on merit rather than heredity. This story is foundational to the development of the concept of the Mandate of Heaven, which holds that Heaven grants the right to rule only to those who rule well. Rulers generally passed on their thrones to their sons, but rebellion and the establishment of a new dynasty were justified if a ruler failed to rule wisely.

Questions

1. What qualities are attributed to the emperor? How are these qualities tied to the emperor's success?
2. Enumerate the qualities that disqualify the various nominees for the throne. Why are they so important? What qualities that might be appropriate are never mentioned?
3. By what logic is filial piety the most important virtue for an emperor to possess?

Book of Documents

Book of Documents based on James Legge, *The Chinese Classics with a Translation, Critical and Exegetical Notes,*

Prolegomena, and Copious Indexes, vol. 3, part 1, *The Shoo King* (Hong Kong: James Legge, 1861), pp. 23–26.

The Canon of Yao from the Book of Tang

Examining into antiquity, we find that the emperor Yao was reverential, enlightened, accomplished, and thoughtful, naturally and without effort. He was sincerely courteous and compliant. The display of these qualities reached to the four extremities of the empire, and extended from earth to heaven. He was able to make the able and virtuous distinguished, and thence proceeded to the love of the nine generations of his kindred [relatives reaching from his great-great grandfather to his great-great grandson], who all became harmonious. He also regulated and polished the gentry of his domain, who all became brightly intelligent. He united and harmonized the myriad States and the common people were amply nourished and prosperous.

The emperor said, "Who will search out for me a man equal to the exigency of my affairs?" Another minister said, "There is the minister of Works [who was responsible for flood control], whose merits have just been displayed in various ways." The emperor said, "Alas! His speech is smooth, but his actions are perverse. He is respectful only in appearance. See! The floods assail the heavens."

[The emperor assigned a new minister to undertake flood control. Nine years later, despite his failure to complete the mission, the emperor offered him the throne:]

The emperor said, "I have been on the throne for seventy years. You can carry out my appointments. I will resign my throne to you." The minister said, "I have not the virtue. I would only disgrace the imperial seat."

The emperor said, "Point out some one among the illustrious, or set forth one from among the poor and mean." All in the court said to the emperor, "There is an unmarried man among the lower people, called Shun of Yu." The emperor said, "Yes, I have heard of him. What is his character?" The minister said, "He is the son of a blind man. His father was obstinately unprincipled, his step-mother was deceitful, his half-brother was arrogant. He has been able, however, by his filial piety to live in harmony with them, and to lead them gradually to self-government, so that they no longer proceed to great wickedness." The emperor said, "I will try him!"

[After three years of observing Shun's behavior, the emperor asked Shun to take the throne. Shun at first refused, but eventually consented and became Yao's successor.]

3

Book of Rites

As important as the rites are in Confucian thinking, few textbooks give examples of specific rites. The *Book of Rites* contains a hodgepodge of sweeping general statements about the meaning and value of the rites as well as very detailed instructions for proper etiquette in various specific situations. The rites probably originated with rules explaining how to present sacrifices to the dead and then how to present and receive gifts among the living. Eventually rites were also developed for the ceremonies of coming of age, marriage, mourning, archery, chariot-driving, audiences with rulers, diplomatic missions, and daily life. Legend attributes much of the *Book of Rites* to the Duke of Zhou and some chapters to Confucius's grandson and other direct disciples, but it probably was compiled during the Western Han (206 BCE–8 CE). Its most famous sections are the two seminal essays, the "Great Learning" and the "Doctrine of the Mean," which were taken separately as two of the "Four Books" chosen by Zhu Xi (1130–1200) to be the core curriculum of Neo-Confucianism. Below are specific prescriptions for the proper behavior and attitude when mourning the death of a parent and in daily greetings, plus an example of a general statement of the value of proper behavior.

Questions

1. Discuss the concept that proper behavior leads to proper feelings.

2. To what extent is there a balance of power between parents and children?
3. Compare and contrast expectations for the relationship between parents and children today with the Confucian norm.

Book of Rites

> Book of Rites based on James Legge, *The Sacred Books of China*, vol. 4, *The Lî Kî (The Book of Rites)*, part 1 (Oxford: Clarendon Press, 1885).

Book 2, Section I, Part I

19. When a father has just died, the son should appear quite overcome, and as if he were at his wits' end; when the corpse has been put into the coffin, he should cast quick and sorrowful glances around, as if he were seeking for something and could not find it; when the interment has taken place, he should look alarmed and restless, as if he were looking for someone who does not arrive; at the end of the first year's mourning, he should look sad and disappointed; and at the end of the second year's, he should have a vague and insecure look.

Part II

24. A disciple asked Confucius saying, 'How should a son conduct himself with reference to the man who has killed his father or mother?' The Master said, 'He should sleep on straw, with his shield for a pillow; he should not take office; he must be determined not to live with the slayer under the same heaven. If he meet him in the market-place or the court, he should not have to go back for his weapon, but instantly fight with him.'

Part III

3. Confucius said, 'In dealing with the dead, if we treat them as if they were entirely dead, that would show a lack of affection, and should not be done; or, if we treat them as if they were entirely alive, that would show a lack of wisdom, and should not be done.'

Book 8, Section I

1. The rules of propriety serve as instruments to form men's characters, and they are therefore prepared on a great scale. Being so, the value of them is very high. They remove from a man all perversity, and increase what is beautiful in his nature. They make him correct, when employed in the ordering of himself; they ensure for him free course, when employed towards others. They are to him what their outer coating is to bamboos, and what its heart is to a pine or cypress. These two are the best of the world of flora. They endure through all the four seasons, without altering a branch or changing a leaf. The superior man observes these rules of propriety, so that all in a wider circle are harmonious with him, and those in his narrower circle have no dissatisfactions with him. Men acknowledge and are affected by his goodness, and spirits enjoy his virtue.

Book 10, Section I

2. Sons [of the elite], in serving their parents, on the first crowing of the cock, should all wash their hands and rinse their mouths, comb their hair, draw over it the covering of silk, fix this with the hairpin, bind the hair at the roots with the headband, brush the dust from that which is left free, and then put on their caps, leaving the ends of the strings hanging down. They should then put on their squarely made black jackets, knee-covers, and girdles, fixing in the last their tablets. From the left and right of the girdle they should hang their articles for use. On the left side, the duster and handkerchief, the knife and whetstone, the small spike, and the metal speculum for getting fire from the sun. On the right, the archer's thimble for the thumb and the armlet, the tube for writing instruments, the knife-case, the larger spike, and the borer for getting fire from wood. They should put on their leggings, and adjust their shoestrings.

3. Sons' wives should serve their parents-in-law as they served their own. At the first crowing of the cock, they should wash their hands, and rinse their mouths; comb their hair, draw over it the covering of silk, fix this with the hairpin, and tie the hair at the roots with the headband. They should then put on the jacket, and over it the sash. On the left side, they should hang the duster and handkerchief, the knife and whetstone, the small spike, and the metal speculum to get fire with; and on the right,

the needle-case, thread, and floss, all bestowed in the satchel, the great spike, and the borer to get fire with from wood. They will also fasten on their necklaces, and adjust their shoestrings.

4. Thus dressed, they should go to their parents and parents-in-law. On getting to where they are, with bated breath and gentle voice, they should ask if their clothes are too warm or too cold, whether they are ill or pained, or uncomfortable in any part; and if they be so, they should proceed reverently to stroke and scratch the place. . . . They will ask whether they want anything, and then respectfully bring it. All this they will do with an appearance of pleasure to make their parents feel at ease.

11. When ordered to do anything by their parents, sons and their wives should immediately respond and reverently proceed to do it. In going forwards or backwards, or turning round, they should be careful and grave; while going out or coming in, while bowing or walking, they should not presume to belch, sneeze, or cough, to yawn or stretch themselves, to stand on one foot, or to lean against anything, or to look askance. They should not dare to spit or snivel, nor, if it be cold, to put on more clothes, nor, if they itch anywhere, to scratch themselves. . . .

14. When sons and their wives have not been filial and reverential, the parents should not be angry and resentful with them, but endeavor to instruct them. If they will not receive instruction, they should then be angry with them. If that anger do no good, they can then drive out the son, and send the wife away, yet not publicly showing why they have so treated them.

15. If a parent has a fault, the son should with bated breath, and bland aspect and gentle voice, admonish him. If the admonition does not take effect, he will be the more reverential and the more filial; and when the father seems pleased, he will repeat the admonition. If he should be displeased with this, rather than allow him to commit an offence against anyone in the neighborhood or countryside, the son should strongly remonstrate. If the parent be angry and more displeased, and beat him till the blood flows, he should not presume to be angry and resentful, but be still more reverential and more filial.

17. Although his parents be dead, when a son is inclined to do what is good, he should think that he will thereby transmit the good name of his parents, and carry his wish into effect. When he is inclined to do what is not good, he should think that he will thereby bring disgrace on the name of his parents, and by no means carry his wish into effect.

4

Analects

CONFUCIUS

The teachings of Kong Fuzi or Kong Qui (551–479 BCE), commonly known in the West as Confucius, had a widespread and lasting effect on Chinese culture. When he was born in northern China, society was disintegrating into competing feudal states after several centuries of order and stability during the first half of the Zhou dynasty (1046–770 BCE). Confucius entered the service of the prince of Lu, a small state in what is now Shandong province. He eventually rose to become police commissioner but left Lu due to an internal power struggle.

Confucius was unsuccessful in finding employment as an adviser to other feudal states, so he devoted himself to teaching. He taught that the welfare of the people and the good of the state depended on an individual's proper conduct in relationships with others and that virtuous individuals taught by example. Virtue was seen as its own reward, and proper conduct ennobled someone more than a high-status birth. Confucius believed that the founders of the Zhou dynasty brought peace and order to the world through their wisdom and virtue and that practicing the rituals they established would restore unity and harmony to society.

Confucius was essentially a moralist who showed little interest in metaphysics or cosmological speculation. Humanity was at the center of his philosophical world; the highest duty was to improve one's character, cultivating the virtues of benevolence, wisdom, courage, integrity, righteousness, conscientiousness, reciprocity, and reverence. His teachings later were adopted as the official doctrine of the Han dynasty (206 BCE–220 CE).

Although Confucius wrote little himself, his disciples and their followers recorded his ideas in the *Lunyu* or *Analects*, which became something every educated person was expected to know. The *Analects* is a random collection of brief quotes attributed to Confucius and anecdotes about him rather than an organized treatise. The selections below are a small sample of them.

Questions

1. What qualities does Confucius believe one should try to cultivate? Are they relevant for today?
2. How does Confucius advise that good government is to be achieved? What part does reverence play in this process?
3. What is Confucius's attitude toward knowledge and learning? Why do you think his teachings emphasized this?
4. According to Confucius, how should one act toward parents or elders? How do these recommendations compare to those of religious traditions in the West?

Analects

Analects based on James Legge, *The Four Books:*
Confucian Analects, the Great Learning,
the Doctrine of the Mean, and the Works of Mencius
(Shanghai: Commercial Press, 1923),
pp. 1–2, 5, 12–13, 16, 18–19, 21, 23, 26, 42–43,
45, 47, 87, 229.

Book 1

1. The Master said: 'Is it not pleasant to learn with a constant perseverance and application? Is it not delightful to have friends coming from distant quarters? Is he not a man of complete virtue, who feels no discomposure though men may take no note of him?'

5. The Master said: 'To rule a country of a thousand chariots, there must be reverent attention to business, and sincerity; economy in expenditure, and love for men; and the employment of the people at the proper seasons.'

6. The Master said: 'A youth, when at home, should be filial, and, abroad, respectful to his elders. He should be earnest and truthful. He should overflow in love to all, and cultivate the friendship of the good. When he has time and opportunity, after the performance of these things, he should employ them in polite studies.' ["Polite studies" refers to ritual, music, archery, horsemanship, writing, and mathematics.]

Book 2

1. The Master said: 'He who exercises government by means of his virtue may be compared to the north polar star, which keeps its place and all the stars turn towards it.'

3. The Master said: 'If the people be led by laws, and order kept by punishments, they will try to avoid the punishment, but have no sense of shame. If they be led by virtue, and order kept by the practice of rites, they will have the sense of shame, and moreover will become good.'

7. The Master said: 'Filial piety today means the support of one's parents. But even dogs and horses are able to do something in the way of support. Without reverence, what is there to distinguish the one support from the other?'

12. The Master said: 'The accomplished scholar is not a utensil.'

13. The Master said: 'The superior man acts before he speaks, and afterwards speaks according to his actions.'

15. The Master said: 'Learning without thought is useless; thought without learning is perilous.'

17. The Master said: 'When you know a thing, to acknowledge that you know it, and when you do not know a thing, to admit that you do not know it; this is knowledge.'

20. The Master said: 'Let a ruler preside over his people with gravity, then they will reverence him. Let him be filial and kind to all, then they will be faithful to him. Let him advance the good and teach the incompetent, then they will eagerly seek to be virtuous.'

24. The Master said: 'To see what is right and not do it is lack of courage.'

Book 3

3. The Master said: 'In festive ceremonies, it is better to be sparing than extravagant. In the ceremonies of mourning, it is better that there be deep sorrow than a minute attention to observances.'

Book 4

5. The Master said: 'Riches and honors are what men desire. If they cannot be gained while following the Way, they should be shunned. Poverty and disrespect are what men dislike. If they cannot be avoided while following the Way, they should be embraced.'

11. The Master said: 'The superior man thinks of virtue; the inferior man thinks of comfort.'

12. The Master said: 'He who acts always thinking of his own advantage will be much murmured against.'

17. The Master said: 'When we see men of worth, we should think of equaling them; when we see men who are worthless, we should turn inwards and examine ourselves.'

18. The Master said: 'In serving his parents, a son may remonstrate with them, but gently; when he sees that they are not inclined to follow his advice, he shows an increased degree of reverence, but does not abandon his purpose; and should they punish him, he does not complain.'

23. The Master said: 'The cautious seldom err.'

25. The Master said: 'Virtue is not left to stand alone. He who practices it will have neighbors.'

Book 7

21. The Master said: 'When I walk along with two others, they may serve as my teachers. I will select their good qualities and follow them, their bad qualities and avoid them.'

Book 15

23. The Master said: 'What you do not want done to yourself, do not do to others.'

5

Mencius

Mencius (372–289 BCE?) was a student of Confucius's grandson who developed Confucian ideas and championed them vis à vis rival philosophies. Like Confucius, he was a teacher who had no luck gaining a post as a royal adviser but whose many followers collected records of his influential teachings and passed them down as the book *Mencius*. Mencius emphasized that human nature is fundamentally good and that the primary duty of government is to benefit the people.

Questions

1. Do any of Mencius's ideas ring true?
2. Which of Mencius's ideas seem impractical?
3. Compare contemporary concepts of leadership with those expressed by Mencius.

Mencius

Mencius based on James Legge, *The Four Books: Confucian Analects, the Great Learning, the Doctrine of the Mean, and the Works of Mencius* (Shanghai: Commercial Press, 1923), pp. 429–432, 444–446, 540–541, 548–552, 851–852, 947–948.

Book I, Part 1

Chapter I.1–6. Mencius went to see King Hui of Liang. The king said, 'Venerable sir, since you have not counted it far to come here, a distance of a thousand *li*, may I presume that you are provided with counsels to profit my kingdom?' Mencius replied, 'Why must your Majesty use that word "profit"? What I am provided with are counsels to benevolence and righteousness, and these are my only topics. If your Majesty say, "What is to be done to profit my kingdom?" the great officers will say, "What is to be done to profit our families?" and the inferior officers and the common people will say, "What is to be done to profit our persons?" Superiors and inferiors will try to snatch this profit the one from the other, and the kingdom will be endangered. . . . There never has been a benevolent man who neglected his parents. There never has been a righteous man who made his sovereign an after consideration. Let your Majesty also say, "Benevolence and righteousness, and let these be your only themes." Why must you use that word—"profit"?'

Chapter V.3–6. [King Hui asked Mencius how to restore his country after having been defeated in battle by three neighboring states.] Mencius answered: 'If your Majesty will indeed dispense a benevolent government to the people, being sparing in the use of punishments and fines, and making the taxes and levies light, causing the fields shall be ploughed deep, and the weeding of them be carefully attended to, and that the strong-bodied, during their days of leisure, shall cultivate their filial piety, fraternal respectfulness, sincerity, and truthfulness, serving thereby, at home, their fathers and elder brothers, and abroad their elders and superiors, you will then have a people who can be employed, with sticks which they have prepared, to oppose the strong mail and sharp weapons of the troops of Qin and Chu. The rulers of those States rob their people of their time, so that they cannot plough and weed their fields, in order to support their parents. Their parents suffer from cold and hunger. Brother, wives, and children are separated and scattered abroad. Those rulers, as it were, drive their people into pit-falls, or drown them. Your Majesty will go to punish them. In such a case, who will oppose your Majesty? In accordance with this is the saying—"The benevolent has no enemy."'

Book II, Part 1

Chapter III.2. Mencius said: 'When one subdues men by force, they do not submit in their hearts. They submit because their strength is not adequate to resist. When one subdues men by virtue, in their hearts' core they are pleased and sincerely submit.'

Chapter VI.1–7 Mencius said: 'All men have a mind which cannot bear to see the sufferings of others. The ancient kings had this commiserating mind, and they, as a matter of course, had likewise a commiserating government. When with a commiserating mind was practiced a commiserating government, to rule the kingdom was as easy a matter as to make anything go round in the palm of your hand. When I say that all men have a mind which cannot bear to see the sufferings of others, my meaning may be illustrated thus: even nowadays, if men suddenly see a child about to fall into a well, they will without exception experience a feeling of alarm and distress. They will feel so, not because they may gain the favor of the child's parents, nor because they seek the praise of their neighbors and friends, nor from a dislike of a reputation of having been unmoved by such a thing. From this case we may perceive that the feeling of commiseration is essential to man, that the feeling of shame and dislike is essential to man, that the feeling of modesty and willing compliance is essential to man, and that the feeling of approving and disapproving is essential to man. The feeling of commiseration is the principle of benevolence. The feeling of shame and dislike is the principle of righteousness. The feeling of modesty and willing compliance is the principle of propriety. The feeling of approving and disapproving is the principle of knowledge. . . . Men have these four principles just as they have their four limbs. . . . Since all men have these four principles in themselves, when men develop them to the fullest extent, the result will be like a fire starting, or an underground spring breaking through the surface of the ground. When these principles are completely developed, they will enable love and protection for all within the four seas. When these principles are not developed, a man will not even be able to serve his parents.'

Book 6, Part 1

Chapter II.1–3. The philosopher Gao said, 'Man's nature is like water whirling round in a corner. Open a passage for it to the east, and it will flow to the east; open a passage for it to the west, and it will flow to the west. Man's nature is indifferent to good and evil, just as the water is indifferent to the east and west.' Mencius replied: 'Water indeed will flow indifferently to the east or west, but will it flow indifferently up or down? The tendency of man's nature to good is like the tendency of water to flow downwards. Everyone has this tendency to good, just as all water flows downwards. Now by striking water and causing it to leap up, you may make it go over your forehead, and, by damming and leading it, you may force it up a hill; but are such movements according to the nature of water? It is the force applied which causes them. Men can be made to do what is not good when their nature is dealt with in this way.'

Book 7, Part1

Chapter XX.1–4. Mencius said: 'The superior man has three things in which he delights, and to be ruler over the kingdom is not one of them. That his father and mother are both alive, and that the condition of his brothers affords no cause for anxiety; this is one delight. That, when looking up, he has no occasion for shame before Heaven, and, below, he has no occasion to blush before men; this is a second delight. That he can get from the whole kingdom the most talented individuals, and teach and nourish them; this is the third delight.'

6

Great Learning

This short essay is found with the *Book of Rites*, but in the twelfth century Zhu Xi (1130–1200) selected it as one of the Four Books that present the essence of Confucian teachings. Between 1313 and 1905, the Four Books were the core of the curriculum required to prepare for the civil service examinations and thus profoundly important in Chinese cultural history. The *Great Learning* was intended to be a practical guide to self-improvement for rulers and government officials, but its tenets can be generalized to any person. It was once attributed to the grandson or a disciple of Confucius, but it is now believed to date from about 200 BCE. The text and the commentary that follows it have long been treated as a single work.

Questions

1. The terms *sincerity*, *rectify*, and *cultivate* have particular meanings in this text. How would you explain these terms?
2. What other values are considered essential?
3. What is the ultimate goal of the elaborate process described here?

Great Learning

> Great Learning based on James Legge, *The Four Books: Confucian Analects, the Great Learning, the Doctrine of the*

Mean, and the Works of Mencius (Shanghai: Commercial Press, 1945), pp. 308–314, 323–324, 326–328.

1. What the Great Learning teaches is to illustrate illustrious virtue; to renovate the people; and to rest in the highest excellence.

2. The point where to rest being known, the object of pursuit is then determined, a calm unperturbedness may be attained to. To that calmness there will succeed a tranquil repose. In that repose there may be careful deliberation, and that deliberation will be followed by the attainment of the desired end.

3. Things have their root and their branches. Affairs have their end and their beginning. To know what is first and what is last will lead near to what is taught in the *Great Learning*.

4. The ancients who wished to illustrate illustrious virtue throughout the kingdom, first ordered well their own States. Wishing to order well their States, they first regulated their families. Wishing to regulate their families, they first cultivated their persons. Wishing to cultivate their persons, they first rectified their hearts. Wishing to rectify their hearts, they first sought to be sincere in their thoughts. Wishing to be sincere in their thoughts, they first extended to the utmost their knowledge. Such extension of knowledge lay in the investigation of things.

5. Things being investigated, knowledge became complete. Their knowledge being complete, their thoughts were sincere. Their thoughts being sincere, their hearts were then rectified. Their hearts being rectified, their persons were cultivated. Their persons being cultivated, their families were regulated. Their families being regulated, their States were rightly governed. Their States being rightly governed, the whole kingdom was made tranquil and happy.

6. From the Son of Heaven down to the mass of the people, all must consider the cultivation of the person the root of everything besides.

7. It cannot be, when the root is neglected, that what should spring from it will be well ordered. It never has been the case that what was of great importance has been slightly cared for, and, at the same time, that what was of slight importance has been greatly cared for.

Commentaries

VI. What is meant by 'making the thoughts sincere' is the allowing no self-deception, as when we hate a bad smell, and as when we love what is beautiful. This is called self-enjoyment. Therefore, the superior man must be watchful over himself when he is alone. There is no evil to which the mean man . . . will not proceed, but when he sees a superior man, he instantly tries to disguise himself, concealing his evil, and displaying what is good. The other beholds him, as if he saw his heart . . . ; of what use is his disguise? This is an instance of the saying: 'What truly is within will be manifested without.' Therefore, the superior man must be watchful over himself when he is alone.

VII. What is meant by 'The cultivation of the person depends on rectifying the mind' may be thus illustrated: If a man be under the influence of passion, he will be incorrect in his conduct. He will be the same, if he is under the influence of terror, or under the influence of fond regard, or under that of sorrow and distress. When the mind is not present, we look and do not see; we hear and do not understand; we eat and do not know the taste of what we eat. This is what is meant by saying that the cultivation of the person depends on the rectifying of the mind.

VIII. What is meant by 'The regulation of one's family depends on the cultivation of his person' is this: Men are partial where they feel affection and love; partial where they despise and dislike; partial where they stand in awe and reverence; partial where they feel sorrow and compassion; partial where they are arrogant and rude. Thus it is that there are few men in the world who love and at the same time know the bad qualities of the object of their love, or who hate and yet know the excellences of the object of their hatred. . . . This is what is meant by saying that if the person be not cultivated, a man cannot regulate his family.

7

Doctrine of the Mean

The "mean" refers to a state of balance that brings humans into harmony with the universe. It is both a philosophical and a moral concept that is meant to guide people toward achieving an ideal life both as individuals and as members of society. The essay is presented as the words of Confucius as recorded by his grandson, but some scholars think it is a later combination of texts dating from about 200 BCE.

Questions

1. Divide the advice in this text into two categories: advice for managing relationships and advice for developing one's character. What are the most important aspects of each? How are they intertwined?
2. How does the use of the word *sincerity* in 17–18 differ from the way we typically use it?

Doctrine of the Mean

> Doctrine of the Mean based on James Legge, *The Four Books: Confucian Analects, the Great Learning, the Doctrine of the Mean, and the Works of Mencius* (Shanghi: Commercial Press, 1923), pp. 349–352, 367–368, 381–396.

Chapter I

1. What Heaven has conferred is called the nature; following this nature is called the Way; the regulation of this Way is called Instruction.

2. The Way may not be left for an instant. If it could be left, it would not be the Way. On this account, the superior man does not wait until he sees things to be cautious, or until he hears things to be apprehensive.

3. There is nothing more visible than what is secret, and nothing more manifest than what is minute. Therefore the superior man is watchful over himself when he is alone.

4. While there are no stirrings of pleasure, anger, sorrow, or joy, the mind may be said to be in the state of Equilibrium. When those feelings have been stirred, and they act in their due degree, there ensues what may be called the state of Harmony. This Equilibrium is the great root from which grow all the human actions in the world, and this Harmony is the universal path that all should pursue.

5. Let the states of equilibrium and harmony exist in perfection, and a happy order will prevail throughout heaven and earth, and all things will be nourished and flourish.

Chapter XIV. Confucius said

1. 'The superior man does what is proper to the station in which he is; he does not desire to go beyond this.

2. 'In a position of wealth and honor, he does what is proper to a position of wealth and honor. In a poor and low position, he does what is proper to a poor and low position. Situated among barbarous tribes, he does what is proper to a situation among barbarous tribes. In a position of sorrow and difficulty, he does what is proper to a position of sorrow and difficulty. The superior man can find himself in no situation in which he is not himself.

3. 'In a high situation, he does not treat with contempt his inferiors. In a low situation, he does not court the favor of his superiors. He rectifies himself, and seeks for nothing from others, so that he has no dissatisfactions. He does not murmur against Heaven, nor grumble against men.

4. 'Thus it is that the superior man is quiet and calm, awaiting destiny as ordained by Heaven, while the inferior man walks dangerous paths, hoping for good luck.

5. 'In archery we have something like the way of the superior man. When the archer misses the center of the target, he turns round and asks for the cause of his failure in himself.'

Chapter XX. Confucius said

3. 'With the right men the growth of government is rapid, just as the growth of vegetation is rapid in the earth; and moreover their government might be called an easily growing reed.

4. 'Therefore the administration of government lies in getting proper men. Such men are to be got by means of the ruler's own character. That character is to be cultivated by following the Way. The Way is cultivated by cherishing benevolence.

5. 'Benevolence is the characteristic element of humanity, and the great exercise of it is in loving relatives. Righteousness is the accordance of actions with what is right, and the great exercise of it is in honoring the worthy. The decreasing measures of the love due to relatives, and the steps in the honor due to the worthy, are produced by the principle of propriety.

6. 'When those in inferior situations do not possess the confidence of their superiors, they cannot retain the government of the people.

7. 'Hence the sovereign may not neglect the cultivation of his own character. Wishing to cultivate his own character, he may not neglect to serve his parents. In order to serve his parents, he may not neglect to acquire knowledge of men. In order to know men, he may not dispense with a knowledge of Heaven.

8. 'The duties of universal obligation are five, and the virtues wherewith they are practiced are three. The duties are those between sovereign and minister, between father and son, between husband and wife, between elder brother and younger brother, and those belonging to the intercourse of friends. Those five are the duties of universal obligation. Knowledge, magnanimity, and fortitude, these three, are the virtues universally binding. . . .

9. 'Some are born with the knowledge of those duties; some know them by study; and some acquire the knowledge after a painful feeling of their ignorance. But the knowledge being possessed, it comes to the same thing. Some practice them with a natural ease; some from a desire for their advantages; and some by strenuous effort. But the achievement being made, it comes to the same thing.

11. 'He who knows these three things, knows how to cultivate his own character. Knowing how to cultivate his own character, he knows how

to govern other men. Knowing how to govern other men, he knows how to govern the kingdom with all its States and families.

12. 'All who have the government of the kingdom with its States and families have nine standard rules to follow: the cultivation of their own characters; the honoring of men of virtue and talents; affection towards their relatives; respect towards the great ministers; kind and considerate treatment of all the officers; dealing with the mass of the people as children; welcoming all kinds of artisans; indulgent treatment of men from a distance, and the kindly cherishing of the princes of the State.

13. 'By the ruler's cultivation of his own character, the duties of universal obligation are set forth. By honoring men of virtue and talents, he is preserved from errors of judgment. By showing affection to his relatives, there is no grumbling nor resentment among his uncles and brethren. By respecting the great ministers he is kept from errors in the practice of government. By kind and considerate treatment of all the officers, they are led to make the most grateful return for his courtesies. By dealing with the mass of the people as his children, they are led to exhort one another to do what is good. By welcoming all kinds of artisans, his resources will be sufficient. By indulgent treatment of men from a distance, they will be attracted to his kingdom. And by kindly cherishing the princes of the States, the whole kingdom is brought to revere him.

14. 'Self-adjustment and purification, with careful regulation of his dress, and the not making a movement contrary to the rules of propriety, this is the way for a ruler to cultivate his person. Discarding slanderers, and keeping himself from the seductions of beauty; making light of riches, and giving honor to virtue, this is the way for him to encourage men of worth and talents. Giving them places of honor and generous compensation, and sharing with them in their likes and dislikes, this is the way for him to encourage his relatives to love him. Giving them numerous officers to carry out their commissions, this is the way for him to encourage the great ministers. Showing confidence in them and giving them generous compensation, this is the way to encourage the body of officers. Requiring service only at the proper times, and not requiring onerous service, this is the way to encourage the people. By daily inspections and monthly examinations, and by awarding them their rations in accordance with their workmanship, this is the way to encourage the artisans. To escort them on their departure and welcome them on their arriving, to commend the good among them, and show compassion to the incompetent, this is the way to treat indulgently men from a distance. . . .

17. 'When those in inferior situations do not obtain the confidence of the sovereign, they cannot succeed in governing the people. There is a way to obtain the confidence of the sovereign; if one is not trusted by his friends, he will not get the confidence of his sovereign. There is a way to be trusted by one's friends; if one is not obedient to his parents he will not be true to his friends. There is a way to being obedient to one's parents; if one, on turning his thoughts in upon himself, finds a want of sincerity, he will not be obedient to his parents. There is a way to the attainment of sincerity in one's self; if a man do not understand what is good, he will not attain sincerity in himself.

18. 'Sincerity is the Way of Heaven. The attainment of sincerity is the Way of men. He who possesses sincerity, is he who, without an effort, hits what is right, and apprehends, without the exercise of thought; he is the sage who naturally and easily embodies the Way. He who attains to sincerity, is he who chooses what is good, and firmly holds it fast.

19. 'To attain sincerity requires extensive study of what is good, accurate inquiry about it, careful reflection on it, the clear discrimination of it, and the earnest practice of it.

20. 'The superior man, while there is anything he has not studied, or while in what he has studied there is anything he cannot understand, will not quit. While there is anything he has not inquired about, or anything in what he has inquired about which he does not know, he will not quit. While there is anything which he has not reflected on, or anything in what he has reflected on which he does not apprehend, he will not quit. While there is anything which he has not discriminated, or his discrimination is not clear, he will not quit. If there be anything which he has not practiced, or his practice fails in earnestness, he will not quit. If another man succeed by one effort, he will use a hundred efforts. If another man succeed by ten efforts, he will use a thousand.

21. 'Let a man proceed in this way, and, though dull, he will surely become intelligent; though weak, he will surely become strong.'

8

Daoist Texts

The two main Daoist texts are *Daodejing* by Laozi (ca. sixth century BCE) and *Zhuangzi* by Zhuangzi (369–285 BCE). In contrast to the straightforward, worldly advice of the *Analects* of Confucius, the two foundational texts of Daoism are enigmatic and provocative. The *Daodejing* (sometimes translated as "The Classic of the Way and the Power") and the *Zhuangzi* encourage freedom from convention, intuitive understanding of the nature of things, and blissful transcendence of mundane cares and worries. The most important concept in the *Daodejing* is *wuwei*, which literally means "non-action," but which implies "acting effortlessly." Acting effortlessly means acting in accordance with cosmic principles so that action is spontaneous and natural. This principle was considered applicable to both matters of state and an individual's daily life.

The *Daodejing* consists of eighty-one brief, poetic, philosophical statements that may have circulated orally before being compiled in the third century BCE. According to tradition, a court archivist in the kingdom of Zhou known as Laozi (Old Master) wrote the *Daodejing* in the sixth century. Having become disgusted with the kingdom's rulers, he decided to leave China and wrote the *Daodejing* when a border guard insisted that he leave behind his teachings.

Zhuangzi was a minor official who lived in the fourth century BCE. His name serves as the title of a book that includes both his work and that of his disciples. The *Zhuangzi* uses anecdotes, parables, and paradox to encourage people to question

"Laozi Riding an Ox" by Zhang Lu (1464–1538), hanging scroll, ink and light color on paper. Laozi is carrying a copy of the *Daodejing. (Wikimedia Commons, National Palace Museum, Taipei)*

society's values, conventional wisdom, and accepted knowledge. Teaching that what hinders our attainment of happiness and freedom is our own mind, Zhuangzi held out the tantalizing promise that we can transcend our self-centered, narrow thinking and gain spiritual freedom by comprehending the Dao.

Daoist texts were never required reading as preparation for civil service exams as the so-called Confucian classics were, but they were widely read and treasured. While Confucian texts focus on how to govern society, beginning with self-control, Daoist writings focus on how people might find freedom from the fetters of society. Scholar-officials who fell out of favor or soured on their official duties often turned to Daoism. Many studied both traditions simultaneously. Daoism also proved attractive to the peasant masses. The idea that one could achieve supernatural powers through harmony with nature led to a popular form of Daoism that mixed superstition, the shamanistic practices of China's northern neighbors, and ancient fertility rituals. Popular Daoism borrowed some of the practices of Indian Yoga, and Daoist practitioners sought longevity and immortality through herbal and mineral elixirs that were, in fact, often poisonous. Daoism thus eventually came to involve magic, alchemy, and fortune-telling. A steady stream of new translations and commentaries shows continuing and international interest in these Daoist texts, especially the *Daodejing*.

Daodejing Questions

1. In what ways does the *Daodejing* criticize society?
2. What values does the *Daodejing* encourage?
3. How does the Sage exert power?
4. What is the Daoist view of how to govern?

Zhuangzi Questions

1. Discuss how we know what we think we know in light of the entries about dreaming of being a butterfly, the happiness of fish, and the death of Zhuangzi's wife.
2. Try applying Zhuangzi's ideas to current issues. What would Zhuangzi think about contemporary problems?
3. Think of other examples of fresh perspectives changing the value of something.
4. Debate the wisdom of Zhuangzi's refusal to accept a government position.

Daoist Texts

Daodejing

Daodejing based on Lionel Giles, *The Sayings of Lao Tzŭ* (London: J. Murray, 1905), pp. 19, 22–24, 30–31, 37, 43–44, 47.

1. THE Dao that can be expressed in words is not the eternal Dao; the name that can be uttered is not its eternal name. Without a name, it is

the Beginning of Heaven and Earth; with a name, it is the Mother of all things. Only one who is eternally free from earthly passions can apprehend its spiritual essence; he who is ever clogged by passions can see no more than its outer form. These two things, the spiritual and the material, though we call them by different names, in their origin are one and the same. This sameness is a mystery, the mystery of mysteries. It is the gate of all spirituality.

2. AMONG mankind, the recognition of beauty as such implies the idea of ugliness, and the recognition of good implies the idea of evil. There is the same mutual relation between existence and non-existence in the matter of creation; between difficulty and ease in the matter of accomplishing; between long and short in the matter of form; between high and low in the matter of elevation; between treble and bass in the matter of musical pitch; between before and after in the matter of priority.

3. NOT exalting worth keeps the people from rivalry. Not prizing what is hard to procure keeps the people from theft. Not to show them what they may covet is the way to keep their minds from disorder. Therefore the Sage, when he governs, empties their minds [of envy] and fills their bellies, weakens their inclinations [toward evil] and strengthens their bones. His constant object is to keep the people without wrong ambitions and without desire, or to prevent those who have wrong ambitions from daring to act. He practices inaction, and nothing remains ungoverned.

5. Nature is not benevolent; with ruthless indifference she makes all things serve their purposes, like the straw dogs we use at sacrifices. The Sage is not benevolent: he utilizes the people with like neutrality. The space between Heaven and Earth, is it not like a bellows? It is empty, yet inexhaustible; when it is put in motion, more and more comes out.

8. The highest goodness is like water, for water is excellent in benefiting all things, and it does not strive. It occupies the lowest place, which men disdain. And therefore it is near to the Dao.

9. He who grasps more than he can hold, would be better without any. If a house is crammed with treasures of gold and jade, it will be impossible to guard them all. He who prides himself upon wealth and honor hastens his own downfall. He who strikes with a sharp point will not himself be safe for long.

10. Dao produces all things; its Virtue nourishes them; its Nature gives them form; its Force perfects them.

Hence there is not a single thing but pays homage to Dao and extols its Virtue. This homage paid to Dao, this extolling of its Virtue, is due to no command, but is always spontaneous.

Thus it is that Dao, engendering all things, nourishes them, develops them, and fosters them; perfects them, ripens them, tends them, and protects them.

Production without possession, action without self-assertion, development without domination, this is its mysterious operation.

11. Thirty spokes unite in one hub; the utility of the cart depends on the hollow center in which the axle turns. Clay is molded into a vessel; the utility of the vessel depends on its hollow interior. Doors and windows are cut out in order to make a house; the utility of the house depends on the empty spaces.

Thus, while the existence of things may be good, it is the non-existent in them that makes them serviceable.

19. Cast off your sageliness, rid yourself of wisdom, and the people will benefit an hundredfold. Discard benevolence and abolish righteousness, and the people will return to filial piety and paternal love. Renounce your scheming and abandon gain, and thieves and robbers will disappear. These three precepts mean that outward show is insufficient, and therefore they bid us be true to our proper nature; to show simplicity, to embrace plain dealing, to reduce selfishness, to moderate desire.

37. Dao is eternally inactive, and yet it leaves nothing undone. If kings and princes could but hold fast to this principle, all things would work out their own reformation. If, having reformed, some still desired to act, I would restrain them with the simplicity of the Nameless Dao. The simplicity of the Nameless Dao brings about an absence of desire. The absence of desire gives tranquility. And thus the Empire will rectify itself.

48. The pursuit of book learning brings about daily increase. The practice of Dao brings about daily loss. Repeat this loss again and again, and you arrive at inaction. Practice inaction, and there is nothing that cannot be done.

Zhuangzi

Zhuangzi based on James Legge, *The Sacred Books of China: The Text of Taoism* (London: Oxford University Press, 1891), part 1, pp. 172–175, 194, 197, 390, 391–392; part 2, pp. 4–5.

From Book 1, Section 7

Huizi spoke to Zhuangzi. 'The king of Wei sent me some seeds of a large gourd, which I sowed. The fruit, when fully grown, could hold hundreds of pounds of anything. I used it to hold water, but it was so heavy that I could not lift it by myself. I cut it in two to make the parts into cups, but they were too wide and unstable and were useless. I knocked them to pieces.'

Zhuangzi replied, 'You were indeed stupid in the use of what was large. There was a man of Song who was skillful at making a salve that prevented hands from getting chapped; and his family for generations had used it in their business of bleaching silk. A stranger heard of it, and proposed to buy the art of the preparation for a hundred ounces of silver. The man's family gathered and considered the proposal. 'We have,' they said, 'been bleaching silk for generations, and have only made a little money. Now in one morning we can sell our art to this man for a hundred ounces of silver. Let's make the deal.' The stranger went away with it to give advice to the king of Wu, who was at war with the state of Yue. The king gave the stranger command of his fleet, and, thanks to the salve, his troops defeated Yue in battle in the winter, and he was granted a portion of the territory taken from Yue. In both cases hands were protected from getting chapped, but in the one case it led to gaining territory and in the other it only enabled the continued bleaching of silk. The difference of result was owing to the different use made of the art. Now you, Sir, had large gourds. Why did you not think of making buoys of them, by means of which you could have floated over rivers and lakes, instead of giving yourself the sorrow of finding that they were useless for holding anything.'

Huizi commented, 'I have a large tree. Its trunk swells out to a large size, but is not fit for a carpenter to apply his line to it. Its smaller branches are knotted and crooked, so that the compass and square cannot be used on them. Though planted on the wayside, a builder would not turn his head to look at it. Your words, Sir, are like the tree, great, but of no use.'

Zhuangzi replied, 'You, Sir, have a large tree and are troubled because it is of no use. Why do you not plant it in a tract where there is nothing else, or in a wide and barren wild? There you might saunter idly by its side, or enjoy untroubled sleep beneath it. No axe would shorten its existence. There would be nothing to injure it. What is there in its uselessness to cause you distress?'

From Book 2, Section 9

Chang Wu-tzu spoke: 'How do I know that the love of life is not a delusion and that the dislike of death is not like a child's losing his way, and not knowing that he is really going home? Lady Li was a daughter of the border Warden of Ai. When she became the hostage of the duke of Jin [in 671 BCE], she wept until the front of her dress was soaked with tears. But when she came to the king's palace, shared with him his luxurious couch, and ate delicacies at his table, then she regretted that she had wept. How do I know that the dead do not repent of their former craving for life?'

From Book 2, Section 11

Formerly, Zhuangzi dreamt that he was a butterfly, a butterfly flying about, feeling that it was enjoying itself. It did not know that it was Zhuangzi. Suddenly he awoke, and was himself again. He did not know whether formerly he had been dreaming that he was a butterfly, or he was now a butterfly dreaming he was Zhuangzi. But between Zhuangzi and a butterfly there must be a difference. This is a case of what is called the Transformation of Things.

From Book 17, Section 11

Zhuangzi was fishing when the king of Chu sent two great officers to him, with the message, 'I wish to trouble you with the charge of all within my territories.' Zhuangzi kept on holding his rod without looking round, and said, 'I have heard that in Chu there is a tortoise-shell, the wearer of which died 3,000 years ago, and which the king keeps, in his ancestral temple, in a hamper covered with a cloth. Was it better for the tortoise to die, and leave its shell to be thus honored? Or would it have been better for it to live, and keep on dragging its tail through the mud?' The two officers said, 'It would have been better for it to live, and draw its tail after it over the mud.' 'Go your way. I will keep on drawing my tail after me through the mud.'

Zhuangzi and Huizi were walking on the dam over the Hao River, when the former said, 'The fish come out, and play about at their ease. That is the enjoyment of fishes.' The other said, 'You are not a fish; how do you know what constitutes the enjoyment of fishes?' Zhuangzi rejoined,

'You are not I. How do you know that I do not know what constitutes the enjoyment of fishes?' Huizi said, "I am not you, and though indeed I do not fully know you, you are certainly not a fish, and that proves you cannot know what constitutes the happiness of fishes.' Zhuangzi replied, 'Let us keep to your original question. You said to me, "How do you know what constitutes the enjoyment of fishes?" You knew that I knew it, and yet you put your question to me. Well, I know it from our enjoying ourselves together by the Hao.'

From Book 18, Section 2

When Zhuangzi's wife died, Huizi went to express his condolences and found Zhuangzi squatting on the ground, drumming on a basin, and singing. Huizi said, 'When a wife has lived with her husband, and brought up children, then dies in her old age, not to wail for her is enough. To drum and sing, is that not excessive?' Zhuangzi replied. 'When she first died, how could I not have been affected? But I reflected on the beginning of her being, before she was born, she had no life, no bodily form, no spirit. Then a change took place and there was spirit. Another change, and there was the bodily form. Another change, and there came birth and life. There is now a change again, and she is dead. The relation between these things is like the procession of the four seasons from spring to autumn, from winter to summer. There now she lies with her face up, sleeping between heaven and earth. If I were to sob and wail for her, it would seem that I did not understand fate. Therefore I restrained myself.'

9

Chinese Poetry

Throughout premodern Chinese history, poetry was a revered art form: every educated person had to be able to recite and compose it. Poetry had multiple functions. Most importantly it was a medium for moral instruction and social commentary, a form of emotional self-expression, an exercise of technical skill, and a way to express views of the world gained through inspiration and intuition.[1] The most common poetic structure was four or eight lines of five or seven words. Rhyme and tonal variations also gave pattern to poetic expression. Vast quantities of Chinese poetry have been preserved. The Tang dynasty (618–906) is considered a golden age of poetry in terms of both quality and quantity. There are 48,000 poems by 2,200 authors in the official compilation of poems from the Tang dynasty. The few poems included here range through a time span of almost 1,000 years and have been selected for their relative accessibility.

Questions

1. Which poems constitute social commentary? What aspects of society are criticized?
2. Which poems reflect emotional self-expression? What emotions are expressed? What techniques enhance the effect of the poems?
3. A few poems advise the reader on how best to live life. What is this ideal lifestyle? What values are implicitly criticized in such poems?

Chinese Poetry

Poems 1, 2, 3, 6.1, 6.2, 6.3, 7 from Arthur Waley, *A Hundred and Seventy Chinese Poems* (London: Constable, 1918), pp. 64, 65, 76, 98, 150, 155, 157.
Poem 4.1 translated by Margaret Helen Childs from *Li Bai ji jiao zhu*, edited by Duiyuan Qu (Shanghai: Shanghai gu ji chu ban she: Xin hua shu dian Shanghai fa xing suo fa xing, 1980), p. 1340.
Poems 4.2, 4.3 from Arthur Waley, *The Poet Li Po AD 702–762* (London: East and West, 1919), pp. 23–24, 25–26.
Poem 5 from *Sunflower Splendor: Three Thousand Years of Chinese Poetry* edited by Wu-chi Liu, and Irving Yucheng Lo (Bloomington: Indiana University Press, 1990), pp. 130–131. Copyright ©1990, Indiana University Press. Reprinted with permission of Indiana University Press.

1. Ji Kiang (223–262)

Ji Kang was a member of a Daoist group of scholar-poets known as the Seven Sages of the Bamboo Grove, who abandoned political careers to pursue simple pleasures. Ji Kang alienated a powerful official and was sentenced to death despite 3,000 students signing a petition to spare him, but his last wish, to play his zither, was granted.

A Daoist Song

I will cast out Wisdom and reject Learning.
My thoughts shall wander in the Great Void.
Always repenting of wrongs done
Will never bring my heart to rest.
I cast my hook in a single stream;
But my joy is as though I possessed a Kingdom.
I loose my hair and go singing;
To the four frontiers men join in my refrain.
This is the purport of my song:
"My thoughts shall wander in the Great Void."

2. Fu Xuan (217–278)

Fu Xuan was a successful scholar-official who wrote several poems expressing sympathy for women and others who suffered injustice.

Woman
How sad it is to be a woman!!
Nothing on earth is held so cheap.
Boys stand leaning at the door
Like Gods fallen out of Heaven.
Their hearts brave the Four Oceans,
The wind and dust of a thousand miles.
No one is glad when a girl is born:
By her the family sets no store.
When she grows up, she hides in her room
Afraid to look at a man in the face.
No one cries when she leaves her home—
Sudden as clouds when the rain stops.
She bows her head and composes her face,
Her teeth are pressed on her red lips:
She bows and kneels countless times.
She must humble herself even to the servants.
His love is distant as the stars in Heaven,
Yet the sunflower bends towards the sun.
Their hearts are more sundered than water and fire—
A hundred evils are heaped upon her.
Her face will follow the years' changes:
Her lord will find new pleasures.
They that were once like the substance and shadow
Are now as far from Hu as from Ch'in [two distant places]
Yet Hu and Ch'in shall sooner meet
Than they whose parting is like Ts'an and Ch'en [two stars].

3. Tao Yuanming (365–427)

Tao Yuanming held both civilian and military posts but resigned in 405 rather than compromise his principles and became a gentleman farmer. He is noted for his descriptions of the natural beauty of his own neighborhood, celebrating such simple pleasures as drinking wine, and for a simple, direct style, even though complexity was fashionable then.

Blaming Sons (An Apology for His Own Drunkenness)
White hair covers my temples,
I am wrinkled and seared beyond repair,
And though I have got five sons,
They all hate paper and brush.

A-shu is eighteen:
For laziness there is none like him.
A-hsuan does his best,
But really loathes the Fine Arts.
Yung-tuan is thirteen,
But does not know "six" from "seven."
T'ung-tzu in his ninth year
Is only concerned with things to eat.
If Heaven treats me like this,
What can I do but fill my cup?

4. Li Bai (701–763)

Li Bai, also known as Li Po), is one of the greatest and most beloved
Chinese poets. Thanks to his fame as a poet, he was invited to serve
at the imperial court of Emperor Xuanzong (r. 712–756), but he was
eccentric and brash. Once, when summoned to court, he sent a message
to the emperor saying he was a god of wine and could not be bothered
to leave his tavern. He lost his post after just three years and spent
much of the rest of his life wandering. His poetry reveals that he was
sensitive to the beauties of nature and cherished serenity and the pleasures of friendship. He is believed to have written several thousand
poems, of which perhaps a thousand are extant. According to legend,
he fell out of a boat and drowned when he drunkenly tried to embrace
the reflection of the moon in the water.

4.1. Thoughts on a Quiet Night

By my bed, bright moonlight.
Is it frost on the ground?
I lift my head and gaze at the bright moon.
I lower my head and long for my home.

4.2. At Ching-hsia, parting from Sung Chih-t'i

Clear as the sky the waters of Hupeh
Far away will join with the Blue Sea;
We whom a thousand miles will soon part
Can mend our grief only with a cup of wine.

"Li Bai Strolling" (thirteenth century) by Liang Kai (ca. 1140–1210), hanging scroll, ink on paper. Renowned for fine facial details coupled with brushstrokes of varied widths in the garment and sometimes said to depict the poet reciting one of his poems. *(Wikimedia Commons, Tokyo National Museum)*

The valley birds are singing in the bright sun;
The river monkeys wail down the evening wind.
And I, who in all my life have seldom wept,
Am weeping now with tears that will never dry.

4.3. *Drinking Alone by Moonlight*

(1) A cup of wine, under the flowering-trees:
I drink alone, for no friend is near.
Raising my cup, I beckon the bright moon,
For he, with my shadow, will make three men.
The moon, alas! is no drinker of wine:
Listless, my shadow creeps about at my side.
Yet with the moon as friend and the shadow as slave
I must make merry before the Spring is spent.
To the songs I sing the moon flickers her beams;
In the dance I weave my shadow tangles and breaks.
While we were sober, three shared the fun;
Now we are drunk, each goes his way.
May we long share our odd, inanimate feast,
And meet at last on the Cloudy River of the Sky [the Milky Way].

(2) In the third month the town of Hsien-yang
Is thick-spread with a carpet of fallen flowers.
Who in Spring can bear to grieve alone?
Who, sober, looks on sights like these?
Riches and Poverty, long or short life,
By the Maker of Things are portioned and disposed.
But a cup of wine levels life and death
And a thousand things obstinately hard to prove.
When I am drunk, I lose Heaven and Earth;
Motionless, I cleave to my lonely bed.
At last I forget that I exist at all,
And at *that* moment my joy is great indeed.

(3) If High Heaven had no love for wine,
There would not be a Wine Star in the sky.
If Earth herself had no love for wine,
There would not be a city called Wine Springs.
Since Heaven and Earth both love wine,
I can love wine, without shame before God.
Clear wine was once called "a Saint;"
Thick wine was once called "a Sage."
Of Saint and Sage I have long quaffed deep,
What need for me to study spirits and immortals?
At the third cup I penetrate the Great Way;

A full gallon—Nature and I are one. . . .
But the things I feel when wine possesses my soul
I will never tell to those who are not drunk.

5. Du Fu (712–770)

Du Fu came from an illustrious family but did not have much success
in gaining official appointments. He traveled a great deal, married
late (752), and endured long separations from his family due to
poverty and the An Lushan rebellion (755). He had some peaceful
years after 760, thanks to the support of friends. His poetry reflects
his deep affection for his family and his concern for ordinary people
who suffered terrible hardships because of political corruption and
warfare.

Recruiting Officer of Shih-hao
At dusk I sought lodging at Shih-hao village,
When a recruiting officer came to seize men at night.
An old man scaled the wall and fled,
His old wife came out to answer the door.
How furious was the officer's shout!
How pitiable was the woman's cry!
I listened as she stepped forward to speak:
"All my three sons have left for garrison duty at Yeh;
From one of them a letter just arrived,
Saying my two sons had newly died in battle.
Survivors can manage to live on,
But the dead are gone forever.
Now there's no other man in the house,
Only a grandchild at his mother's breast.
The child's mother has not gone away;
She has only a tattered skirt for wear.
An old woman, I am feeble and weak,
But I will gladly leave with you tonight
To answer the urgent call at Ho-yang—
I can still cook morning gruel for your men."

The night drew on, but talking stopped;
It seemed I heard only half-concealed sobs.
As I got back on the road at daybreak,
Only the old man was there to see me off.

"Traveling Early in Clouds and Sun" (early fifteenth century) by Xie Jin (1369–1415), hanging scroll, ink on paper. *(Wikimedia Commons, Shanghai Museum)*

6. *Bai Juyi (772–846)*

Bai Juyi, also known as Po Juyi), was a relatively successful scholar-bureaucrat, despite a propensity to earn disfavor by speaking his mind.

Like Du Fu, he was a strong humanitarian and often criticized society and the government. Bai Juyi is known for his simple, straightforward style, which made him widely popular in China as well as in Korea and Japan.

6.1 After Lunch

After lunch—one short nap.
On waking up—two cups of tea.
Raising my head, I see the sun's light
Once again slanting to the south-west.
Those who are happy regret the shortness of the day;
Those who are sad tire of the year's sloth.
But those whose hearts are devoid of joy or sadness
Just go on living, regardless of "short" or "long."

6.2. Being Visited By a Friend During Illness

I have been ill so long that I do not count the days;
At the southern window, evening—and again evening.
Sadly chirping in the grasses under my eaves
The winter sparrows morning and evening sing.
By an effort I rise and lean heavily on my bed;
Tottering I step towards the door of the courtyard.
By chance I meet a friend who is coming to see me;
Just as if I had gone specially to meet him.
They took my couch and placed it in the setting sun;
They spread my rug and I leaned on the balcony-pillar.
Tranquil talk was better than any medicine;
Gradually the feelings came back to my numbed heart.

6.3. The Big Rug

That so many of the poor should suffer from cold what can
    we do to prevent?
To bring warmth to a single body is not much use.
I wish I had a big rug ten thousand feet long,
Which at one time could cover up every inch of the City.

"Rising Moon" by Sun K'o-hung (1555–1610), detail of handscroll, ink and color on paper. *(Wikimedia Commons, National Palace Museum, Taipei)*

7. *Su Shi (1037–1101)*

Su Shi, (also known as Su Dongpo), was a well-respected and successful scholar-official, even though he was often exiled to provincial posts due to political power struggles. He wrote on a very wide variety of topics and was a noted painter as well as poet.

On the Birth of His Son
Families, when a child is born
Want it to be intelligent.
I, through intelligence,
Having wrecked my whole life,
Only hope the baby will prove
Ignorant and stupid.
Then he will crown a tranquil life
By becoming a Cabinet Minister.

Note

1. James J.Y. Liu, *The Art of Chinese Poetry* (Chicago: University of Chicago Press, 1962), pp. 65, 70, 77, 81–82.

10

The West Chamber

WANG SHIFU

There are innumerable stories of love between promising scholars and women of both high and ignoble birth. *The West Chamber* is one of the most enduringly popular. The best-loved version is a play written by Wang Shifu during the Yuan (or Mongol) dynasty (1279–1368). It is based on an autobiographical short story written by the poet and scholar-official Yuan Chen (779–831) in which a young scholar, Chang, eventually spurns the love of the beautiful and loyal Ying-ying.

In Wang's greatly expanded and melodramatic version, Ying-ying is journeying with her mother, brother, and maid to bury her recently deceased father, but they have stopped at a temple along the way due to dangerous conditions in the region.

"Court Women on Horseback" (twelfth century) attributed to Li Gonglin (1049–1106) after work by Zhang Xuan (eighth century), detail of handscroll, ink and color on silk. Upper-class women in China like Lady Guoguo and her sisters, pictured here, were able to enjoy riding. *(Wikimedia Commons, National Palace Museum, Taipei)*

Chang, also traveling, catches sight of her, falls in love, and exchanges love poems with her. When a powerful local bandit demands that Ying-ying marry him, she offers to sacrifice herself for her family's safety. Ying-ying's mother promises to marry her daughter to whatever man can save them, although she had hoped to marry the girl to a cousin. To Ying-ying's delight, Chang earns the right to marry her by soliciting the help of his powerful friend, General Tu, but Ying-ying's mother reneges on her promise. Hung Niang, Ying-ying's maid, who cannot bear to see the young couple's despair, intercedes by leading Chang to Ying-ying. Ying-ying, an obedient daughter, is furious at this lack of propriety and rebuffs Chang, but she has a change of heart the next day when she learns how much Chang's unrequited love for her is causing him to suffer. She agrees to meet him again and allows him to make love to her. Ying-ying's mother is furious, but Hung Niang points out that the only way to avoid shame now is to let the couple marry. Ying-ying's mother only insists that Chang pass his examination and gain an official position first.

The themes of love at first sight, courtship undertaken via poetic love letters, forbidden love, and maidservants serving as accomplices to lovesick men are common themes in East Asian literature. This story is both touching and comic as Hung Niang takes the initiative when Chang is virtually incapacitated by lovesickness and as Ying-ying, surprising everyone, scolds Chang, despite her love for him, for his impertinence in courting her against her mother's wishes. Summarized or explanatory portions are given in italics.

Questions

1. To what extent do the standards of feminine beauty found here differ from those of today?
2. What do you think of a man who needs help from a maid to succeed in courting his beloved? Of a woman as changeable as Ying-ying?

The West Chamber

Excerpts from *The West Chamber: A Medieval Drama* by Wang Shifu, translated by Henry H. Hart (Stanford, CA:

From Act 1

From Chang's description of himself

Ah! How I have labored and worried
In the examination hall!
I have rubbed enough black ink-sticks
To wear through an iron slab. . . .
For ten years I have studied,
In the light of the glowworm and the snow.[1]
. . . But the times are out of joint,
And I cannot reach the goal
To which all men aspire,
Though like a bookworm I have bored
In every book and broken volume
And even in collections of old and scattered leaves.

From Chang's description of Ying-ying at his first glimpse

Suddenly I behold the consequences of my life five hundred years ago.[2] Though I have seen thousands of people, never have I been so thrilled as at the sight of this beautiful maid! My . . . [vision is] blurred, my confused lips find difficulty in speaking. My soul is dashed to bits, and flies through half the heavens. . . . Can it be that I have come upon one of the immortals? She can be serious or smiling, with her face like the breezes of spring. She is indeed worthy to be adorned with enameled flowers of kingfisher blue. Her eyebrows are curved like the crescent moon, and touch the tresses at her temples. She blushes ere she speaks. Like the bursting open of the cherry and the crimson peach are her red lips. Her teeth are like pure white jade moist with dew. She stands silent for a while. Now she begins to speak, like the oriole flitting among the flowers.

When she takes even a single step,
How I adore her!
When she sways her waist and moves her limbs,
How charming! How she thrills me!
A thousand wiles, ten thousand different graces has she.

From Act 3

Chang and Ying-ying exchange verses from a distance while in a temple garden

Chang
Tonight the moon shines in all its glory.
The shadows of the flowers of spring are calm and peaceful.
As I look upon the brilliant surface of the moon,
Can I not see the goddess who has her home therein?

Ying-ying
Behind my maidenly screen are solitude and silence.
There is no way for me to enjoy the fragrant spring.
Why does not he who sings so loudly
Take pity on my long-drawn sighs?

From Act 11

Hung Niang encourages Chang to climb the wall of the garden to meet Ying-ying

See how the light clouds veil the flowery moon.
It is like a silver lantern with a crimson paper shade.
The flowers and tiny willow buds
Bow down to form a screen,
And the green moss will serve you as a bed of rich brocade.
The night is calm and silent,
The courtyard is deserted, and peace reigns everywhere.

The branches are heavy laden with fair blossoms.
She is very young.
Allay her fears with soothing words,
And use caressing speech.
Win her with gentle wooing.
Remember, she is no woman of the streets,
No faded willow blossom by the dusty roadside wall.
Pluck her as you would the cassia flower,
And bow low before her,
For she is a woman, beautiful as flawless jade.
Be not satisfied with gazing at her face,
White though it be as the dawning of the spring,
Nor at the clustered clouds of hair
That gather at her brow,
Dark though that hair may be
As the wing of blackest crow. . . .
The time has come.
Lay aside your troubles, great and small,
And, banishing the deep furrows from your brow,
Prepare to receive your beloved in your arms.

Act 12

Hung Niang describes Ying-ying as Chang awaits her

Her eyebrows are dark
As the lines of mountains far away.
Her eyes are brilliant, far more brilliant
Than the clearest autumn pools.
Her skin is like the thickest of white cream.
Her waist is slender as the willow,
Her glance is full of charm,
Tender and loving is her heart,
And all her manners are alluring.
In character she is calm but firm,
And she has no need to seek
Artifices to enhance her beauty.
Best of all, to save a man from sorrow
She is as powerful as white-robed Kuan Yin,[3]
Our Lady of All Mercies.

"Plate with the Heroine of the *Romance of the Western Chamber*" from Jingdezhen (ca. 1680–1700), hard-paste porcelain with underglaze of cobalt. Other types of art, such as painting and ceramics, often took themes and motifs from literature. *(Wikimedia Commons, Gardiner Museum, Toronto)*

From Act 13

Chang describes waiting for Ying-ying

> If she is really coming
> She has left her room by now.
> And when she comes she will bring with her
> Springtime to this cold cell.
> If she comes not it will be
> As though I had cast a stone

In the depths of the great ocean
To stir it up—in vain. . . .
Promise me to come at dusk,
And to remain until the dawn.
It seems a full half-year
That I have waited for this night,
And all this time my lot has been
An irksome one to bear.
I was patient in my illness, though sick nigh unto death.
I think of those long days
When nothing passed my lips save tea and broth,
And all because of you, my best beloved.
I strengthened my sad heart, endured in silence,
And only by severest self-control
Did I hold my body and spirit as they were.
If I called in a geomancer he would say
That half a year of such utter sadness
Would need full ten years of peace and calm
To restore again the chariot of my lacerated soul.

Chang describes their intimacy

But one glance, O incomparable lady,
And my ills are nine-tenths cured.
When last we met, and you abused me roundly,
Who would believe that today you could be so changed?
When you show this proof of your affection,
I could bow low in humble adoration.
Though I have not the grace of Sung Yu,
Nor the beauty of P'an An,
Nor yet the brilliant talent of Tzu Chien,
Have pity, little lady, on this wanderer
 . . . .
Her tiny silken shoe
Is but an inch or two in length,[4]
And my open hand can span her willow waist.
She blushes in confusion, and will not lift her head,
As she reclines upon the fine embroidered pillow.
Her cloud-like hair is unbound,

And her pins of gold have fallen.
The disorder of her headdress but enhances her every charm.
Now I loosen her silken garments, and remove her slender
    girdle.
And sweet scent of musk and orris[5]
Now perfume my lonely room.
She still seems to wish to try me,
Will she not turn her face to mine?

. . . .

I press close to my body her fragrant breast of jade. . . .
Her willow-slim form stirs gently.
The flower is half-awakened.
And the pearly drops of dew
Have caused the peony to open wide its petals.
One draught, and my limbs are all atremble,
And I am happy as a fish
Disporting in the stream,
Or as a butterfly who sips
The evanescent fragrance of the flowers.
You the while seem half-reluctant, yet half-willing.
Filled with love and wonderment
I gently kiss your crimson mouth.
I hold you as my heart and my possession,
And your spotless purity is mine forevermore.
I had forgotten food and thought of sleep;
My heart longed but to die.
If my will had not been firm and steadfast,
How could I have endured life until this hour
When I fulfill my wildest dreams of joy?
For this night I have drained the cup
Of desire, love, and passion,
And now my soul soars upward
To the ninth heaven of delight.
Alas, that I was forced to wait until today, beloved!
See my body, thin with grief,
And my bones as weak as threshed and beaten straw.
But I dare not even think
Of the joys of this wondrous night of love.
The dew now dampens the fragrant earth,
And the wind no longer stirs on the silent stair.

The moon still lights my chamber,
And the clouds veil the tower of Yang T'ai.
My soul is illumined with a bright white light,
And I look at you more closely.
To make sure that you are real
And not a vision that will fade and vanish soon.

Notes

1. These are references to two fourth-century students who were so poor they could not afford a lamp and instead studied by the light reflected from snow outside (Sun K'ang) and by the light of fireflies collected and kept in a gauze bag (Che Yin).

2. Chang is suggesting that he has met Ying-ying in a previous lifetime.

3. Kuan Yin or Guanyin (in India, Avalokiteshvara; in Japan, Kannon) is a bodhisattva of supreme compassion.

4. This is a reference to the practice of foot-binding, which began during the Song dynasty (960–1126). A bound foot was four or five inches long.

5. Orris is an alternate term for iris.

11

Journey to the West

WU CHENG'EN

Journey to the West, by Wu Cheng'en (1505–1580), was inspired by the travels of the monk Xuanzang (602–664), who left China in secret and traveled to India in search of Buddhist texts. He faced many dangers along the way, but also received invaluable support from Buddhist believers during this fifteen-year sojourn. He returned to China in 645 with well over 600 documents, which greatly influenced the subsequent development of Buddhist thought and practice in China. In this fantastic version, the monk (also known as Sanzang) is portrayed as timid and totally dependent upon three primary companions: a temperamental monkey (Sun Wukong) and a lazy pig, who frequently clash, and a reliable river monster. The novel is full of comic moments and vividly described battles involving all sorts of supernatural powers. This story has been retold in many formats (plays, films, video games, etc.) and is often titled *Monkey*. The selections and synopses below present the story through the first fifteen of one hundred chapters. Summaries of missing sections are given in italics.

Questions

1. Various aspects of Chinese culture are blended in this story. Identify Confucian, Daoist, and Buddhist elements and explain the hierarchy they are given.
2. What makes Monkey such an interesting character?

"Chinese Buddhist Pilgrim Hsuan-Tsang [Xuanzang]" (nineteenth century), ink and color on paper. Inexpensive images such as this were popular religious souvenirs and talismans. (*Wikimedia Commons, Brooklyn Museum*)

Journey to the West

Excerpts from Wu Cheng'en, translated by W.J.F. Jenner, *Journey to the West* (Beijing: Foreign Languages Press, 1982), pp. 4–5, 10–13, 36–37, 243, 264, 273–280. See also Wu Cheng'en, translated by Anthony C. Yu, *The Journey to the West* (Chicago: University of Chicago Press, 2012).

After a description of the origin of the universe, the story turns to an explanation of Monkey's origins.

There was once a magic stone on the top of this mountain, which was thirty-six feet five inches high and twenty-four feet round. It was thirty-six feet five inches high to correspond with the 365 degrees of the heavens, and twenty-four feet round to match the twenty-four divisions of the solar calendar. On top of it were nine apertures and eight holes, for the Nine Palaces and the Eight Trigrams. There were no trees around it to give shade, but magic fungus and orchids clung to its sides. Ever since Creation began it had been receiving the truth of Heaven, the beauty of Earth, the essence of the Sun and the splendor of the Moon; and as it had been influenced by them for so long it had miraculous powers. It developed a magic womb, which burst open one day to produce a stone egg about the size of a ball.

When the wind blew on this egg it turned into a stone monkey, complete with the five senses and four limbs. When the stone monkey had learnt to crawl and walk, he bowed to each of the four quarters. As his eyes moved, two beams of golden light shot towards the Pole Star Palace and startled the Supreme Heavenly Sage, the Greatly Compassionate Jade Emperor of the Azure Vault of Heaven, who was sitting surrounded by his immortal ministers on his throne in the Hall of Miraculous Mist in the Golden-gated Cloud Palace. When he saw the dazzling golden light he ordered Thousand-mile Eye and Wind-accompanying Ear to open the Southern Gate of Heaven and take a look. The two officers went out through the gate in obedience to the imperial command, and while one observed what was going on the other listened carefully. Soon afterwards they reported back:

"In obedience to the Imperial Mandate your subjects observed and listened to the source of the golden light. We found that at the edge of the country of Aolai, which is east of the ocean belonging to the Eastern Continent of Superior Body, there is an island called the Mountain of Flowers and Fruit. A magic stone on the top of this mountain produced a magic egg, and when the wind blew on this egg it turned into a stone monkey which bowed to each of the four quarters. When he moved his eyes, golden light shot towards the Pole Star Palace; but now that he is eating and drinking, the golden light is gradually dying."

In his benevolence and mercy the Jade Emperor said, "Creatures down below are born of the essence of heaven and earth: there is nothing remarkable about him."

Thanks to being clever and bold, the monkey is crowned King by his fellow monkeys, and he enjoys life with his subjects until one day he falls prey to somber thoughts.

"Although I'm happy now," the Monkey King replied, "I'm worried about the future. That's what's getting me down." The other monkeys laughed and said, "Your Majesty is being greedy. We have parties every day; we live in a mountain paradise, in an ancient cave in a divine continent. We are spared the rule of unicorns, the domination of phoenixes, and the restraints of human kings. We are free to do just as we like—we are infinitely lucky. Why make yourself miserable worrying about the future?" To this the Monkey King replied, "Yes, we don't have to submit to the laws and regulations of human kings, and we don't live in terror of the power of birds and beasts. But the time will come when we are old and weak, and the underworld is controlled by the King of Hell. When the time comes for us to die, we won't be able to go on living among the Blessed, and our lives will have been in vain." All the monkeys covered their faces and wept as every one of them thought about death.

Suddenly a gibbon jumped out from their ranks and shrieked in a piercing voice, "If Your Majesty is thinking so far ahead, this is the beginning of enlightenment. Now of the Five Creatures, there are only three that do not come under the jurisdiction of the King of Hell." "Do you know which they are?" asked the Monkey King. "Yes," the ape replied. "They are the Buddhas, the Immortals and the Sages. They are free from the Wheel of Reincarnation. They are not born and they do not die. They are as eternal as Heaven and Earth, as the mountains and the rivers." "Where do they live?" the Monkey King asked. "Only in the human world," the ape replied, "in ancient caves on magic mountains." The Monkey King was delighted to hear this. "I shall leave you all tomorrow," he said, "and go down the mountain. If I have to, I'll roam the corners of the oceans and go to the edge of the sky to find these three kinds of beings and discover the secret of eternal youth that will keep us out of the clutches of the King of Hell forever." Goodness! Because of these words he was to learn how to be free from the Wheel of Reincarnation and become the Great Sage Equaling Heaven. All the monkeys clapped with approval and said, "Great! Great! Tomorrow we'll climb all over the mountain and get lots of fruit to give Your Majesty a really big banquet to send you off."

The Monkey King sailed away and after many days came to the Southern Continent.

He saw humans by the coast, fishing, hunting geese, gathering clams, and extracting salt. He went up to them, leaping around and making faces, which so scared them that they dropped their baskets and nets and fled in all directions as fast as they could. The Monkey King grabbed one of them who was a poor runner, stripped him of his clothes, and dressed himself in them like a human. He swaggered through the provinces and prefectures, learning human behavior and human speech in the market places. Whether he was eating his breakfast or going to bed at night he was always asking about Buddhas, Immortals and Sages, and seeking the secret of eternal youth. He observed that the people of the world were too concerned with fame and fortune to be interested in their fates.

The Monkey King traveled for many years until he found an Immortal with whom to study. The Immortal bestowed upon the Monkey King the name Sun Wukong or Monkey Awakened to Emptiness. Monkey spent several years studying and was finally granted the secret of Immortality and, after a few more years, the spells for seventy-two transformations so he would be able to escape the dangers of thunderbolts, fire, and wind. Monkey also learned how to soar through the clouds, but one day the Immortal found him using his magical abilities to entertain others and sent him home. Monkey found that a demon had been harassing his subjects and confronted him.

"You insolent demon," shouted the Monkey King. "Your eyes may be big but you can't see who I am." The demon king laughed at him. "You don't even stand four feet from the ground, you're still in your twenties, and you've got no weapon in your hand. What sort of mad courage makes you challenge me to a fight?" "You insolent demon," retorted Sun Wukong, "how blind you are. You may think I'm small, but I can grow easily enough. You may think I'm unarmed, but I could pull the moon down from the sky with my two hands. Don't worry, old Sun Wukong will sock you one." Sun Wukong gave a jump and leapt into the air, taking a swing at his face. The demon king put out his hand to stop him and said, "Look how big I am, you dwarf. If you use your fists, I'll use my sword. But I'd only make myself look ridiculous if I killed you with a sword. Wait till I've put my sword down and then I'll give you a display of boxing." "Well said," exclaimed Sun Wukong, "spoken like a man. Come on then." The demon king dropped his guard to throw a punch, and Sun Wukong rushed in towards him, punching and kicking. When he spread out his hand it was enormous, and when he clenched his fist it was very hard. Sun Wukong hit the demon king in the ribs, kicked his backside, and smashed several of his joints. The demon king seized his steel sword that was as big as a plank, and swung it at Sun Wukong's skull. Sun Wukong dodged the blow, and the sword only split air. Seeing how ugly the demon king had turned, Sun Wukong used his magic art of getting extra bodies. He pulled out one of his hairs, popped it in his mouth, chewed it up, and blew it out into the air, shouting, "Change!" It turned into two or three hundred little monkeys, who all crowded round him.

Sun Wukong now had an immortal body, and there was no magic transformation of which he was not capable. Since he had followed the Way he could change each of the eighty-four thousand hairs on his body into anything he wanted. The little monkeys were too quick and nimble for sword or spear. Look at them, leaping forwards and jumping backwards, rushing up and surrounding the demon king, grabbing him, seizing him, poking him in the backside, pulling at his feet, punching him, kicking him, tearing his hair out, scratching at his eyes, twisting his nose, all picking him up together and throwing him to the ground. They went on until they had beaten him to a pulp. Sun Wukong snatched his sword from him, told the little monkeys to get out of the way, and brought it down on the crown of his head, splitting it into two.

Having saved his countrymen, Monkey armed them but felt the need for a suitable weapon for himself. Monkey bullied Dragon King of the Eastern Sea into handing over a miraculous 13,500-pound piece of iron that anchored the Milky Way. Monkey magically shrank it to a manageable size for a cudgel (later he shrinks it to the size of a needle and keeps it behind his ear) and then he demanded a suit of armor as well. Having returned home well armed, Monkey dreamed that his soul was brought to the underworld, but he beat up his escorts and intimidated the Ten Kings who judge the dead. The Ten Kings showed him that the Register of Life and Death indicated that he would die at age 342. Monkey crossed out the names of all the monkeys in the Register and went home. Subsequently the Dragon King and the Ten Kings submitted complaints about Monkey to the Jade Emperor, who decided to summon Monkey to heaven rather than risk a ruckus by trying to arrest him. Monkey was made Protector of the Horses and he happily took up his duties until he found out it was a lowly post and stormed out of heaven in a rage. Monkey defiantly decided to call himself "Great Sage Equaling Heaven" and defeated the heavenly army that was sent to arrest him. The Jade Emperor decided to appease Monkey by awarding him the title he wanted and building a palace for him in heaven. Soon Monkey was given the task of guarding the Peach Orchard, but he ate all the best peaches and then stole the food and drink intended for the Feast of Peaches. In a drunken state he stumbled upon the palace of Laozi and ate up a great supply of pills of immortality. Sobering up, he realized he was in serious trouble and fled heaven. The Jade Emperor, now determined to capture Monkey, sent a vast army, but Monkey fought them off. The Emperor then dispatched a disciple of the Bodhisattva Guanyin, who also failed to subdue Monkey.

The next step was to commission the god Erlang, the most powerful warrior in heaven. On the verge of defeat by Erlang, Monkey resorted to flight and transformations to hide himself but was finally cornered and captured. Efforts to execute Monkey failed; Monkey withstood being burned in Laozi's furnace for forty-nine days and then escaped. Finally the Buddha tricked Monkey into making a bet he could not win and then imprisoned him under Five Elements Mountain. There Monkey was fed iron pellets and given molten copper to drink until he had served his sentence, when he would be freed.

Five hundred years later the Buddha recruited Guanyin to find someone to come and gather up scripture to take to the East where people are greedy and violent. As Guanyin traveled east, she encountered a monster in the River of Flowing Sands. He had been made into a monster as punishment for having smashed a crystal dish in heaven and he was adding to his karmic debt by devouring travelers. Guanyin proposed that the monster promise to aid the scripture seeker in order to earn forgiveness. Then Guanyin met another monster in the shape of a pig, who was being punished for getting drunk and flirting with the moon goddess. He was also given the opportunity to serve the scripture seeker. When Guanyin came upon Monkey, still imprisoned under the mountain, he told her he had repented and he too agreed to become a disciple of the scripture seeker.

The text of Journey to the West *then turns to the story of the birth of Xuanzang. His father placed first in the civil service examinations and was awarded the post of district prefect but was murdered by a ferryman on his way to take up his post. The murderer assumed the father's identity, but the corpse was preserved by a dragon king and later resuscitated. Xuanzang's mother gave birth while the murderer was away and abandoned her baby, setting him afloat on a river. An abbot rescued the boy and raised him to become a monk. In a story too complicated to summarize here, Xuanzang found his mother and the murderer was eventually brought to justice. After another complex side story in which emperor Taizong died and returned to life, Guanyin appeared and told the emperor to send a scripture seeker to the West. Xuanzang volunteered.*

At court the next morning Taizong assembled his civil and military officials and wrote out the document Xuanzang would need to fetch the scriptures, stamping it with the imperial seal that gave the right to travel freely. When an imperial astrologer reported that this day was under an auspicious star for setting out on a long journey, the Tang Emperor was delighted. A eunuch official came in to report, "The Imperial Younger Brother, the Master of the Law,[1] awaits a summons outside the palace doors." Calling him into the throne hall, Taizong said, "Brother, today is a lucky one for starting on a journey, and here is the pass that will let you through the checkpoints. I am also giving you a golden bowl with which you may beg for food on your journey, in addition to choosing two experienced travelers to accompany you and presenting you with a horse to carry you on your long journey. You may now set out."

The emperor gave Xuanzang the name Sanzang, or Tripitaka, which referred to the three categories of Buddhist scripture, and Sanzang set out with two attendants and a packhorse. After some days they were captured by demons and the two attendants were eaten. Sanzang was saved by the planet Venus, which appeared as an old man and freed him. Not long after that, Sanzang came upon the mountain where Monkey was imprisoned.

"Are you the fellow sent to the Western Heaven by the Emperor of the East to fetch the scriptures?" asked the monkey. "Yes, I am," Sanzang replied. "Why do you ask?" "I am the Great Sage Equaling Heaven who wrecked the Heavenly Palace five hundred years ago. The Lord Buddha put me under this mountain for my criminal insubordination. Some time ago the Bodhisattva Guanyin went to the East on the Buddha's orders to find someone who could fetch the scriptures. When I asked her to save me she told me that I was to give up evil-doing, return to the Buddha's Law, and do all I could to protect the traveler when he went to the Western Paradise to worship Buddha and fetch the scriptures; she said that there'll be something in it for me when that's done. Ever since then I've been waiting day and night with eager anticipation for you to come and save me, Master. I swear to protect you on your way to fetch the scriptures and to be your disciple."

Sanzang released Monkey from the mountain prison and they set off. One of the first things Monkey did was to kill a tiger and use the hide as a kilt. Then one day six brigands attempted to rob them. Sanzang fell off his horse from fear, but Monkey was unperturbed.

Waving their spears and swords they rushed him, hacking wildly at his face. Seventy or eighty blows crashed down on him, but he simply stood in the middle of them, ignoring everything. "What a monk!" the bandits said. "He's a real tough nut." "I think we've seen enough of that," said Brother Monkey with a smile. "Your hands must be tired after all that bashing. Now it's my turn to bring out my needle for a bit of fun." "This monk must have been an acupuncturist," said the bandits. "There's nothing wrong with us. Why is he talking about needles?"

Taking the embroidery needle from his ear, Brother Monkey shook it in the wind, at which it became an iron cudgel as thick as a rice bowl. With this in his hand he said, "Stick around while I try my cudgel out." The terrified bandits tried to flee in all directions, but Monkey raced after them, caught them all up, and killed every one of them. Then he stripped the clothes off them, took their money, and went back with his face wreathed in smiles. "Let's go, master; I've wiped those bandits out," he said. "Even though they were highwaymen, you're really asking for trouble," Sanzang replied. "Even if they had been arrested and handed over to the authorities, they wouldn't have been sentenced to death. You may know a few tricks, but it would be better if you'd simply driven them away. Why did you have to kill them all? Even taking a man's life by accident is enough to stop someone from becoming a monk. A person who enters the religious life *"Spares the ants when he sweeps the floor, Covers the lamps to save the moth."*[2] What business did you have to slaughter the lot of them, without caring which of them were the guilty and which were innocent? You haven't a shred of compassion or goodness in you. This time it happened in the wilds, where nobody will be able to trace the crime. Say someone offended you in a city and you turned murderous there. Say you killed and wounded people when you went berserk with that club of yours. I myself would be involved even though I'm quite innocent." "But if I hadn't killed them, they'd have killed you, master," protested Sun Wukong. "I am a man of religion, and I would rather die than commit murder," said Sanzang. "If I'd died, there'd only have been me dead, but you killed six of them, which was an absolute outrage. If the case were taken to court, you couldn't talk your way out of this even if the judge were your own father." "To tell you the truth, master, I don't know how many people I killed when I was the monster who ruled the Mountain of Flowers and Fruit," said Sun Wukong, "but if I'd acted your way I'd never have become the Great Sage Equaling Heaven." "It was precisely because you acted with such tyrannical cruelty among mortals and committed the most desperate crimes against Heaven that you got into trouble five hundred years ago," retorted Sanzang. "But now you have entered the faith, you'll never reach the Western Heaven and never become a monk if you don't give up your taste for murder. You're too evil, too evil."

Monkey, who had never let himself be put upon, flared up at Sanzang's endless nagging. "If you say that I'll never become a monk and won't ever reach the Western Heaven, then stop going on at me like that. I'm going back." Before Sanzang could reply, Monkey leapt up in a fury, shouting, "I'm off." Sanzang looked up quickly, but he was already out of sight. All that could be heard was a whistling sound coming from the east. Left on his own, the Priest nodded and sighed to himself with great sadness and indignation. "The incorrigible wretch," he reflected. "Fancy disappearing and going back home like that just because I gave him a bit of a telling-off. So that's that. I must be fated to have no disciples or followers. I couldn't find him now even if I wanted to, and he wouldn't answer if I called him. I must be on my way." So he had to strive with all his might to reach the West, looking after himself with nobody to help.

As Sanzang proceeded alone Guanyin appeared to him, gave him a brocade tunic and hat for Monkey, and taught him a spell that caused a band in the hat to tighten, thereby giving him control over his impetuous disciple.

Let us turn to Sun Wukong, who after leaving his master went straight back to the Eastern Ocean on his somersault cloud. Putting his cloud away, he parted the waters and went straight to the undersea palace of crystal. His approach had alarmed the dragon king, who came out to welcome him and took him into the palace, where they sat down. When they had exchanged courtesies the dragon king said, "I'm sorry that I failed to come and congratulate you on the end of your sufferings, Great Sage. I take it that you are returning to your old cave to put your immortal mountain back in order." "That's what I wanted to do," Monkey replied. "But I've become a monk instead." "A monk? How?" the dragon king asked. "The Bodhisattva of the Southern Sea converted me. She taught me to work for a good reward later by going to the West with the Tang Priest from the East, visiting the Buddha, and becoming a monk. And my name has been changed to Brother Monkey." "Congratulations, congratulations," said the dragon king. "You've turned over a new leaf and decided to be good. But in that case why have you come back to the East instead of going West?" Monkey laughed. "Because that Tang Priest doesn't understand human nature. He started nagging away at me about a few small-time highwaymen I killed, and said that everything about me was wrong. You know how I can't stand people going on at me, so I left him to come home to my mountain. I looked in on you first to ask for a cup of tea." "Delighted to oblige," said the dragon king, and his dragon sons and grandsons came in with some fragrant tea which they presented to Monkey.

The dragon king urged Monkey to do the right thing.

"Great Sage, if you don't protect the Tang Priest with all your might, and if you reject his instruction, then you might as well stop trying to win yourself a good later reward, because it will mean you're only an evil Immortal after all." Monkey hummed and hawed, but said nothing. "Great Sage," said the dragon king, "you must make your mind up. Don't ruin your future for the sake of an easy life now." "Enough said. I'll go back and look after him," replied Sun Wukong.

Monkey hurried back to the Tang Priest.

Monkey saw the Tang Priest sitting gloomily beside the path. He went up to him and said, "Why aren't you traveling, master? What are you still here for?" Sanzang looked up. "Where have you been?" he asked. "I couldn't move without you, so I had to sit here and wait till you came back." "I went to visit the Old Dragon King of the Eastern Sea to ask him for some tea," Monkey replied. "Disciple, a religious man shouldn't tell lies. How can you say that you went to drink tea at the dragon king's place when you haven't been gone two hours?" "I can tell you quite truthfully," replied Monkey with a smile, "that with my somersault cloud I can cover thirty-six thousand miles in a single bound. That's how I got there and back." "When I spoke to you a little severely you resented it and went off in a huff," said Sanzang. "It was all right for a clever person like you—you begged yourself some tea. But I couldn't go, and had to stay here hungry. You ought to be sorry for me." "If you're hungry, master, I'll go and beg you some food," suggested Monkey. "No need," his master replied, "there are still some dry provisions in my bundle. . . . Take that bowl and fetch some water. When we've eaten some of it we can be on our way."

Opening the bundle, Brother Monkey found some scones made of coarse flour, which he took out and gave to his master. He also noticed the dazzling brocade tunic and the hat with inlaid golden patterns. "Did you bring this tunic and hat with you from the east?" he asked. Sanzang had to make something up on the spot. "I used to wear them when I was young. With that hat on you can recite scriptures without ever having been taught them, and if you wear that tunic you can perform the rituals without any practice." "Dear master, please let me wear them," Monkey pleaded. "I don't know whether they'll fit you, but if you can get them on, you can wear them." Monkey . . . found that it was a perfect fit. Then he put the hat on his head. As soon as he had the hat on, Sanzang stopped eating and silently recited the Band-tightening Spell. "My head aches, my head aches," cried Brother Monkey, but his master went on and recited the spell several times more. Monkey, now rolling in agony, tore the hat to shreds, and Sanzang stopped reciting the spell for fear he would break the golden band. The moment the spell stopped the pain finished. Reaching up to feel his head, Monkey found something like a golden wire clamped so tightly around it that he could not wrench or snap it off. It had already taken root there. He took the needle out of his ear, forced it inside the band, and pulled wildly at it. Sanzang, again frightened that he would snap it, started to recite the spell once more. The pain was so bad this time that Monkey stood on his head, turned somersaults, and went red in the face and ears. His eyes were popping and his body went numb. Seeing the state he was in, Sanzang had to stop, and the pain stopped again too. "Master," said Monkey, "what a curse you put on me to give me a headache like that." "I didn't put a curse on you, I recited the Band-tightening Spell," Sanzang replied. "Say it again and see what happens," said Monkey, and when Sanzang did as he asked, Monkey's head ached again. "Stop, stop," he shouted, "the moment you started reciting it my head ached. Why did you do it?" "Will you accept my instruction now?" Sanzang asked. "Yes," Monkey replied. "Will you misbehave again in future?" "I certainly won't," said Monkey.

Although he had made this verbal promise, he was still nurturing evil thoughts, and he shook his needle in the wind till it was as thick as a rice bowl. He turned on the Tang Priest, and was on the point of finishing him off when the terrified Sanzang recited the spell two or three more times. The Monkey dropped his cudgel and fell to the ground, unable to raise his arm, "Master," he shouted, "I've seen the light. Stop saying the spell, please stop." "How could you have the perfidy to try to kill me?" asked Sanzang. "I'd never have dared," said Brother Monkey, adding, "who taught you that spell, master?" "An old lady I met just now," replied Sanzang. Monkey exploded with rage. "Tell me no more," he said, "I'm sure and certain the old woman was that Guanyin. How could she do this to me? Just you wait. I'm going to the Southern Sea to kill her." "As she taught me this spell," Sanzang replied, "she's bound to know it herself. If you go after her and she recites it, that will be the end of you." Seeing the force of his argument, Monkey changed his mind and gave up the idea of going. He knelt down and pleaded pitifully, "Master, she's used this to force me to go with you to the West. I shan't go to make trouble for her, and you must recite scriptures instead of saying that spell all the time. I promise to protect you, and I shall always be true to this vow." "In that case you'd better help me back on the horse," Sanzang replied. Monkey, who had been plunged into despair, summoned up his spirits, tightened the belt round his brocade tunic, got the horse ready, gathered up the luggage, and hurried off towards the West. If you want to know what other stories there are about the journey, then listen to the explanation in the next installment.

"Probably Avalokiteshvara (Guanyin), the Bodhisattva of Mercy" (ca. 591–618) cast bronze with gilding. Statuettes like this were made for home worship or even carried by pilgrims. (Los Angeles County Museum of Art)

Notes

1. It is a great honor for the Tang Emperor Taizong to address Xuanzang in this manner.

2. This appears to be a fragment of a song or poem.

12

Outlaws of the Marsh

SHI NAI'AN AND LUO GUANZHONG

Outlaws of the Marsh by Shi Nai'an and Luo Guanzhong (also known as *Water Margin*, and *All Men Are Brothers*, and *Men of the Marshes*) is a lengthy novel written in the fourteenth century but based on events that occurred during the reign of Huizong, a Song dynasty emperor (r. 1101–1125). Song Jiang became the leader of 108 chiefs who gathered at Liangshan, a mountain surrounded by marshes in what is now Shandong province, to escape corruption, injustice, or poverty. There they amassed an army of thousands and fought off government troops with bold strategies and wily tricks. Eventually they surrendered to the government and were commissioned to fight other rebels or foreign invaders. Summaries of missing sections are given in italics.

Questions

1. Compare and contrast Song Jiang's character with that of a hero in Western culture.
2. The battle scenes describe a wide variety of tactics. What are some of the most effective ones?
3. What are the attitudes of the combatants as the fighting begins? What are the attitudes of captor and captive after a battle?

Outlaws of the Marsh

> Excerpts from Shi Nai'an and Luo Guanzhong, translated
> by Sidney Shapiro, *Outlaws of the Marsh* (Beijing: Foreign
> Languages Press, 1980), pp. 271–273, 881–882, 886–893,
> 895–897, 937–938.

The first several chapters introduce various corrupt government offi-
cials and their victims, who become outlaws. The following excerpt
introduces Song Jiang, who is on duty when Police Inspector Ho Tao
arrives to enlist the local magistrate's aid in capturing a thief named
Chao Gai. Ho Tao is waiting in a teahouse for a late morning recess
to end when the waiter points out the clerk on duty that day.

From Chapter 18

Ho Tao looked. Emerging from the magistracy was a man whose
family name was Song. His formal given name was Jiang, his popular
given name was Kongming. A third son, he was born in the county's
Song Family Village. Because he was short and swarthy, everyone
called him Dark Song Jiang. And since he was filial to his parents,
and was a chivalrous man, generous to friends, he was also known as
the Filial and Gallant Dark Third Master. Above him, his father was
still alive, though his mother had died early. Below him was a younger
brother Song Jing, known as the Iron Fan who, with their father, the
Venerable Song, ran the farm in the village and lived on the fruits of
their fields.

Song Jiang was a clerk of the county magistrate's court in Yuncheng.
He wrote legibly and well, and was familiar with administrative proce-
dures. Especially fond of playing with weapons, he was adept at many
forms of fighting. He made friends only in the gallant fraternity, but he
helped anyone, high or low, who sought his aid, providing his guest with
food and lodging in the family manor, tirelessly keeping him company,
and giving him travelling expenses when he wanted to leave. Song Jiang
scattered gold about like dust! He never refused a request for money.
He was always making things easy for people, solving their difficulties,
settling differences, saving lives. He provided the indigent with funds for
coffins and medicines, gave charity to the poor, assisted in emergencies,
helped in cases of hardship.

And so he was famed throughout the provinces of Shandong and Hebei, and was known to all as the Timely Rain, for like the rain from the heavens he brought succor to every living thing.

As Song Jiang walked from the magistracy with an attendant, Inspector Ho crossed the street to meet him.

"Won't you join me for some tea, sir Clerk?"

Song Jiang could tell from his appearance that Ho Tao was in the police.

"Where are you from, brother?" he queried courteously.

"If I may have the pleasure of your company in the tea-house we can talk there."

"As you wish, sir."

The two men entered the tea-house and sat down. Song Jiang told the attendant to wait outside. Then he turned to the inspector.

"May I presume to ask brother's name?"

"I am Ho Tao, a mere police inspector of Jizhou Prefecture. May I dare to ask your name, sir Clerk?"

"Forgive me for not having recognized you, Inspector. I'm a small official called Song Jiang."

Ho Tao fell to his knees and kowtowed. "I have long known your fame, but never had the honor of meeting you."

"You overwhelm me. Please sit at the head of the table."

"An insignificant person like me—I wouldn't dream of it!"

"As a member of our superior organization and a guest from afar, you must, Inspector."

They argued politely for a few moments. Then Song Jiang took the host's seat and Ho Tao's the guest's.

"Waiter," called the clerk, "two cups of tea." The refreshments soon came and both men drank.

"What instructions from above do you bring to our humble county, Inspector?" asked Song Jiang.

"I'll speak frankly. It concerns several important people here."

"It couldn't be about a robbery?"

"I've brought a sealed order. I trust you will help me carry it out."

"How could I do otherwise with an emissary from our superiors? Which robbery does it involve?"

"You're the keeper of the official records, sir Clerk. There's no harm in telling you. On Yellow Earth Ridge, which is under our prefect's jurisdiction, a band of eight robbers drugged fifteen men who were bringing birthday gifts from Governor Liang of Daming, the Northern Capital, to Premier Cai and made off with eleven loads of gold and jewels of an estimated value of a hundred thousand strings of cash. We've caught Bai Sheng, the accomplice. He says the other seven, the actual robbers, are all in this county. The Premier has sent an aide to our prefecture with orders to remain until we've caught them. We hope you'll give us every assistance."

"Of course we'll apprehend the criminals and turn them over. We'd do that on your orders, Inspector, to say nothing of orders from the Premier himself. Who are the seven named by Bai Sheng?"

"The leader is Ward Chief Chao of East Bank. To tell you the truth, we don't know the names of the other six. We beg your utmost diligence."

Song Jiang was shocked. He said to himself: "Chao Gai is one of my dearest friends! This crime he's committed is a capital offense! I must save him. If they capture him he's sure to die!"

Concealing his anxiety, Song Jiang said: "That dirty scoundrel. Everyone in the county hates him. So now he's come to this. We'll make him pay!"

"Please help us apprehend him."

"There won't be any difficulty. 'Easy as catching turtles in a jug. Just stretch out your hand,' as the old saying goes. But you'll have to present your order to the magistrate when the court is in session. He will read it and send men to make the arrest. I'm only a clerk. I couldn't assume responsibility for an important matter like this. What if word leaked out!"

"You're quite right. Please lead me in."

"The magistrate has been busy all morning and he's taking a short rest. If you'll wait a bit, court will be resumed soon. I'll call you."

"I hope you'll help us accomplish our mission, come what may."

"Naturally. That goes without saying. I must go home to attend to a few things. I'll be right back. Please sit and rest a while."

Song Jiang rushes to Chao Gai's home to warn him. Chao Gai and his accomplices flee to a village on the edge of Liangshan Marsh where they thoroughly defeat a large force led by Ho Tao by taking advantage of their knowledge of the marsh. Chao Gai and his men then join the outlaws already living in Liangshan Marsh, but their arrival precipitates a power struggle among them. Chao Gai is recruited to become the new leader of all the outlaws in the marsh. Meanwhile, Song Jiang's wife learns that her husband aided Chao Gai and tries to blackmail him but Song Jiang kills her and flees. Song Jiang is caught and exiled for the murder, but has relative freedom while in exile. One day after drinking too much, he writes a poem which the authorities interpret as threatening to lead a rebellion and he is sentenced to death. Chao Gai and his men rescue Song Jiang from execution and so Song Jiang joins the outlaws. In the next section, Marshal Gao urges the emperor to send a force against the outlaws because his cousin was killed when the outlaws attacked the city of Gaotang. The outlaws face their most serious threat so far.

From Chapter 55

"Let those with business present their petitions," intoned the chief of ceremonies.

Marshal Gao stepped forward and spoke. "Of late Chao Gai and Song Jiang, leaders of the bandits in Liangshan Marsh in Jizhou Prefecture, have committed a series of terrible crimes, plundering cities and robbing government granaries. In savage hordes they slaughtered government troops in Jizhou and ran riot in Jiangzhou and Wuweijun. Most recently, they wiped out the entire city of Gaotang and walked off with everything in the granary and treasury. They are like a canker in our vitals. If we don't quell them quickly they will grow so strong that we shall be unable to control them. I beseech Your Majesty to act."

The emperor was shocked. He ordered Gao to assemble an army, arrest the culprits, thoroughly purge the Marsh, and kill all such persons.

"We don't need a large army to deal with those petty outlaws. If Your Majesty will grant me a certain man, he will take care of them," said Gao.

"If you consider him so useful, he must be good. Have him go at once. Let us hear news of victory soon and we shall raise him in rank and reward him well. He will be given a high and important post."

"He is the direct descendant of Huyan Zan, the general from Hedong who won fame at the start of the dynasty. His name is Huyan Zhuo. He wields two steel rods and is a man of peerless courage. At present he is garrison commander of Runing Shire, and has under him many crack soldiers and brave officers. With the services of this man we can restore order to Liangshan Marsh. If given good officers and skilled troops and placed at their head, he will swiftly clean out the lair and return victorious."

Huyan Zhuo recruits two outstanding district garrison commanders, Han Tao and Peng Qi, to lead this expedition against the outlaws. [The names of those fighting for the imperial government are italicized to help the reader keep track of the numerous characters.]

"Along the River During the Qing Ming Festival" by Zhang Zeduan (1085–1145), detail of handscroll, ink on silk. The Song dynasty capital of Bianjing, the gate of which is shown here, was one of the largest cities in the world at the time with more than 400,000 people. *(Wikimedia Commons, Palace Museum, Beijing)*

To the mountain stronghold came a far-posted scout with a report of the approaching troops. Chao Gai and Song Jiang, together with Military Advisor Wu Yong, magic expert Gong-sun Sheng, and the various other chieftains, had been feasting daily in celebration with Chai Jin. When they heard that Two Rods *Huyan Zhuo* of Runing was leading an army of infantry and cavalry to attack, they conferred on strategy.

"I've heard of him," said Wu Yong. "He's a direct descendant of Huyan Zan, the general from Hedong who helped establish the dynasty. His skill with weapons is superb. When he wields those two steel rods of his no one can come near him. We must use our most competent and courageous officers. To capture him we'll have to apply first force and second guile."

Before the words were out of his mouth, Black Whirlwind Li Kui spoke up. "I'll nab the wretch for you!"

"You'd never do it," said Song Jiang. "I have a plan of my own. We'll ask Qin Ming the Thunderbolt to fight the first bout, Panther Head Lin Chong the second, Hua Rong the third, Ten Feet of Steel the fourth, and Sickly General Sun Li the fifth. These bouts must come one right after the next, like the spokes of a spinning wheel. I myself will head ten brothers who will command our main divisions. On the left will be Zhu Tong, Lei Heng, Mu Hong, Huang Xin and Lü Fang. On the right will be Yang Xiong, Shi Xiu, Ou Peng, Ma Lin and Guo Sheng. Our water approaches will be defended by boats under the command of Li Jun, Zhang Heng, Zhang Shun and the three Ruan brothers. Li Kui and Yang Lin will lead two columns of infantry and lie in ambush as reinforcements."

Shortly thereafter, Qin Ming went down the mountain with a unit of men and horses. They set up a battle position on a broad plain.

Although it was already winter, the weather was pleasantly warm. The next day, they saw in the distance the approaching government troops. The van, led by Ever-Victorious General *Han Tao,* made camp and built surrounding palisades. There was no fighting that night.

The two armies faced each other at dawn the following day. Horns blared, and the thunder of drums shook the heavens. On Song Jiang's side Qin Ming the Thunderbolt rode forth from the arch of pennants, his wolf-toothed mace athwart his mount. On the opposite side at the arch of pennants appeared *Han Tao,* leader of the van. Holding his lance crosswise, he gave his horse rein and shouted at his foe.

"We heavenly hosts have arrived! But instead of surrendering, you dare to resist! You're asking to die! I'll fill in your marsh and pulverize your Mount Liangshan! I'll capture you rebellious bandits, take you to the capital, and have you smashed to bits!"

Qin Ming was a hot-tempered man. Without a word, he clapped his steed, and rode straight at *Han Tao,* flourishing his mace. *Han Tao* kicked up his horse, levelled his lance, and galloped to meet him. They fought over twenty rounds, and *Han Tao* began to weaken. He turned to go. From behind him came *Huyan Zhuo,* commander of the main contingent. He saw that *Han Tao* was being bested, and he charged forth on the snowy-hoofed black steed the emperor had given him, roaring and waving his steel rods.

Qin Ming recognized him, and prepared to do battle. But Lin Chong the Panther Head cantered up, calling: "Rest a while, commander. Let me go three hundred rounds with this fellow, then we'll see."

Lin Chong levelled his serpent-decorated lance and charged *Huyan.* Qin Ming wheeled his mount to the left and rode out of sight behind a bend. The new adversaries were evenly matched. The lance and rods interwove in flowery patterns for more than fifty rounds, but neither man could vanquish the other.

Hua Rong appeared for the third bout. At the entrance to the field of combat he called: "Rest a while, General Lin Chang. Watch me capture the lout."

Panther Head turned his horse and departed. *Huyan* had seen enough of his high-powered use of weapons. He let him go and returned to his own position, while Lin Chong disappeared around a bend with his men. *Huyan* was already among his rear column when Hua Rong emerged with lance at the level. *Peng Qi* the Eyes of Heaven General, astride a glossy brown piebald that could run a thousand *li* in a day, rode towards Hua Rong. Holding crosswise his three-pointed, two-edged, four-holed, eight-ringed weapon, Peng shouted: "Traitorous robber! You're devoid of all morality! Let's fight this one to a finish!"

Hua Rong was furious. Without a word, he clashed with *Peng Qi*. More than twenty rounds they battled. *Huyan* could see that *Peng* was weakening. He gave his horse rein and engaged Hua Rong.

Before they had fought three rounds, the girl warrior Ten Feet of Steel rode out for the fourth round. "Rest a while, General Hua Rong," she cried. "Watch me take this oaf!"

Hua Rong led his contingent off to the right and departed round a bend. Even before the battle between *Peng Qi* and Ten Feet of Steel approached a decisive stage, Sun Li the Sickly General, who would fight the fifth bout, had already arrived. He had reined his horse at the edge of the field of combat and was watching the two contestants.

They fought in a cloud of dust with murderous intensity, one with a long-handled sabre, the other with a pair of swords. For over twenty rounds they battled. Then the girl separated her blades and rode off. *Peng Qi*, eager for glory, gave chase. Ten Feet of Steel hung her swords on the pommel of her saddle. From inside her robe she pulled out a red lariat bearing twenty-four gold hooks. She let *Peng Qi* draw near, then suddenly twisted around and flung the rope. The noose landed squarely on him before he could ward it off, and he was dragged from his horse. Sun Li yelled a command, and his men rushed forward and grabbed the fallen rider.

Huyan, enraged, galloped to the rescue. Ten Feet of Steel lapped her steed and met him. The seething *Huyan* would have swallowed her down in one gulp, if he could. They battled more than ten rounds, *Huyan* increasingly frantic because he couldn't defeat the girl. "What a spitfire," he fretted. "After all this fighting, she's still so tough!"

Impatiently, he feinted and let her close in, then raised his steel rods and started to bring them down. The swords were still in their resting place when the rod in *Huyan's* right hand was only a hair away from the girl's forehead. But Ten Feet of Steel was clear of eye and swift of hand. A sword sprang into her right fist, flew up and warded off the blow with a clang of metal and a shower of sparks.

The girl galloped back towards her own position. *Huyan* raced in pursuit. Sun Li promptly levelled his lance, intercepted *Huyan* and engaged him in fierce combat. Song Jiang moved up with his ten divisions and deployed them in battle formation. Ten Feet of Steel and her contingent, meanwhile, had ridden away down the slope.

Song Jiang was very pleased that *Peng Qi* the Eyes of Heaven General had been taken. He rode to the front to watch Sun Li and *Huyan* do battle. Sun Li sheathed his lance and went at *Huyan* with the steel rod ribbed like bamboo, which had been hanging from his wrist. Now, both were wielding rods of steel. Even their style of dress was similar. Sun Li wore a five-cornered iron helmet bound in place by a red silk band around his forehead, a white-flowered black silk robe flecked with jade green, and darkly gleaming gold embossed armor. He rode a black stallion, and wielded a bamboo-shaped steel rod with dragon's eyes. Truly, a bolder picture than Yuchi Gong, that hero of old.

As to *Huyan Zhuo*, he wore a high pointed five-cornered helmet bound round the forehead by gold-flecked yellow silk, a black robe with sequins of seven stars, and darkly gleaming armor of over-lapping leaf. He rode the snowy-hoofed black stallion given him by the emperor, and wielded two octagonal steel rods polished bright as water. The one in his left hand weighed twelve catties, the one in his right thirteen. He indeed resembled his ancestor Huyan Zan.

Left and right over the field of combat they fought for more than thirty rounds, with neither man the victor.

When *Han Tao* saw *Peng Qi* captured, he quickly gathered the rear column and led them forward in a headlong rush. Song Jiang, afraid that they would break through, pointed his whip, and his ten commanders moved their divisions up to meet them, the last two spreading out in an enveloping pincers. *Huyan* hurriedly wheeled his columns around and each engaged their adversaries.

Why didn't the Liangshan warriors win total victory? Because of *Huyan's* "Armored Cavalry." Both horses and men wore chainmail. The battle steeds were draped to their hoofs, the soldiers protected to the eyes. Although Song Jiang's animals were equipped with some cover, this consisted mainly of red-tasseled net masks, copper bells, and plumes.

The arrows sped by his archers were easily deflected by the chainmail. And all three thousand of *Huyan's* cavalry were armed with bows. They spewed flights of arrows which discouraged the men of Liangshan from coming any closer.

Song Jiang hastily had the horns sound the call to withdraw. *Huyan* also pulled his forces back twenty *li*, where they made camp.

The Song Jiang army encamped west of the mountain and settled their horses. At Song Jiang's command, his swordsmen hustled *Peng Qi* forward. Shouting for them to fall back, Song Jiang rose and untied his captive's bonds, then escorted him into the headquarters tent. He seated *Peng Qi* as a guest and kowtowed. *Peng Qi* at once returned the courtesy.

"I am your prisoner. By rights I should be killed. Why are you treating me with such courtesy, General?"

"Most of us are hunted men who have taken temporary shelter in the Marsh. The imperial court has sent you, General, here to arrest us. The proper thing for me would be to submit and be bound. But I fear for my life. And so I've criminally clashed with you. I beg your forgiveness for my presumptuousness."

"I have long known of your fraternal devotion and righteousness, of your aid to the endangered and your succor to the needy. But I never expected such chivalry! If you will spare my miserable life, I will serve you with every breath in my body!"

That day Song Jiang had the Eyes of Heaven General *Peng Qi* escorted to the mountain fortress to be introduced to Chao Gai and given refuge there. After rewarding his three armies, he conferred with his commanders on the military situation.

Meanwhile, *Huyan Zhuo* discussed with *Han Tao* how to vanquish Liangshan Marsh.

"Today, those louts moved forward in a quick covering action when they saw us coming at them," said *Han Tao*. "Tomorrow, we ought to hit them with our entire cavalry. That way, a big victory will be guaranteed."

"Exactly what I had in mind. I just wanted to make sure you agreed."

Huyan then ordered that all three thousand of the cavalry be stretched out in a single line, divided into troops of thirty, and that all the horses in each troop be connected together by chains. On nearing the foe, the men were to use arrows at a distance and their lances when they got close, and drive relentlessly ahead. The three thousand armored cavalry would become one hundred platoons, each locked in solid formation. Five thousand infantry would follow as support.

"Don't challenge them in person, tomorrow," *Huyan* admonished *Han Tao*. "You and I will stay behind with the reinforcements. When the fighting starts, we'll rush them from three sides."

It was decided they would go into action the next day at dawn.

The following day Song Jiang set five troops of cavalry to the fore, backed by the ten divisions, with two contingents to left and right lying in ambush.

Qin Ming rode forth and challenged *Huyan*. But the imperial troops only shouted, and no one appeared. The five Liangshan cavalry units spread out in a line. Qin Ming was in the center, Lin Chong and Ten Feet of Steel were on the left, Hua Rong and Sun Li were on the right. The ten divisions under Song Jiang stood to the rear, a dense mass of men and horses. About a thousand imperial foot soldiers were arrayed opposite. Although they beat their drums and yelled, not a single man rode out to joust.

Song Jiang grew suspicious. He quietly gave the order for his rear forces to withdraw, then rode up to Hua Rong's contingent to look. Suddenly, a volley of cannon fire erupted from the opposite side. The thousand imperial foot soldiers separated into two sections and platoons of linked cavalry poured through in an enveloping three-sided phalanx. Arrows winged from both flanks. The middle bristled with long lances.

Startled, Song Jiang ordered his archers to reply. But how could they withstand this assault? Every animal in the thirty-horse platoons galloped together, unable to hold back even if it wanted to. From all over the hills and plains the linked cavalry charged.

Song Jiang's forward five cavalry units were thrown into a panic. They couldn't stem the tide. The rear divisions, also unable to make a stand, broke and ran. Song Jiang raced away on his horse, guarded by his ten commanders.

A platoon of imperial linked cavalry closed in after them. Li Kui, Yang Lin and their men rose out of their ambush in the reeds and drove them off. Song Jiang fled to the water's edge. Li Jun, Zhang Heng, Zhang Shun and the three Ruan brothers were waiting with war boats. Song Jiang hurriedly boarded one of the craft and ordered them to rescue the chieftains and get them into the boats, quickly.

A platoon of linked cavalry rode right up to the river and showered the craft with arrows, but shields blocked the arrows and no one was hurt. The boats were rowed hastily to Duck's Bill Shore, where everyone disembarked. In the fort there a count was made. They had lost more than half their effectives. Fortunately all of the chieftains had been saved, although several of their mounts had been killed.

Shortly thereafter, Shi Yong, Shi Qian, Sun Xin and Mistress Gu arrived. "The imperial infantry swarmed all over us," they reported. "They levelled our inns and houses. If our boats hadn't rescued us, we would have been captured."

Song Jiang consoled them and took stock of his commanders. Six had arrow wounds—Lin Chong, Lei Heng, Li Kui, Shi Xiu, Sun Xin and Huang Xin. Innumerable lesser chieftains had also been struck by arrows or otherwise wounded.

When Chao Gai learned of this, he came down the mountain with Wu Yong and Gongsun Sheng. They found Song Jiang frowning and depressed.

"Don't fret, brother," Wu Yong said soothingly. "Both victory and defeat are common fare for the soldier. Why worry? We'll work out a good plan to deal with that linked cavalry."

Chao Gai ordered the naval forces to strengthen the shore stockades, repair the boats, and guard the beaches day and night. He urged Song Jiang to return to the mountain stronghold and rest. But Song insisted on remaining at the fort on Duck's Bill Shore. He agreed only that the wounded commanders should go up and recuperate.

The imperial forces are encouraged by their success and plan to push their advantage by employing a cannon expert, Ling Zhen, to enable them to attack the outlaws' lair from a distance.

Song Jiang, in the Duck's Bill Shore fort, conferred with Wu Yong on how to achieve a breakthrough on the battlefield. But they could not think of anything.

A spy entered and reported: "The Eastern Capital has sent a cannoneer, *Ling Zhen*, Heaven-Shaking Thunder. He's set up guns near the river and he's getting ready to bombard our forts."

"It doesn't matter," said Wu Yong. "Our mountain stronghold is surrounded by a marsh which is full of creeks and ponds. It's a long way from the river. Even if he has guns that can reach the sky, he'll never hit it. We'll just abandon this fort on Duck's Bill Shore and let him shoot. Then we'll talk some more."

Song Jiang left the fort and returned to the mountain stronghold. Chao Gai and Gongsun Sheng escorted him to Fraternity Hall.

"How are we going to crack the enemy?" they asked.

Almost before the words were out of their mouths, they heard the boom of artillery at the foot of the mountain. Three cannon balls were fired. Two landed in the river. A third scored a direct hit on the Duck's Bill Shore fort.

Song Jiang watched glumly. The other leaders blanched.

"If *Ling Zhen* could be inveigled to the river we could nab him," said Wu Yong. "Then we could discuss what to do about the enemy."

"We'll send Li Jun, Zhang Heng, Zhang Shun and the three Ruan brothers in charge of six boats. Zhu Tong and Lei Heng will be on the opposite shore," said Chao Gai. And he told what each would do.

The six naval leaders received their orders and divided into two units. Li Jun and Zhang Heng took forty or fifty good swimmers in two fast craft and slipped across through the reeds. Backing them were Zhang Shun and the three Ruan brothers with another forty or so men in a fleet of small boats. On reaching the shore, Li Jun and Zhang Heng and their men, shouting and yelling, charged up to the cannon mountings and knocked them over.

Soldiers hurriedly reported this to *Ling Zhen*, who at once took two Fireball cannon and his lance, mounted his horse, and hastened to the scene with a thousand soldiers. Only then did Li Jun and Zhang Heng and their men leave. *Ling Zhen* chased them as far as the reedy shore, where a line of forty small craft, manned by a hundred or more sailors, were moored.

Li and Zhang went aboard, but didn't cast off. When *Ling Zhen* and his force came in sight, everyone on the boats shouted and jumped into the water.

Ling Zhen's men seized the boats. Zhu Tong and Lei Heng, on the opposite shore, began yelling and pounding drums. *Ling Zhen* ordered his soldiers to board the craft and go across and get them.

When the boats reached the middle of the river, Zhu Tong and Lei Heng struck a gong loudly. Forty or fifty swimmers rose from beneath the waves and pulled the plugs from sterns. Water flooded the craft. Strong hands capsized many of the boats, dumping the soldiers into the river.

Ling Zhen made haste to go back, but his craft's rudder had already been removed under water. Two of the chieftains clambered aboard. With one quick rock, they turned it bottom up. *Ling Zhen* landed in the water. He was grabbed by Ruan the Second from below and dragged ashore. There, other chieftains who were waiting had him bound and taken up the mountain.

Over two hundred soldiers were captured. More than half of the remainder had been drowned. The few who escaped with their lives reported to *Huyan Zhuo*. He hastily mustered his forces and galloped to the rescue. But the boats had already crossed to Duck's Bill Shore. It was too far for arrows. Besides, the raiders were gone.

Ling Zhen is invited to join the outlaws and agrees to do so. To finally defeat Huyan's linked cavalry, the outlaws recruit a man who knows how to make barbed lances and a man to teach them how to use them. With the help of these men's weapons and tactics and the cannoneer, the outlaws ambush and rout Huyan's forces and eventually capture Huyan himself by luring him into a trap.

Song Jiang returned to camp and took his seat. Knife-wearing attendants pushed *Huyan Zhuo* before him. Song immediately rose and ordered that his bonds be removed. He personally conducted *Huyan* to a chair and greeted him respectfully.

"Why are you doing this?" *Huyan* asked.

"Would I be ungrateful to the imperial court?" Song Jiang retorted. "I was hard pressed by corrupt officials and forced to commit a crime. I've had to seek refuge in this marsh while awaiting an imperial pardon. I never expected to stir into action so mighty a general, for whom I have such great admiration. It was very wrong of me, and I beg your forgiveness."

"I am your prisoner. Ten thousand deaths would be too light punishment. Yet you treat me with such courtesy!"

"Never would I presume to harm you. Heaven is my witness."

"Is it your wish, respected brother, that I should go to the Eastern Capital and ask for a royal pardon to bring to your mountain?"

"You couldn't possibly do that, General! Marshal Gao is a narrow-hearted villain. He forgets a man's large accomplishments and remembers only his small failings. You've lost a lot of troops, money and grain. He'd surely hold you culpable. *Han Tao, Peng Qi* and *Ling Zhen* have all joined our band. If you don't scorn our mountain stronghold as too humble, I'd be happy to relinquish to you my place as chieftain. When the court has use for us and issues its imperial pardon, we can once again serve our country with our utmost efforts."

Huyan hesitated for several minutes. But, firstly, since he was one of the stars of Heavenly Spirits, he naturally was of the same chivalrous mentality. And, secondly, he was overwhelmed by Song Jiang's courtesy and reasonableness. With a sigh, he knelt.

"It's not that I lack loyalty to the government. But your exceeding gallantry leaves me no choice but to agree. I'll follow you faithfully. The situation being what it is, there's no alternative."

13

Short Stories

Lu Xun

"Lu Xun" (1930), photograph. *(Wikimedia Commons)*

Lu Xun (1881–1936) was born into a family of scholar-officials that lost all its power and wealth due to corruption and illness. He had a traditional education in the Confucian classics before turning to Western science and literature. He was studying to become a medical doctor when he decided he could best help a weak and backward China by writing literature that might inspire its people to change. He became the most celebrated author of his time, a leader in the movement to create realistic fiction in the vernacular; he also wrote essays and prose poetry and worked as an editor and translator. His works of social criticism focused on the crushing cruelty and ignorance in Chinese society, but he hoped his writing would help lead the way to a better future for China.

"Kong Yiji" was first published in March 1919 and "A Small Incident" in July 1920. Dark as these two stories are, they are more positive than most of Lu Xun's work.

Questions

1. The narrator reports that Kong was lazy and too fond of drinking. What else can be said about Kong's character?
2. Why did the narrator give a handful of coins to the policeman for the rickshaw man in the story "A Small Incident"?
3. What social ills are depicted in these stories?

Short Stories by Lu Xun

> Short Stories: "Kong Yiji" and "A Small Incident" from Lu Xun, translated by Xianyi Yang and Gladys Yang, *Lu Xun, Selected Works* (Beijing: Foreign Languages Press, 2003), pp. 52–57, 76–78. See also Lu Xun, translated by Julia Lovell, *The Real Story of Ah-Q and Other Tales of China: The Complete Fiction of Lu Xun* (London: Penguin Books, 2009).

Kong Yiji

The layout of Luzhen's taverns is unique. In each, facing you as you enter, is a bar in the shape of a carpenter's square where hot water is kept ready for warming rice wine. When men come off work at midday and in the evening they spend four coppers on a bowl of wine—or so they did twenty years ago; now it costs ten—and drink this warm, standing by the bar, taking it easy. Another copper will buy a plate of salted bamboo shoots or peas flavoured with aniseed to go with the wine, while a dozen will buy a meat dish; but most of the customers here belong to the short-coated class,[1] few of whom can afford this. As for those in long gowns,[2] they go into the inner room to order wine and dishes and sit drinking at their leisure.

At the age of twelve I started work as a pot-boy in Prosperity Tavern at the edge of the town. The boss put me to work in the outer room, saying that I looked too much of a fool to serve long-gowned customers. The short-coated customers there were easier to deal with, it is true, but among them were quite a few pernickety ones who insisted on watching for themselves while the yellow wine was ladled from the keg, looked for water at the bottom of the wine-pot, and personally inspected the pot's immersion into the hot water. Under such strict surveillance, diluting the wine was very hard indeed. Thus it did not take my boss many days to decide that this job too was beyond me. Luckily I had been recommended by somebody influential, so he could not sack me. Instead I was transferred to the dull task of simply warming wine.

After that I stood all day behind the bar attending to my duties. Although I gave satisfaction at this post, I found it somewhat boring and monotonous. Our boss was a grim-faced man, nor were the customers much pleasanter, which made the atmosphere a gloomy one. The only times when there was any laughter were when Kong Yiji came to the tavern. That is why I remember him.

Kong Yiji was the only long-gowned customer who used to drink his wine standing. A big, pallid man whose wrinkled face often bore scars, he had a large, unkempt and grizzled beard. And although he wore a long gown it was dirty and tattered. It had not by the look of it been washed or mended for ten years or more. He used so many archaisms in his speech that half of it was barely intelligible. And as his surname was Kong, he was given the nickname Kong Yiji from *kong*, *yi*, *ji*, the first three characters in the old-fashioned children's copybook. Whenever he came in, everyone there would look at him and chuckle. And someone was sure to call out:

"Kong Yiji! What are those fresh scars on your face?"

Ignoring this, he would lay nine coppers on the bar and order two bowls of heated wine with a dish of aniseed-peas. Then someone else would bawl:

"You must have been stealing again!"

"Why sully a man's good name for no reason at all?" Kong Yiji would ask, raising his eyebrows.

"Good name? Why, the day before yesterday you were trussed up and beaten for stealing books from the Ho family. I saw you!"

At that Kong Yiji would flush, the veins on his forehead standing out as he protested, "Taking books can't be counted as stealing. . . . Taking books . . . for a scholar . . . can't be counted as stealing." Then followed such quotations from the classics as "A gentleman keeps his integrity even in poverty," together with a spate of archaisms which soon had everybody roaring with laughter, enlivening the whole tavern.

From the gossip that I heard, it seemed that Kong Yiji had studied the classics but never passed the official examinations and, not knowing any way to make a living, he had grown steadily poorer until he was almost reduced to beggary. Luckily he was a good calligrapher and could find enough copying work to fill his rice bowl. But unfortunately he had his failings too: laziness and a love of tippling. So after a few days he would disappear, taking with him books, paper, brushes and ink-stone. And after this had happened several times, people stopped employing him as a copyist. Then all he could do was resort to occasional pilfering. In our tavern, though, he was a model customer who never failed to pay up. Sometimes, it is true, when he had no ready money, his name would be chalked up on our tally-board; but in less than a month he invariably settled the bill, and the name Kong Yiji would be wiped off the board again.

After Kong Yiji had drunk half a bowl of wine, his flushed cheeks would stop burning. But then someone would ask:

"Kong Yiji, can you really read?"

When he glanced back as if such a question were not worth answering, they would continue, "How is it you never passed even the lowest official examination?"

At once a grey tinge would overspread Kong Yiji's dejected, discomfited face, and he would mumble more of those unintelligible archaisms. Then everyone there would laugh heartily again, enlivening the whole tavern.

At such times I could join in the laughter with no danger of a dressing-down from my boss. In fact he always put such questions to Kong Yiji himself, to raise a laugh. Knowing that it was no use talking to the men, Kong Yiji would chat with us boys. Once he asked me: "Have you had any schooling?"

When I nodded curtly he said, "Well then, I'll test you. How do you write the *hui*[3] in aniseed-peas?"

Who did this beggar think he was, testing me! I turned away and ignored him. After waiting for some time he said earnestly:

"You can't write it, eh? I'll show you. Mind you remember. You ought to remember such characters, because you'll need them to write up your accounts when you have a shop of your own."

It seemed to me that I was still very far from having a shop of my own; in addition to which, our boss never entered aniseed-peas in his account-book. Half amused and half exasperated, I drawled, "I don't need you to show me. Isn't it the *hui* written with the element for grass?"

Kong Yiji's face lit up. Tapping two long finger-nails on the bar, he nodded. "Quite correct!" he said. "There are four different ways of writing *hui*. Do you know them?"

But my patience exhausted, I scowled and moved away. Kong Yiji had dipped his finger in wine to trace the characters on the bar. When he saw my utter indifference his face fell and he sighed.

Sometimes children in the neighbourhood, hearing laughter, came in to join in the fun and surrounded Kong Yiji. Then he would give them aniseed-peas, one apiece. After eating the peas the children would still hang round, their eyes fixed on the dish. Growing flustered, he would cover it with his hand and bending forward from the waist would say, "There aren't many left, not many at all." Straightening up to look at the peas again, he would shake his head and reiterate, "Not many, I do assure you. Not many, nay, not many at all." Then the children would scamper off, shouting with laughter.

That was how Kong Yiji contributed to our enjoyment, but we got along all right without him too.

One day, shortly before the Mid-Autumn Festival[4] I think it was, my boss who was slowly making out his accounts took down the tally-board. "Kong Yiji hasn't shown up for a long time," he remarked suddenly. "He still owes nineteen coppers." That made me realize how long it was since we had seen him.

"How could he?" rejoined one of the customers. "His legs were broken in that last beating up."

"Ah!" said my boss.

"He'd been stealing again. This time he was fool enough to steal from Mr. Ding, the provincial-grade scholar. As if anybody could get away with that!"

"So what happened?"

"What happened? First he wrote a confession, then he was beaten. The beating lasted nearly all night, and they broke both his legs."

"And then?"

"Well, his legs were broken."

"Yes, but after?"

"After? . . . Who knows? He may be dead."

My boss asked no further questions but went on slowly making up his accounts.

After the Mid-Autumn Festival the wind grew daily colder as winter approached, and even though I spent all my time by the stove I had to wear a padded jacket. One afternoon, when the tavern was deserted, as I sat with my eyes closed I heard the words:

"Warm a bowl of wine."

It was said in a low but familiar voice. I opened my eyes. There was no one to be seen. I stood up to look out. There below the bar, facing the door, sat Kong Yiji. His face was thin and grimy—he looked a wreck. He had on a ragged lined jacket and was squatting cross-legged on a mat which was attached to his shoulders by a straw rope. When he saw me he repeated:

"Warm a bowl of wine."

At this point my boss leaned over the bar to ask, "Is that Kong Yiji? You still owe nineteen coppers."

"That . . . I'll settle next time." He looked up dejectedly. "Here's cash. Give me some good wine."

My boss, just as in the past, chuckled and said: "Kong Yiji, you've been stealing again!"

But instead of a stout denial, the answer simply was: "Don't joke with me."

"Joke? How did your legs get broken if you hadn't been stealing?"

"I fell," whispered Kong Yiji. "Broke them in a fall." His eyes pleaded with the boss to let the matter drop. By now several people had gathered round, and they all laughed with the boss. I warmed the wine, carried it over, and set it on the threshold. He produced four coppers from his ragged coat pocket, and as he placed them in my hand I saw that his own hands were covered with mud—he must have crawled there on them. Presently he finished the wine and, to the accompaniment of taunts and laughter, slowly pushed himself off with his hands.

A long time went by after that without our seeing Kong Yiji again. At the end of the year, when the boss took down the tally-board he said, "Kong Yiji still owes nineteen coppers." At the Dragon-Boat Festival[5] the next year he said the same thing again. But when the Mid-Autumn Festival arrived he was silent on the subject, and another New Year came round without our seeing any more of Kong Yiji.

Nor have I ever seen him since—no doubt Kong Yiji really is dead.

A Small Incident

Six years have slipped by since I came from the country to the capital. During that time the number of so-called affairs of state I have witnessed or heard about is far from small, but none of them made much impression. If asked to define their influence on me, I can only say they made my bad temper worse. Frankly speaking, they taught me to take a poorer view of people every day.

One small incident, however, which struck me as significant and jolted me out of my irritability, remains fixed even now in my memory.

It was the winter of 1917, a strong north wind was blustering, but the exigencies of earning my living forced me to be up and out early. I met scarcely a soul on the road, but eventually managed to hire a rickshaw to take me to S-Gate. Presently the wind dropped a little, having blown away the drifts of dust on the road to leave a clean broad highway, and the rickshaw man quickened his pace. We were just approaching S-Gate when we knocked into someone who slowly toppled over.

It was a grey-haired woman in ragged clothes. She had stepped out abruptly from the roadside in front of us, and although the rickshaw man had swerved, her tattered padded waistcoat, unbuttoned and billowing in the wind, had caught on the shaft. Luckily the rickshaw man had slowed down, otherwise she would certainly have had a bad fall and it might have been a serious accident.

She huddled there on the ground, and the rickshaw man stopped. As I did not believe the old woman was hurt and as no one else had seen us, I thought this halt of his uncalled for, liable to land him in trouble and hold me up.

"It's all right," I said. "Go on."

He paid no attention—he may not have heard—but set down the shafts, took the old woman's arm and gently helped her up.

"Are you all right?" he asked.

"I hurt myself falling."

I thought: I saw how slowly you fell, how could you be hurt? Putting on an act like this is simply disgusting. The rickshaw man asked for trouble, and now he's got it. He'll have to find his own way out.

But the rickshaw man did not hesitate for a minute after hearing the old woman's answer. Still holding her arm, he helped her slowly forward. Rather puzzled by this I looked ahead and saw a police-station. Because of the high wind, there was no one outside. It was there that the rickshaw man was taking the old woman.

Suddenly I had the strange sensation that his dusty retreating figure had in that instant grown larger. Indeed, the further he walked the larger he loomed, until I had to look up to him. At the same time he seemed gradually to be exerting a pressure on me which threatened to overpower the small self hidden under my fur-lined gown.

Almost paralyzed at that juncture I sat there motionless, my mind a blank, until a policeman came out. Then I got down from the rickshaw.

The policeman came up to me and said, "Get another rickshaw. He can't take you any further."

On the spur of the moment I pulled a handful of coppers from my coat pocket and handed them to the policeman. "Please give him this," I said.

The wind had dropped completely, but the road was still quiet. As I walked along thinking, I hardly dared to think about myself. Quite apart from what had happened earlier, what had I meant by that handful of coppers? Was it a reward? Who was I to judge the rickshaw man? I could give myself no answer.

Even now, this incident keeps coming back to me. It keeps distressing me and makes me try to think about myself. The politics and the fighting of those years have slipped my mind as completely as the classics I read as a child. Yet this small incident keeps coming back to me, often more vivid than in actual life, teaching me shame, spurring me on to reform, and imbuing me with fresh courage and fresh hope.

Notes

1. "The short-coated class" is a reference to manual laborers.
2. Wearing a long gown is a signal that one is a scholar.
3. A Chinese character meaning "aniseed."
4. The fifteenth day of the eighth lunar month.
5. The fifth day of the fifth month.

14

Essays

MAO ZEDONG

"Portrait of Mao Zedong at Tiananmen Gate," attributed to Zhang Zhenshi (1914–1992) and a committee of artists, weighs 1.5 tons and is generally replaced yearly or if vandalized. The current image was painted by Ge Xiaoguang (b. 1953). *(Wikimedia Commons)*

Mao Zedong (1893–1976) was born into a relatively well-off farming family in Hunan province and was educated in the city of Changsha, Hunan, where he was exposed to the socially progressive ideas of China's New Culture Movement. In 1919 he moved to Beijing, where he joined a Marxist study group that went on to found the Chinese Communist Party (CCP) two years later. Although the CCP's initial approach to transforming Chinese society was focused on organizing the urban working class into a revolutionary force, Mao was among the first party members to realize the extent of the political power that China's vast and impoverished rural population might wield if the party could help the peasants to seize it. In his "Report on an Investigation of the Peasant Movement in Hunan," Mao articulated many of the principles that would later guide the CCP as it led a successful, peasant-based revolution against the ruling Guomindang (Kwangtung), or Nationalist, Party in the late 1940s. "Preserve the Style of Plain Living and Hard Struggle," written twenty-two years later, just before the CCP came to power in October 1949, articulates an additional set of fundamental Maoist principles. Taken together, these two pieces highlight the main tenets of Maoist thought and reveal the ideology that guided CCP policy from the mid-1930s, when Mao rose to ascendancy within the party, until his death in September 1976. If you consult the footnotes at the end of this section, you will notice the careful use of approved Communist terminology to describe past events in Chinese history. No other way of interpreting or describing past events would have been permissible in China in the early 1970s.

Questions

1. In his report on the Hunan peasant movement, what group of people does Mao see as having great revolutionary potential, and what is it about their world that he thinks they might want to change?
2. Class struggle became an important theme in Maoist movements. What does Mao have to say about class in these documents? In what ways is class connected to tradition?
3. According to Mao, what virtues should good Communists have, and how can they stay on the right path?
4. What fundamental principles of Maoist thought can you identify in these readings?

Essays by Mao Zedong

Essays by Mao Zedong from *Selected Readings from the Works of Mao Tse-tung* (Peking: Foreign Languages Press, 1971), pp. 23–39, 362–363.

Report on an Investigation of the Peasant Movement in Hunan.[1] March 1927

The Importance of the Peasant Problem

During my recent visit to Hunan[2] I made a first-hand investigation of conditions in the five counties of Hsiangtan, Hsianghsiang, Hengshan, Liling and Changsha. In the thirty-two days from January 4 to February 5, I called together fact-finding conferences in villages and county towns, which were attended by experienced peasants and by comrades working in the peasant movement, and I listened attentively to their reports and collected a great deal of material. Many of the hows and whys of the peasant movement were the exact opposite of what the gentry in Hankow and Changsha are saying. I saw and heard of many strange things of which I had hitherto been unaware. I believe the same is true of many other places, too. All talk directed against the peasant movement must be speedily set right. All the wrong measures taken by the revolutionary authorities concerning the peasant movement must be speedily changed. Only thus can the future of the revolution be benefited. For the present upsurge of the peasant movement is a colossal event. In a very short time, in China's central, southern and northern provinces, several hundred million peasants will rise like a mighty storm, like a hurricane, a force so swift and violent that no power, however great, will be able to hold it back. They will smash all the trammels that bind them and rush forward along the road to liberation. They will sweep all the imperialists, warlords, corrupt officials, local tyrants and evil gentry into their graves. Every revolutionary party and every revolutionary comrade will be put to the test, to be accepted or rejected as they decide. There are three alternatives. To march at their head and lead them? To trail behind them, gesticulating and criticizing? Or to stand in their way and oppose them? Every Chinese is free to choose, but events will force you to make the choice quickly.

Get Organized!

The development of the peasant movement in Hunan may be divided roughly into two periods with respect to the counties in the province's central and southern parts where the movement has already made much headway. The first, from January to September of last year, was one of organization. In this period, January to June was a time of underground activity, and July to September, when the revolutionary army was driving out Chao Heng-ti[3] one of open activity. During this period, the membership of the peasant associations did not exceed 300,000–400,000, the masses directly under their leadership numbered little more than a million, there was as yet hardly any struggle in the rural areas, and consequently there was very little criticism of the associations in other circles. Since their members served as guides, scouts and carriers of the Northern Expeditionary Army, even some of the officers had a good word to say for the peasant associations. The second period, from last October to January of this year, was one of revolutionary action. The membership of the associations jumped to two million and the masses directly under their leadership increased to ten million. Since the peasants generally enter only one name for the whole family on joining a peasant association, a membership of two million means a mass following of about ten million. Almost half the peasants in Hunan are now organized. In counties like Hsiangtan, Hsianghsiang, Liuyang, Changsha, Liling, Ninghsiang, Pingkiang, Hsiangyin, Hengshan, Hengyang, Leiyang, Chenhsien and Anhua, nearly all the peasants have combined in the peasant associations or have come under their leadership. It was on the strength of their extensive organization that the peasants went into action and within four months brought about a great revolution in the countryside, a revolution without parallel in history.

Down With the Local Tyrants and Evil Gentry!
All Power to the Peasant Associations!

The main targets of attack by the peasants are the local tyrants, the evil gentry and the lawless landlords, but in passing they also hit out against patriarchal ideas and institutions, against the corrupt officials in the cities and against bad practices and customs in the rural areas. In force and momentum the attack is tempestuous; those who bow before it survive and those who resist perish. As a result, the privileges which the feudal landlords enjoyed for thousands of years are being shattered to pieces. Every bit of the dignity and prestige built up by the landlords is being swept into the dust. With the collapse of the power of the landlords, the peasant associations have now become the sole organs of authority and the popular slogan "All power to the peasant associations" has become a reality. Even trifles such as a quarrel between husband and wife are brought to the peasant association. Nothing can be settled unless someone from the peasant association is present. The association actually dictates all rural affairs, and, quite literally, "whatever it says, goes." Those who are outside the associations can only speak well of them and cannot say anything against them. The local tyrants, evil gentry and lawless landlords have been deprived of all right to speak, and none of them dares even mutter dissent. In the face of the peasant associations' power and pressure, the top local tyrants and evil gentry have fled to Shanghai, those of the second rank to Hankow, those of the third to Changsha and those of the fourth to the county towns, while the fifth rank and the still lesser fry surrender to the peasant associations in the villages.

"Here's ten yuan. Please let me join the peasant association," one of the smaller of the evil gentry will say.

"Ugh! Who wants your filthy money?" the peasants reply.

Many middle and small landlords and rich peasants and even some middle peasants, who were all formerly opposed to the peasant associations, are now vainly seeking admission. Visiting various places, I often came across such people who pleaded with me, "Mr. Committeeman from the provincial capital, please be my sponsor!"

In the Ching Dynasty, the household census compiled by the local authorities consisted of a regular register and "the other" register, the former for honest people and the latter for burglars, bandits and similar undesirables. In some places the peasants now use this method to scare those who formerly opposed the associations. They say, "Put their names down in the other register!"

Afraid of being entered in the other register, such people try various devices to gain admission into the peasant associations, on which their minds are so set that they do not feel safe until their names are entered. But more often than not they are turned down flat, and so they are always on tenterhooks; with the doors of the association barred to them, they are like tramps without a home or, in rural parlance, "mere trash." In short, what was looked down upon four months ago as a "gang of peasants" has now become a most honourable institution. Those who formerly prostrated themselves before the power of the gentry now bow before the power of the peasants. No matter what their identity, all admit that the world since last October is a different one.

"It's Terrible!" Or "It's Fine!"

The peasants' revolt disturbed the gentry's sweet dreams. When the news from the countryside reached the cities, it caused immediate uproar among the gentry. Soon after my arrival in Changsha, I met all sorts of people and picked up a good deal of gossip. From the middle social strata upwards to the Kuomintang right-wingers, there was not a single person who did not sum up the whole business in the phrase, "It's terrible!" Under the impact of the views of the "It's terrible!" school then flooding the city, even quite revolutionary-minded people became downhearted as they pictured the events in the countryside in their mind's eye; and they were unable to deny the word "terrible." Even quite progressive people said, "Though terrible, it is inevitable in a revolution." In short, nobody could altogether deny the word "terrible." But, as already mentioned, the fact is that the great peasant masses have risen to fulfil their historic mission and that the forces of rural democracy have risen to overthrow the forces of rural feudalism. The patriarchal-feudal class of local tyrants, evil gentry and lawless landlords has formed the basis of autocratic government for thousands of years and is the cornerstone of imperialism, warlordism and corrupt officialdom. To overthrow these feudal forces is the real objective of the national revolution. In a few months the peasants have accomplished what Dr. Sun Yat-sen wanted, but failed, to accomplish in the forty years he devoted to the national revolution. This is a marvelous feat never before achieved, not just in forty, but in thousands of years. It's fine. It is not "terrible" at all. It is anything but "terrible." "It's terrible!" is obviously a theory for combating the rise of the peasants in the interests of the landlords; it is obviously a theory of the landlord class for preserving the old order of feudalism and obstructing the establishment of the new order of democracy, it is obviously a counter-revolutionary theory. No revolutionary comrade should echo this nonsense. If your revolutionary viewpoint is firmly established and if you have been to the villages and looked around, you will undoubtedly feel thrilled as never before. Countless thousands of the enslaved—the peasants—are striking down the enemies who battened on their flesh. What the peasants are doing is absolutely right; what they are doing is fine! "It's fine!" is the theory of the peasants and of all other revolutionaries. Every revolutionary comrade should know that the national revolution requires a great change in the countryside. The Revolution of 1911[4] did not bring about this change, hence its failure. This change is now taking place, and it is an important factor for the completion of the revolution. Every revolutionary comrade must support it, or he will be taking the stand of counter-revolution.

The Question of "Going Too Far"

Then there is another section of people who say, "Yes, peasant associations are necessary, but they are going rather too far." This is the opinion of the middle-of-the-roaders. But what is the actual situation? True, the peasants are in a sense "unruly" in the countryside. Supreme in authority, the peasant association allows the landlord no say and sweeps away his prestige. This amounts to striking the landlord down to the dust and keeping him there. The peasants threaten, "We will put you in the other register!" They fine the local tyrants and evil gentry, they demand contributions from them, and they smash their sedan-chairs. People swarm into the houses of local tyrants and evil gentry who are against the peasant association, slaughter their pigs and consume their grain. They even loll for a minute or two on the ivory-inlaid beds belonging to the young ladies in the households of the local tyrants and evil gentry. At the slightest provocation they make arrests, crown the arrested with tall paper-hats, and parade them through the villages, saying, "You dirty landlords, now you know who we are!" Doing whatever they like and turning everything upside down, they have created a kind of terror in the countryside. This is what some people call "going too far," or "exceeding the proper limits in righting a wrong," or "really too much." Such talk may seem plausible, but in fact it is wrong. First, the local tyrants, evil gentry and lawless landlords have themselves driven the peasants to this. For ages they have used their power to tyrannize over the peasants and trample them underfoot; that is why the peasants have reacted so strongly. The most violent revolts and the most serious disorders have invariably occurred in places where the local tyrants, evil gentry and lawless landlords perpetrated the worst outrages. The peasants are clear-sighted. Who is bad and who is not, who is the worst and who is not quite so vicious, who deserves severe punishment and who deserves to be let off lightly the peasants keep clear accounts, and very seldom has the punishment exceeded the crime. Secondly, a revolution is not a dinner party, or writing an essay, or painting a picture, or doing embroidery; it cannot be so refined, so leisurely and gentle, so temperate, kind, courteous, restrained and magnanimous.[5] A revolution is an insurrection, an act of violence by which one class overthrows another. A rural revolution is a revolution by which the peasantry overthrows the power of the feudal landlord class. Without using the greatest force, the peasants cannot possibly overthrow the deep-rooted authority of the landlords which has lasted for thousands of years. The rural areas need a mighty revolutionary upsurge, for it alone can rouse the people in their millions to become a powerful force. All the actions mentioned here which have been labelled as "going too far" flow from the power of the peasants, which has been called forth by the mighty revolutionary upsurge in the countryside. It was highly necessary for such things to be done in the second period of the peasant movement, the period of revolutionary action. In this period it was necessary to establish the absolute authority of the peasants. It was necessary to forbid malicious criticism of the peasant associations. It was necessary to overthrow the whole authority of the gentry, to strike them to the ground and keep them there. There is revolutionary significance in all the actions which were labelled as "going too far" in this period. To put it bluntly, it is necessary to create terror for a while in every rural area, or otherwise it would be impossible to suppress the activities of the counter-revolutionaries in the countryside or overthrow the authority of the gentry. Proper limits have to be exceeded in order to right a wrong, or else the wrong cannot be righted.[6] Those who talk about the peasants "going too far" seem at first sight to be different from those who say "It's terrible!" as mentioned earlier, but in essence they proceed from the same standpoint and likewise voice a landlord theory that upholds the interests of the privileged classes. Since this theory impedes the rise of the peasant movement and so disrupts the revolution, we must firmly oppose it.

The "Movement of the Riffraff"

The right-wing of the Kuomintang says, "The peasant movement is a movement of the riffraff, of the lazy peasants." This view is current in Changsha. When I was in the countryside, I heard the gentry say, "It is all right to set up peasant associations, but the people now running them are no good. They ought to be replaced!" This opinion comes to the same thing as what the right-wingers are saying; according to both it is all right to have a peasant movement (the movement is already in being and no one dare say otherwise), but they say that the people running it are no good and they particularly hate those in charge of the associations at the lower levels, calling them "riffraff." In short, all those whom the gentry had despised, those whom they had trodden into the dirt, people with no place in society, people with no right to speak, have now audaciously lifted up their heads. They have not only lifted up their heads but taken power into their hands. They are now running the township peasant associations (at the lowest level), which they have turned into something fierce and formidable. They have raised their rough, work-soiled hands and laid them on the gentry. They tether the evil gentry with ropes, crown them with tall paper-hats and parade them through the villages. (In Hsiangtan and Hsianghsiang they call this "parading through the township" and in Liling "parading through the fields.") Not a day passes but they drum some harsh, pitiless words of denunciation into these gentry's ears. They are issuing orders and are running everything. Those who used to rank lowest now rank above everybody else; and so this is called "turning things upside down."

Vanguards of the Revolution

Where there are two opposite approaches to things and people, two opposite views emerge. "It's terrible!" and "It's fine!," "riffraff" and "vanguards of the revolution"—here are apt examples.

We said above that the peasants have accomplished a revolutionary task which had been left unaccomplished for many years and have done an important job for the national revolution. But has this great revolutionary task, this important revolutionary work, been performed by all the peasants? No. There are three kinds of peasants, the rich, the middle and the poor peasants. The three live in different circumstances and so have different views about the revolution. In the first period, what appealed to the rich peasants was the talk about the Northern Expeditionary Army's sustaining a crushing defeat in Kiangsi, about Chiang Kai-shek's being wounded in the leg[7] and flying back to Kwangtung,[8] and about Wu Pei-fu's[9] recapturing Yuehchow. The peasant associations would certainly not last and the Three People's Principles[10] could never prevail, because they had never been heard of before. Thus an official of the township peasant association (generally one of the "riffraff" type) would walk into the house of a rich peasant, register in hand, and say, "Will you please join the peasant association?" How would the rich peasant answer? A tolerably well-behaved one would say, "Peasant association? I have lived here for decades, tilling my land. I never heard of such a thing before, yet I've managed to live all right. I advise you to give it up!" A really vicious rich peasant would say, "Peasant association! Nonsense! Association for getting your head chopped off! Don't get people into trouble!" Yet, surprisingly enough, the peasant associations have now been established several months, and have even dared to stand up to the gentry. The gentry of the neighbourhood who refused to surrender their opium pipes were arrested by the associations and paraded through the villages. In the county towns, moreover, some big landlords were put to death, like Yen Jung-chiu of Hsiangtan and Yang Chih-tse of Ninghsiang. On the anniversary of the October Revolution, at the time of the anti-British rally and of the great celebrations of the victory of the Northern Expedition, tens of thousands of peasants in every township, holding high their banners, big and small, along with their carrying-poles and hoes, demonstrated in massive, streaming columns. It was only then that the rich peasants began to get perplexed and alarmed. During the great victory celebrations of the Northern Expedition, they learned that Kiukiang had been taken, that Chiang Kai-shek had not been wounded in the leg and that Wu Pei-fu had been defeated after all. What is more, they saw such slogans as "Long live the Three People's Principles!" "Long live the peasant associations!" and "Long live the peasants!" clearly written on the "red and green proclamations." "What?" wondered the rich peasants, greatly perplexed and alarmed, "'Long live the peasants!' Are these people now to be regarded as emperors?"[11] So the peasant associations are putting on grand airs. People from the associations say to the rich peasants, "We'll enter you in the other register," or, "In another month, the admission fee will be ten yuan a head!" Only under the impact of all this are the rich peasants tardily joining the associations,[12] some paying fifty cents or a yuan for admission (the regular fee being a mere ten coppers), some securing admission only after asking other people to put in a good word for them. But there are quite a number of die-hards who have not joined to this day. When the rich peasants join the associations, they generally enter the name of some sixty or seventy year-old member of the family, for they are in constant dread of "conscription." After joining, the rich peasants are not keen on doing any work for the associations. They remain inactive throughout.

How about the middle peasants? Theirs is a vacillating attitude. They think that the revolution will not bring them much good. They have rice cooking in their pots and no creditors knocking on their doors at midnight. They, too, judging a thing by whether it ever existed before, knit their brows and think to themselves, "Can the peasant association really last?" "Can the Three People's Principles prevail?" Their conclusion is, "Afraid not!" They imagine it all depends on the will of Heaven and think, "A peasant association? Who knows if Heaven wills it or not?" In the first period, people from the association would call on a middle peasant, register in hand, and say, "Will you please join the peasant association?" The middle peasant would reply, "There's no hurry!" It was not until the second period, when the peasant associations were already exercising great power, that the middle peasants came in. They show up better in the associations than the rich peasants but are not as yet very enthusiastic; they still want to wait and see. It is essential for the peasant associations to get the middle peasants to join and to do a good deal more explanatory work among them.

The poor peasants have always been the main force in the bitter fight in the countryside. They have fought militantly through the two periods of underground work and of open activity. They are the most responsive to Communist Party leadership. They are deadly enemies of the camp of the local tyrants and evil gentry and attack it without the slightest hesitation. "We joined the peasant association long ago," they say to the rich peasants, "why are you still hesitating?" The rich peasants answer mockingly, "What is there to keep you from joining? You people have neither a tile over your heads nor a speck of land under your feet!" It is true the poor peasants are not afraid of losing anything. Many of them really have "neither a tile over their heads nor a speck of land under their feet." What, indeed, is there to keep them from joining the associations? According to the survey of Changsha County, the poor peasants comprise 70 percent, the middle peasants 20 percent, and the landlords and the rich peasants 10 percent of the population in the rural areas. The 70 percent, the poor peasants, may be sub-divided into two categories, the utterly destitute and the less destitute. The utterly destitute,[13] comprising 20 percent, are the completely dispossessed, that is, people who have neither land nor money, are without any means of livelihood, and are forced to leave home and become mercenaries or hired labourers or wandering beggars. The less destitute,[14] the other 50 percent, are the partially dispossessed, that is, people with just a little land or a little money who eat up more than they earn and live in toil and distress the year round, such as the handicraftsmen, the tenant-peasants (not including the rich tenant-peasants) and the semi-owner peasants. This great mass of poor peasants, or altogether 70 percent of the rural population, is the backbone of the peasant associations, the vanguard in the overthrow of the feudal forces and the heroes who have performed the great revolutionary task which for long years was left undone. Without the poor peasant class (the "riffraff," as the gentry call them), it would have been impossible to bring about the present revolutionary situation in the countryside, or to overthrow the local tyrants and evil gentry and complete the democratic revolution. The poor peasants, being the most revolutionary group, have gained the leadership of the peasant associations. In both the first and second periods almost all the chairmen and committee members in the peasant associations at the lowest level were poor peasants (of the officials in the township associations in Hengshan County the utterly destitute comprise 50 percent, the less destitute 40 percent, and poverty-stricken intellectuals 10 percent). Leadership by the poor peasants is absolutely necessary. Without the poor peasants there would be no revolution. To deny their role is to deny the revolution. To attack them is to attack the revolution. They have never been wrong on the general direction of the revolution. They have discredited the local tyrants and evil gentry. They have beaten down the local tyrants and evil gentry, big and small, and kept them underfoot. Many of their deeds in the period of revolutionary action, which were labelled as "going too far," were in fact the very things the revolution required. Some county governments, county headquarters of the Kuomintang and county peasant associations in Hunan have already made a number of mistakes; some have even sent soldiers to arrest officials of the lower-level associations at the landlords' request. A good many chairmen and committee members of township associations in Hengshan and Hsianghsiang Counties have been thrown in jail. This mistake is very serious and feeds the arrogance of the reactionaries. To judge whether or not it is a mistake, you have only to see how joyful the lawless landlords become and how reactionary sentiments grow, wherever the chairmen or committee members of local peasant associations are arrested. We must combat the counter-revolutionary talk of a "movement of riffraff" and a "movement of lazy peasants" and must be especially careful not to commit the error of helping the local tyrants and evil gentry in their attacks on the poor peasant class. Though a few of the poor peasant leaders undoubtedly did have shortcomings, most of them have changed by now. They themselves are energetically prohibiting gambling and suppressing banditry. Where the peasant association is powerful, gambling has stopped altogether and banditry has vanished. In some places it is literally true that people do not take any articles left by the wayside and that doors are not bolted at night. According to the Hengshan survey, 85 percent of the poor peasant leaders have made great progress and have proved themselves capable and hard-working. Only fifteen percent retain some bad habits. The most one can call these is "an unhealthy minority," and we must not echo the local tyrants and evil gentry in undiscriminatingly condemning them as "riffraff." This problem of the "unhealthy minority" can be tackled only under the peasant associations' own slogan of "strengthen discipline," by carrying on propaganda among the masses, by educating the "unhealthy minority," and by tightening the associations' discipline; in no circumstances should soldiers be arbitrarily sent to make such arrests as would damage the prestige of the poor peasants and feed the arrogance of the local tyrants and evil gentry. This point requires particular attention.

Preserve the Style of Plain Living and Hard Struggle.[15]
March 5, 1949

Very soon we shall be victorious throughout the country. This victory will breach the eastern front of imperialism and will have great international significance. To win this victory will not require much more time and effort, but to consolidate it will. The bourgeoisie doubts our ability to construct. The imperialists reckon that eventually we will beg alms from them in order to live. With victory, certain moods may grow within the Party—arrogance, the airs of a self-styled hero, inertia and unwillingness to make progress, love of pleasure and distaste for continued hard living. With victory, the people will be grateful to us and the bourgeoisie will come forward to flatter us. It has been proved that the enemy cannot conquer us by force of arms. However, the flattery of the bourgeoisie may conquer the weak-willed in our ranks. There *may* be some Communists who were not conquered by enemies with guns and were worthy of the name of heroes for standing up to these enemies, but who cannot withstand sugar-coated bullets; they will be defeated by sugar-coated bullets. We must guard against such a situation. To win country-wide victory is only the first step in a long march of ten thousand *li*. Even if this step is worthy of pride, it is comparatively tiny; what will be more worthy of pride is yet to come. After several decades, the victory of the Chinese people's democratic revolution, viewed in retrospect, will seem like only a brief prologue to a long drama. A drama begins with a prologue, but the prologue is not the climax. The Chinese revolution is great, but the road after the revolution will be longer, the work greater and more arduous. This must be made clear now in the Party. The comrades must be helped to remain modest, prudent and free from arrogance and rashness in their style of work. The comrades must be helped to preserve the style of plain living and hard struggle. We have the Marxist-Leninist weapon of criticism and self-criticism. We can get rid of a bad style and keep the good. We can learn what we did not know. We are not only good at destroying the old world, we are also good at building the new. Not only can the Chinese people live without begging alms from the imperialists, they will live a better life than that in the imperialist countries.

Notes

1. "Report on an Investigation of the Peasant Movement in Hunan" consists of eight parts, the full text of which is included in the *Selected Works of Mao Tse-tung*, Eng. ed. (Peking: Foreign Language Press, 1967), Vol. I, pp. 23–39.

2. Hunan Province was then the center of the peasant movement in China.

3. Chao Heng-ti, the ruler of Hunan at the time, was the agent of the Northern warlords. He was overthrown by the Northern Expeditionary Army in 1926.

4. The Revolution of 1911 was the bourgeois revolution which overthrew the autocratic regime of the Ching Dynasty. On October 10 of that year, a section of the Ching Dynasty's New Army which was under revolutionary influence staged an uprising in Wuchang, Hupeh Province. The existing bourgeois and petty-bourgeois revolutionary societies and the broad masses of the workers, peasants, and soldiers responded enthusiastically, and very soon the rule of the Ching Dynasty crumbled. In January 1912 the Provisional Government of the Republic of China was set up in Nanking, with Sun Yat-sen as the Provisional President. Thus China's feudal monarchic system which had lasted for more than 2,000 years was brought to an end. The idea of a democratic republic had entered deep in the hearts of the people. But the bourgeoisie which led the revolution was strongly conciliationist in nature. It did not mobilize the peasant masses on an extensive scale to crush the feudal rule of the landlord class in the countryside, but instead handed state power over to the Northern warlord Yuan Shih-kai under imperialist and feudal pressure. As a result the revolution ended in defeat.

5. These were the virtues of Confucius, as described by one of his disciples.

6. The old Chinese phrase, "exceeding the proper limits in righting a wrong," was often quoted for the purpose of restricting people's activities; reforms that remained within the framework of the established order were to be permitted, but activities aiming at the complete destruction of the old order were to be forbidden. Actions within this framework were regarded as "proper," but those that aimed at completely destroying the old order were described as "exceeding the proper limits." It is a convenient doctrine for reformists and opportunists in the revolutionary ranks. Comrade Mao Tsetung refuted this kind of reformist doctrine. His remark in the text that "Proper limits have to be exceeded in order to right a

wrong, or else the wrong cannot be righted" meant that the mass revolutionary method, and not the revisionist-reformist method, had to be taken to end the old feudal order.

7. Chiang Kai-shek had not yet been fully exposed as a counter-revolutionary in the winter of 1926 and the spring of 1927 when the Northern Expeditionary Army was marching into the Yangtse valley, and the peasant masses still thought that he was for the revolution. The landlords and rich peasants disliked him and spread the rumour that the Northern Expeditionary Army had suffered defeats and that he had been wounded in the leg. Chiang Kai-shek came to be fully revealed as a counter-revolutionary on April 12, 1927, when he staged his counter-revolutionary coup d'état in Shanghai and elsewhere, massacring the workers, suppressing the peasants and attacking the Communist Party. The landlords and rich peasants then changed their attitude and began to support him.

8. Kwangtung was the first revolutionary base in the period of the First Revolutionary Civil War (1924–1927).

9. Wu Pei-fu was one of the best-known of the Northern warlords. Together with Tsao Kun, who was notorious for his rigging of the presidential election in 1923 by bribing members of parliament, he belonged to the Chihli (Hopei) clique. He supported Tsao as the leader and the two were generally referred to as "Tsao-Wu." In 1920 after defeating Tuan Chi-jui, warlord of the Anhwei clique, Wu Pei-fu gained control of the Northern warlord government in Peking as an agent of the Anglo-American imperialists; it was he who gave the orders for the massacre, on February 7, 1923, of the workers on strike along the Peking-Hankow Railway. In 1924 he was defeated in the war with Chang Tso-lin (commonly known as the "war between the Chihli and Fengtien cliques"), and he was thereupon ousted from the Peking regime. In 1926 he joined forces with Chang Tso-lin at the instigation of the Japanese and British imperialists, and thus returned to power. When the Northern Expeditionary Army drove northward from Kwangtung in 1926, he was the first foe to be overthrown.

10. The Three People's Principles were the principles and the programme put forward by Sun Yat-sen on the questions of nationalism, democracy and people's livelihood in China's bourgeois-democratic revolution. In the manifesto adopted by the Kuomintang at its First National Congress in 1924 Sun Yat-sen restated the Three People's Principles. Nationalism was interpreted as opposition to imperialism and active support was expressed for the movements of the workers and peasants. Thus the old Three People's Principles were transformed into the new Three People's Principles characterized by the Three Great Policies, that is, alliance with Russia, co-operation with the Communist Party, and assistance to the peasants and workers. The new Three People's Principles provided the political basis for the co-operation between the Communist Party of China and the Kuomintang during the First Revolutionary Civil War period.

11. The Chinese term for "long live" is *wansui*, literally "ten thousand years," and was the traditional salute to the emperor; it had become a synonym for "emperor."

12. Rich peasants should not have been allowed to join the peasant associations, a point which the peasant masses did not yet understand in 1927.

13. Here the "utterly destitute" means the farm labourers (the rural proletariat) and the rural lumpen-proletariat.

14. The "less destitute" means the rural semi-proletariat.

15. This is the tenth part of the report to the Second Plenary Session of the Seventh Central Committee of the Communist Party of China, the full text of which is included in the *Selected Works of Mao Tse-tung*, Eng. ed. (Peking: Foreign Language Press, 1969), Vol. IV, pp. 361–375.

15

The Old Gun

Mo Yan

Mo Yan, whose real name is Guan Moye (1955–) won the Nobel Prize for Literature in 2012. He was born in a village in Shandong province. The start of the Cultural Revolution (1966–1976) put an end to his schooling and he became a farm worker at the age of eleven. At eighteen he went to work in a cotton factory. He joined the People's Liberation Army in 1976 and published his first story in 1981 while still a soldier. His pen name, Mo Yan, means "Don't Speak" and refers to his parents' warning him as a boy to be quiet in public due to political dangers. His novels and short stories, usually set in rural China, are rich in description, often nonlinear, and sometimes contain magical realism. They reflect the harshness of poverty and constrictive social pressures, but also contain humor and fortitude. He is best known for his novel *Red Sorghum* (1986), which was made into an internationally acclaimed film (1987). "The Old Gun" was written in 1985.

Questions

1. The narrator, Dasuo, tells stories within the story of his grandmother and father. What does Dasuo have in common with them, besides the gun?
2. What do the choices these characters make reveal about their lives?
3. How does the author build suspense?

The Old Gun

The Old Gun by Mo Yan, translated by Duncan Hewitt, first published in Renditions Paperback: *Explosions and Other Stories* (Hong Kong: Research Centre for Translations, Chinese University of Hong Kong, 1991), pp. 59–75. Used with permission of the Research Centre for Translation, The Chinese University of Hong Kong.

As he swung the gun down from his right shoulder with his index-finger-less right hand, he was caught in a ray of golden sunlight. The sun was sinking rapidly in a smooth shallow arc; fragmentary sounds like those of a receding tide rippled from the fields, along with an air of desolation by turns pronounced and faint. Gingerly he placed the gun on the ground among the patches of coin-shaped moss, feeling a sense of distress as he saw how damp the earth was. The long-barreled, home-made musket, its butt mahogany, lay unevenly on the soggy ground; beside it the evening sun picked out a fallen sorghum ear on which a great cluster of delicate, tender golden shoots had sprouted, casting discolouring shadows onto the black gun-barrel and deep-red butt. He took the powder-horn from around his waist, at the same time slipping off his black jacket to reveal a raw-boned torso. He wrapped the gun and the powder-horn in the jacket and laid them on the ground, then took three paces forward. Bending down, he stretched out his sun-drenched arms and dragged out one sheaf from among the great clump of sorghum stalks.

The autumn floods had been heavy and the land, water-logged for thousands of hectares, looked like an ocean. In the water the sorghum held high its crimson heads; whole platoons of rats scurried across them as nimbly as birds in flight. By harvest time the water was at chest height, and the people waded in and took the ears of sorghum away on rafts. Red-finned carp and black-backed grass carp appeared from nowhere to dart about among the green aerial roots of the sorghum stalks. Now and again an emerald green kingfisher shot into the water, then shot back out with a tiny glistening fish in its beak. In August the flood waters gradually subsided, revealing roads covered in mud. On the low-lying land the water remained, forming pools of all shapes and sizes. The cut sorghum stalks could not be hauled away; they were dragged out of the water and stacked on the road or on the higher ground around the edges of the pools. A glorious sunlight shone on the low-lying plains. For miles around there was hardly a village; the pools sparkled; the clumps of sorghum stood like clusters of blockhouses.

Silhouetted against the bright warm sun and a big expanse of water, he dragged aside sheaf after sheaf of sorghum, piling them up at the edge of the pool until he had made a square hide half a man's height. Then he picked up the gun, jumped into the hide and sat down. His head came just level with the top of the hide. From outside he was invisible, but through the holes he had left he could clearly see the pool and the sand-bar which rose in its middle like a solitary island; he could see the rosy sky and the brown earth, too. The sky seemed very low; the sun's rays daubed the surface of the water a deep red. The pool stretched away into the hazy dusk, sparkling brilliantly, darts of radiance dancing around its edge like a ring of warm eyelashes. On the sand-bar in the pool, by now a pale shade of blue, clumps of yellow reeds stood solemnly upright. The sand-bar itself, surrounded by flickering light, seemed gently adrift. The hazier the surroundings grew, the brighter the water gleamed, and the more pronounced the impression that the sand-bar was drifting—he felt that it was floating towards him, floating nearer, until it was only a few steps away and he could have jumped onto it. They still hadn't arrived on the sand-bar; he gazed uneasily at the sky once more, thinking it's about time, they ought to be here by now.

He had no idea where they came from. That day the workers had spent the whole afternoon shifting sorghum stalks. When the team leader said time to down tools, the men headed for home by the dozen, their long shadows swaying as they went. He had rushed over here to relieve himself when suddenly he caught sight of them. It was as though he had been punched in the chest—his heart faltered for a moment before it resumed beating. His eyes were dazzled by the great flock of wild ducks landing on the sand-bar. Every night for two weeks he hid among the sorghum sheafs watching them; he observed that they always arrived, cawing loudly, at around this time of the evening, as if they had come flying from beyond the sky. Before landing they would circle elegantly above the pool, like a great grey-green cloud now unfurling, now rolling back . . . When they descended onto the sand-bar, their wings beating the air, he was beside himself with excitement. Never before had he come across so many wild ducks on such a small piece of land, never . . .

They still weren't here—by now they really should have been. They weren't here *yet* . . . or they weren't coming? He was feeling anxious, even began to suspect that what he had seen before had been just an illusion—all along he had never quite believed there could really be such a large flock of wild ducks in this place. He had often heard

"Water Fowl" (1301) by Chen Lin (ca. 1260–1320), handscroll, ink and light colors on paper. The image of ducks in the reeds was a popular one as it symbolized the wish for positive examination results. *(Wikimedia Commons, National Palace Museum, Taipei)*

the old people in the village telling tales of heavenly ducks, but the ducks in the stories were always pure white, and this flock of wild ducks was not. The ones with pretty green feathers on their heads and necks, a white ring round their throats and wings like blue mirrors— weren't they drakes? Those with golden-brown bodies, dappled with dark brown markings—weren't they females? They certainly weren't heavenly ducks, for they left little green and brown feathers all over the sand-bar. He felt greatly reassured at the sight of these feathers. He sat down, picked up his jacket and shook it open, revealing the gun and the shiny powder-horn. The gun lay peacefully on top of the sorghum stalks, its body gleaming dark-red, almost the colour of rust. In the past red rust had covered it several times and had eaten away at the metal, leaving it pocked and pitted. Now, though, there was no rust—he had sandpapered it all away. The gun lay there twisted like a hibernating snake; at any moment, he felt, it might wake up, fly into the air and start thrashing the sorghum stalks with its steel tail. When he stretched out his hand to touch the gun, his first sensation was an iciness in his fingertips, and the chill spread to his chest and made him shiver for a long while. The sun was sinking faster now, its shape altering all the while, flattening out and distorting, like a semi-fluid sphere hitting a smooth steel surface. Its underside was a flat line, its curved surfaces under extreme tension; at last they burst and the bubbling icy red liquid meandered away in every direction. A trance-like calm descended on the pool as the crimson liquid seeped down, turning its depths into a thick red broth, while the surface remained crystal clear and blindingly bright. Suddenly, he caught sight of a gold-hooped dragonfly suspended from a tall, withered blade of grass, its bulging eyes like purple gems, turning now to the left, now to the right, refracting light as they did so.

He reached for the gun and laid it across his legs, its body stretching out behind him along the right-angle of his thighs and belly; the barrel peeped out from beneath his chin at the pale grey southern sky. He opened the lid of the powder-horn, then pulled from his pocket a long, thin measuring cylinder which he filled with gunpowder. He poured this measure into the gun barrel, the smooth sound it made as it fell echoed from the muzzle. He then took a pinch of iron shot from a small iron box and tipped it into the muzzle of the gun; from inside the barrel there came a clatter. Now he pulled out a long rod from below the barrel and tamped down the mixture of gunpowder and shot with its uneven head. He moved as gingerly as if he were scratching a drowsy tiger's itch, nerve-ends tingling, heart pounding. As soon as he had put the third measure of gunpowder and the third handful of shot into the barrel, an icy cold clutched him; beads of cold sweat broke out on his forehead. His hands were trembling as he took out the cotton-wool stopper he had prepared for the purpose and plugged the mouth of the gun. He felt starving, his whole body limp. He snapped a piece of grass from the ground, rubbed the mud from it, put it into his mouth and began to chew on it, but this only made his hunger worse. . . .

Just then, though, he heard the whistle of wings beating the air above the water-flats. He had to hurry and complete his final task of preparation: attaching the percussion cap. He pulled back the protruding head of the hammer, revealing a nipple-shaped protuberance connected to the gun barrel. There was a round groove in the top of the protuberance with a tiny hole in its centre. With great care he tore away several layers of paper from around the golden percussion cap, then fitted it into this groove. The percussion cap contained yellow gunpowder; as soon as the hammer struck it, this would explode, igniting the powder in the barrel and sending a fiery snake leaping from the muzzle, slender at first, then bigger until finally the gun looked like an iron broom. This gun had hung on the pitch-black gable in their house for so long that he had learned the mystery of its workings as if by revelation. Two days before, when he took it down and rubbed it clean of the rust which pocked its surface, he was actually completely at ease with it.

The wild ducks were here. At first they circled a hundred metres up in the air, wings beating. They dived and climbed, merged, then scattered again, hurtling down from all directions to skim across the sparkling surface of the reddened water. He got to his knees, holding his breath, eyes glued to the circle upon circle of purple radiance. Gently he edged the barrel of the gun through the gap in the sorghum stalks, heart pounding crazily. The wild ducks were still whirling around in circles of ever-changing size; it was almost as if the water-flats were spinning with them. Several times, some of the green-feathered drakes almost flew straight into the muzzle of his gun; he caught a glimpse of their pale green beaks and the gleam of cunning in their black eyes. The sun had grown wider and flatter still, turning black around the edges, its centre still like molten iron, crackling and spitting sparks.

The ducks suddenly started calling, the "quack quack quack" of the drakes merging with the "quack quack quack" of the females in a great cacophony. He knew they were about to land—after observing them minutely for a dozen days now he knew they always cried out just before they landed. It was only a few moments since their silhouettes had first appeared in the sky, but already he felt as if an extremely long time had passed; the violent cramps in his stomach reminded him again of his hunger. At last the ducks descended, only extending their purple legs and stretching their wings out flat when they were almost on the ground. Their snowy tails fluffed out like feathery fans, they hit the ground at such speed that the momentum made them stagger a couple of paces. Suddenly the mud was no longer brown: countless suns shimmered in the ducks' brilliant plumage as the entire flock waddled to and fro, carrying the sunlight with it.

Stealthily he raised the gun, rested the butt on his shoulder, and trained the muzzle on the increasingly dense pack of ducks. Another piece had vanished from the sun, which looked distorted, bizarre. Some of the wild ducks had settled on the ground, some were standing, some flew a little way, then landed again. It's time, he thought,

I should open fire, but he didn't do it. As he ran his hand over the trigger he suddenly realized his great disadvantage, recalling with a sense of pain his index finger: two of the joints were missing, the last one alone remained, a gnarled tree stump squatting between his thumb and his middle finger.

He was only six years old when his mother came back from his father's funeral, dressed in mourning—a long white cotton gown with a hempen cord tied around the waist, her hair flowing loose. Her eyelids were so swollen they were transparent, her eyes merely narrow slits from which her tear-stained, darkling gaze flashed out. She called out his name: "Dasuo, come here." He approached her with trepidation. She grabbed hold of his hand and gulped twice, craning her neck as though trying to swallow something hard. "Dasuo, your dad's died, do you realize that?" she said. He nodded, and heard her carry on, "Your dad's died. When you die you can never come back to life, do you realize that?" He gazed perplexedly at her, nodding energetically all the while. "You know how your dad died?" she asked. "He was shot with this gun; this gun was handed down from your grandmother. You're never to touch it: I'm going to hang it on the wall; you're going to look at it every day. And when you look at it you should think of your father, and study hard so you can live a decent life and bring a bit of credit to your ancestors." He wasn't sure how well he understood his mum's words, but he carried on nodding energetically.

And so the gun hung in their house on the gable, which was stained black and shiny by the smoke of decades. Every day he saw it. Later, when he went up from first to second grade, his mum hung a paraffin lamp on the gable every evening to give him enough light to study by. Whenever he saw the black characters in the books his head started spinning, and he couldn't help thinking of the gun and the story behind it. The wind off the desolate plain seeped through the lattice window, buffeting the flames in the oil lamp; the flames looked like the head of a writing brush, with wisps of black smoke shimmering at its tip. Though he appeared intent on his books, he was always aware of the spirit of the gun; he even seemed to hear it clicking. He felt like you do when you see a snake—wanting to look but scared at the same time. The gun hung there, barrel pointing down, butt upwards, a gloomy black glow emanating from its body. The powder-horn hung alongside, tangled up with it, its slender waist resting against the hammer. It was red-gold in colour, its big end facing downwards, its small end upwards. How high the gun and the powder-horn hung, how beautiful they looked hanging there—an ancient gun and an ancient powder-horn hanging on an ancient gable, tormenting his soul.

One evening he climbed up on a high stool and took the gun and the powder-horn down. Holding them up to the lamp-light, he inspected them carefully; the leaden weight of the gun in his hands brought him an acute sense of grief. Just at this moment, his mum walked in from the other room. She was not yet forty, but her hair was already grey, and she said: "Dasuo, what are you doing?" He just stood there blankly, the gun in one hand and the powder-horn in the other. "Where did you come in your class exams?" she asked him. "Second from bottom," he replied. "You good-for-nothing! Hang that gun back up!" He replied stubbornly, "No, I want to go and kill . . ." His mum slapped him round the face and said, "Hang it up. The only thing you're going to do is get on with your studies, and don't you forget it." He hung the gun on the wall. His mum went over to the stove, picked up a chopper and told him calmly, "Hold out your index finger." He stretched it out obediently. She pressed the finger onto the edge of the *kang*,[1] he began to squirm with fear. "Don't move," she told him. "Now remember this, you're never to touch that gun again." She raised the chopper . . . it fell in a flash of cold steel, a violent jolt surged from his fingertips up to his shoulders, his vertebrae arched with the strain. Blood oozed slowly from the severed finger. His mother was weeping as she staunched the wound with a handful of lime. . . .

As he looked at the stub of his finger with its single joint, his nose began to twitch. How many days had he gone without meat now? Couldn't remember exactly; but he could distinctly remember all the meat he had eaten in the past. He seemed never to have eaten his fill of meat. The first time he caught sight of those plump wild ducks, meat was the first thing he thought of. The next thing he thought of was the gun—he had come out in goose-pimples all over as he recalled how his mum had chopped off his finger at the joint because of it. But in the end, yesterday afternoon, he had taken the gun down. Its body was covered in dust, as thick as a coin, and it was enmeshed from top to bottom in a tangle of spider's webs. The leather strap, chewed through by insects, snapped as soon as he touched it. There was still a lot of gunpowder in the horn—when he poured it out to dry he discovered a golden percussion cap. He picked up this single percussion cap, hands trembling with excitement. The first thing that came into his mind was his father: he felt how lucky he was, for where would you get one of these percussion caps nowadays? . . . I haven't got any money, even if I had some I still wouldn't be able to get a meat coupon; I'm thick, even if I wasn't I still wouldn't get a chance to go to school, and anyway what use would it be? Looking at the stump of his finger, he tried to console himself. His mum had only chopped off the tip, but afterwards the wound had turned septic and he had lost another section—hence its present state. As he thought of all these things, he became filled with hatred for this flock of wild ducks with all their fine feathers. I'm going to kill you, kill the lot of you if it's the last thing I do! Then I'll eat you, chew your bones to a pulp and swallow them down. He imagined how crispy and aromatic their bones must be. He stretched his middle finger into the trigger guard.

Still he didn't pull the trigger. This was because another gaggle of wild ducks was swirling down from the sky in another spinning cloud of colour. There was a great commotion among the ducks on the sand-bar. Some stamped their feet, some took off; it was hard to tell whether they were expressing welcome or anger towards their fellows. He gazed irritably at the flurry of birds and gently withdrew the gun. The sun had grown pointed like a sweet potato, its rays now dark green and brilliant purple. The ducks' activity startled the gold-hooped dragonfly into flight. It skimmed low across the surface of the water and came to rest on his hide, its six legs clamped fast to a sorghum leaf, its long golden-hooped tail dangling down. He saw the two bright beads of light in its eyes. The flock of wild ducks was gradually regrouping and growing calmer. On the water's surface, shattered by their claws, concentric ripples spread out, creating new ripples where they collided.

The two flocks of ducks had merged into one. If I had a big net, he thought, and suddenly flung it over them . . . but he knew he had no net, just a gun. Gingerly he removed the percussion cap, pulled out the cotton-wool stopper, and poured three more measures of gunpowder and three more measures of shot into the muzzle. . . . Once more he took aim at the ducks, his heart filled with a primitive blood-lust. . . . Such a huge flock of ducks, such a slender gun barrel. . . . He edged stealthily back once more and poured another two cylinders of gun-powder into the muzzle, then plugged it again. The barrel was almost full now, and when he lifted the gun up he felt how heavy it was. His trembling middle finger pressed on the trigger—at the split second of firing he closed his eyes.

The head of the hammer struck the golden percussion cap with a click, but no shot rang out. The rings on the water's surface seemed to be slowly contracting; the purple vapour which hung between heaven and earth was denser than ever, the red glow fading fast, the brightness of the water's surface undiminished but gradually assuming a deeper hue. Clustered together, the ducks looked so solid, beautiful, warm, their soft, clean plumage dazzling. Their cunning eyes seemed to be staring disdainfully at the muzzle of his gun, as if in mockery of his impotence. He took out the percussion cap, glancing at the mark left on the firing plate by the hammer. A warm breath of putrid air wafted over from the flock of ducks; their bodies gave off a soft, smooth sound as they rubbed against each other. He replaced the percussion cap, not believing that this could really have happened. Dad, Granny, hadn't it fired for them at the first attempt? It was ten or more years since his dad died, but his story was still common currency in the village. He could dimly recall a very tall man with a pitted face and yellow whiskers.

His dad's story had been so widely repeated that it had already taken on the status of a legend among the villagers: he had only to close his eyes for it to unfold in all its detail. It began on the grey dirt road to the fields, with his dad setting out with a throng of hard-headed peasants to sow the sorghum, a heavy wooden seed-drill across his shoulders. The road was lined with mulberry trees, their out-stretched leaves as big as copper coins. Birds were chattering; the grass along the roadside was very green. The water in the ditches lay deep, patches of frogspawn shimmered on the pale yellow reeds. Dad was panting noisily under the weight of the seed-drill, when a bicycle suddenly shot out of nowhere and crashed sidelong into him. He staggered a few paces but didn't fall over, unlike the bicycle which did. Dad flung down his seed-drill, picked up the bicycle, then picked up its rider. The latter was a short-arsed individual; as soon as he tried to walk his knee-joints began cracking. Dad greeted him respectfully, Officer Liu.

Officer Liu said: Have you gone blind, you dog?
Dad said: Yes, the dog is blind, don't be angry sir.
Liu: You dare to insult me? You sonofabitch bastard!
Dad: Officer, it was you who bumped into me.
Liu: Up yours!
Dad: Don't swear, sir, it was you who bumped into me.
Liu: x x x x.
Dad: You're being unreasonable, sir. Even in the old society there were honest officials who listened to reason.
Liu: What, are you saying the New Society is worse than the old society?
Dad: I never said that.

Liu: Counter-revolutionary! Renegade! I'll blow you away! Officer Liu pulled a Mauser from his waistband and pointed the gaping black muzzle at dad's chest.
Dad: I haven't done anything to deserve the death penalty.
Liu: Near as damn it you have.
Dad: Go on then, shoot me.
Liu: I didn't bring any bullets.
Dad: Fuck off then!
Liu: Maybe I can't shoot you, but there's nothing to stop me beating you up.

Officer Liu leapt at Dad like an arrow, knees cracking, and stabbed straight at the bridge of his nose with the long barrel of the pistol. Black blood began to trickle slowly from Dad's nostrils. The peasants pulled him away, and some of the older ones tried to placate Officer Liu. Officer Liu said angrily: I'll let you off this once. Dad was standing to one side, wiping away the blood with his fingers; he lifted them up and inspected them carefully. Liu said: That'll teach you some respect.

Dad: My friends, you all saw it, you'll be my witnesses—He wiped his face vigorously a couple of times, it was covered in blood—Old Liu, fuck your ancestors to the eighth generation.

As Dad stomped towards him, Old Liu raised his gun, and shouted: Come any nearer and I'll shoot. Dad said: You won't get a peep out of that gun. Dad seized Old Liu's wrist, wrested the gun away from him and flung it viciously into the ditch, sending spray flying high into the air. Clasping Old Liu by the scruff of the neck, he shook him backwards and forwards for a moment, then took aim at his buttocks and gave them a gentle kick. Officer Liu plunged headfirst into the ditch, buttocks skywards; his head lodged in the sludge and his legs splashed noisily in the water. The crowd of onlookers turned pale; some edged away, others rushed down into the ditch to drag the officer out. One old man said to Dad: Quick, nephew, run for it! Dad said: Fourth uncle, we'll meet again on the road to the yellow springs.[2] And he strode off towards home.

Officer Liu was extracted by the locals, weeping and wailing like a baby. He begged the crowd to find his gun for him, and at least a dozen of them went down into the ditch. Their searching hands stirred up plenty of mud, but they couldn't find the gun.

Dad felt among the dust on the beam and pulled down a long oil-paper sack, from which he withdrew a long, twisted gun. His eyes were glistening with tears. You mean we've still got a gun in the house? Mum asked him in astonishment. Dad said: Haven't you heard how my mum shot my dad? This was the gun she used. Mum was wide-eyed with fear. Get rid of it quick, she said. Dad said: No. Mum said: What are you going to do? Dad said: Kill someone. He now took down a powder-horn with a narrow waist, and a tin box, and deftly filled the gun with powder and shot. Dad said: Make sure that Dasuo studies hard. Make sure that he looks at this gun every day, just looks, mind, you're not to let him touch it. Have you got that? Mum said: Are you crazy? Dad pointed the gun at her: Get back!

Dad walked into the pear-orchard. The blossom on the trees was like a layer of snow. He hung the gun from a tree, muzzle downwards, and tied a thin piece of string to the hammer. Then he lay on his back on the ground and put the muzzle into his mouth. Eyes wide, he gazed at the golden bees and gave a sharp tug on the string. Pear blossom swirled down like snowflakes. A few bees fell to the ground, dead.

He pulled the trigger again, but still there was no report. He sat down, disheartened. The sun lay across the horizon like a doughnut, its colour the same deep-fried golden brown. The pool had shrunk even smaller, the fringes of the plain grew even hazier, the white half-moon was already visible. In the distance, on a clump of reeds, insects sparkled with a green light. The ducks tucked their beaks under their wings and gazed mockingly at him. They were so close to him, getting even closer now as the sky grew darker. His stomach protested bitterly; countless roast ducks, dripping with oil, flashed before his eyes. He pulled the trigger again and again, until the percussion cap was knocked out of shape by the hammer and embedded itself inextricably in the groove. He slumped disconsolately against the hide, like an animal which had just been filleted; the sorghum stalks cracked beneath him. The wild ducks paid not the slightest heed to the noise; they were silent, motionless, a heap of dappled cobble-stones. The sun disappeared, taking with it all the reds and greens, all shades of colour, leaving a world returned to its original state of grey and white. The crickets and cicadas beat their wings, their chirring merging into a constant drone. On the verge of tears, he stared up at the alfalfa-coloured vault of the sky, casting a sidelong glance, filled with hatred, at the gun. Was this decrepit old gun really the same one? Could such a foul-looking old wreck really have such an extraordinary history?

But when Wang Laoka started telling his tales of the old days, it really was as if they were unfolding before the villagers' eyes, and so everyone young and old loved to listen to him talking. Wang Laoka told them:

THE OLD GUN 131

In the days of the Republic, none of the three counties controlled these parts—there were more bandits round here than hairs on a cow's back; men, women, they'd all turn violent at the drop of a hat, they'd kill a man as calmly as slicing a melon. Have you heard the story of Dasuo here's granny? Well, Dasuo's granddad was a compulsive gambler who lived off Dasuo's granny—that little woman was tough, she built up a home from nothing, all by herself, and that ain't easy for a woman. She sweated her guts out for three years and managed to buy a few dozen hectares of land, even a couple of horses. And what a beauty she was, Dasuo's granny, people called her "the queen of the eight villages." Lovely pointed bound feet she had, a fringe like a curtain of black silk. To protect her house and home she swapped a stone and two pecks of grain for a gun. Now this gun had a long, long barrel and a mahogany butt, and they say that in the dead of night the hammer used to start clicking. She used to sling that gun across her back and ride off into the fields on her big horse to hunt foxes. A dead-shot she was—always shot 'em right up the arse. But then she got sick, a terrible thing, she was in a fever for seven whole weeks of seven whole days. Dasuo's granddad saw his chance—off he went roistering with whores and gambling to his heart's content: he lost all their land, even lost those two fine steeds. When the winner came to collect the horses, Dasuo's granny was lying on the *kang*, gasping for breath. Dasuo's dad was just a lad of five or six then, and when he saw that some people were trying to lead their horses away, he yelled: Mum, someone's taking the horses! The second she heard this, Dasuo's granny rolled straight off the *kang*, grabbed the gun from the wall, and dragged herself painfully into the courtyard. And what right have you to take out the horses, pray? she shouted. The two fellers leading the horses knew that this woman took no prisoners, so they said: Your man lost these horses to our boss, lady. She said: Since that's the case, might I trouble you two brothers to bring my man to see me, there's something I'd like to say to him. Dasuo's granddad—his name was Santao—was so afraid of his wife he was skulking outside the door, too scared to come in. But when he heard her shouting he knew it was too late to chicken out. He plucked up courage, did his best to look tough, marched into the courtyard, thrust out his chest and said: Hot today, isn't it. Dasuo's granny smiled and said: You lost the horses, didn't you? Santao said: Sure did. She said: So, you lost the horses, what are you going to lose next? Santao said: I'm going to lose you. She said: Good old Santao. Fate must bring enemies together, it was really my luck to marry you. You've lost my horses, lost my land, forty-nine days I've been lying here sick and you haven't so much as brought me a bowl of water. And now you think you can lose me—I reckon I'd rather lose you first. On this day next year, Santao, I'll bring the child to your grave and burn paper money for you. . . . The words were hardly out of her mouth when there was a great boom; the courtyard filled with a red flash . . . and his granddad was dead. . . .

When he heard this story his dad was still alive. He asked his dad where the gun was, but his dad screamed furiously at him: You get the hell out of here.

The half-moon was becoming brighter, fireflies flitted unhurriedly, tracing a series of green-tinted arcs across his face. The pool had assumed a somber, dim, steely grey hue, but the sky was not yet completely black—he could still make out the pale green eyes of the gold-hooped dragonflies. The chirring of the insects came in bursts, each close on the heels of the last. The damp air congealed and wafted heavenwards. He wasn't watching the flock of ducks any more, he was thinking only about eating duck, again feeling the sharp contractions in his stomach. The image of the hunter with dead ducks slung all around his body became superimposed on the image of the woman warrior on horseback, her gun slung over her shoulder; at last they merged with that of the decent man under a covering of pear blossoms.

The sun had finally gone out. All that remained was a strip of fading golden warmth on the western horizon. The tip of the half-moon was rising in the south-west, scattering a tender feeling as soft as water. Mist rose from the pool like so many clumps of vegetation, the wild ducks shimmered in and out of sight through the gaps in the mist, and the splashing of big fish echoed from the water. He stood up, as if drunk or in a trance, and flexed his stiff, numb joints. He strapped on the powder-horn, slung the gun over his shoulder and strode out of the hide. Why doesn't anything happen when I pull the trigger? He swung the gun down, cradled it in his arms and stared at it. It shimmered with a blue glow in the moonlight. Why don't you fire? he thought. He cocked the hammer and casually pulled the trigger.

The low, rumbling explosion rolled in waves across the autumn fields and a ball of red light lit up the water-flats and the wild ducks. Shreds of iron and shards of wood hurtled through the air; the ducks took off in startled flight. He toppled slowly to the ground, trying with all his strength to open his eyes. He seemed to see the ducks floating down around him like rocks, falling onto his body, piling up into a great mound, pressing down on him so that it became difficult to breathe.

Notes

1. A kang is a sleeping platform with a flue from a stove in a neighboring room running through it for warmth.
2. A reference to death.

Part II

Japan

The influence of political, social, and economic developments on literary trends and in the arts is visible in Japan from the very beginning. The Japanese state came into being in the fifth century, and among the earliest literary works are poems by early emperors celebrating the beauty of the land they ruled. This appreciation for specific natural sites in the four seasons is also one of the hallmarks of Japanese art.

In 710 CE, the imperial clan stopped relocating the capital each time an emperor died and settled down in the city of Nara for the rest of the eighth century. The oldest book in Japan, *Record of Ancient Matters* (*Kojiki*), completed in 712, contains myths and historical information that establishes the legitimacy of the ruling imperial dynasty by describing it as having descended from gods who created the islands of Japan by stirring the sea with a spear. The imperial family further consolidated its power when it moved the capital to the city of Heian-kyo (now Kyoto) in 794. Here the imperial clan and the aristocracy who helped it govern flourished for almost 400 years. Literacy in Chinese language and culture was necessary then for recording government documents and writing poetry until the adoption in the ninth century of a simple phonetic script (now known as *hiragana*). Vernacular literature then developed as did a Japanese style of painting depicting the lives of courtiers in bright, opaque colors.

Only aristocrats had the time and resources to read and write for pleasure. Their main interest was poetry, and they recorded the poems they had composed and received in diaries and anthologies. As they commented about the situations that inspired their poems, narrative fiction focusing on personal issues developed. Three of the most interesting texts from the tenth century (which could not be included in this anthology) are *The Ise Stories: Ise monogatari*,[1] *The Tosa Diary*,[2] and *The Kagerō Diary*.[3] *The Ise Stories* contains anecdotes relating the many amorous adventures of the great poet Ariwara no Narihira. In *The Tosa Diary*, a retiring provincial governor uses the persona of a woman in his retinue to record his feelings as he returns to the capital, leaving behind a daughter who had died very young. *The Kagerō Diary* was written by the second wife of a prominent statesman. It describes the early days of her marriage when she savors her husband's attention, her despair as her bond with her husband weakens, and the peace of mind she eventually gains by focusing on the careers of her son and stepdaughter.

At the peak of centralized aristocratic power, when the Fujiwara clan dominated the political scene largely through its skillful manipulation of marriage politics, came what most agree is the first novel in the history of the world, *The Tale of Genji*. Unique in depth and scope, its influence has been vast and long-lasting. The glory of the wealth and power of the ruling class was dampened, however, by the Buddhist perspective that we should be mindful of the evanescence of all things. Buddhism was officially adopted in Japan as a state religion in the mid-sixth century when Korean officials recommended Buddhist rites as ensuring prosperity and warding off illness and other calamities. It took several centuries for the Buddhist teachings that address individual fears about suffering and death to permeate Japanese society, but gradually hope for either enlightenment through one's own efforts, as in Zen Buddhism, or salvation via reincarnation in a paradise became widespread. It was commonly believed that salvation was dependent upon one's faith in Amida Buddha (Sanskrit: Buddha Amitābha) at the moment of death, but also it was understood that the paths to both enlightenment and salvation included practicing compassion for all living beings and abandoning worldly desires for material wealth, happiness, and fame. These ideas become especially noticeable in literature of the Kamakura (1185–1333) and

Muromachi (1336–1568) periods as the power of the aristocracy waned, that of the military clans waxed, and armed conflict increased. Painting at this time was once again heavily influenced by Chinese culture, as seen in the landscapes of the fifteenth-century Zen monk Tenshō Shūbun.

Another trend was a transformation of poetry and the performing arts as warrior leaders and some commoners accumulated enough wealth to allow them the leisure to pursue the arts. The aristocrats lost their political power, but they never lost the prestige that emanated from their proximity to the imperial family and so they became the custodians of culture. To survive economically, they became teachers of poetry, music, and etiquette for people of common origin. Poetry in turn became less elegant and restrained and more vibrant and fun. What evolved was a hugely popular new form—linked verse—which is composed in a group setting by individuals who take turns adding lines to create one long poem with unpredictable twists and turns in meaning. Conversely, the origins of the performance art of Noh was in folk music and agricultural rituals, but after the shogun Ashikaga Yoshimitsu (1358–1408) took the boy actor Ze'ami (1363–1443) under his wing, Noh lost its rustic aspects and became a highly stylized and elegant art form.

Frequent and widespread fighting between independent domains under the control of powerful samurai families plagued Japan throughout most of the fifteenth and sixteenth centuries. The literature of that time consists of short tales on a wide range of themes, including religious inspiration and common people rising in the world, especially through poetic ability.[4]

In the late 1500s, Japan was unified by the military might of three men, Oda Nobunaga (1534–1582), Toyotomi Hideyoshi (1536–1598), and Tokugawa Ieyasu (1543–1616), and the capital moved to Edo (now Tokyo). Their exploits inspired the 1975 novel *Shogun*, by the American James Clavell, but did not lead to the creation of literature of particular interest in Japan itself. Instead, stories and plays by, for, and about townspeople and city life emerged. The most prominent of these are known as *ukiyo-zōshi*, stories of the floating world, referring to the world of transitory pleasures to be found in the company of courtesans and actors. Ihara Saikaku had immediate success with his erotic fiction, beginning with *The Life of an Amorous Man*, which is practically a guidebook to the licensed brothels of the day. In the world of art, *ukiyo-e*, pictures of the floating world, included portraits of geisha, actors, and sumo wrestlers as well as famous places. Woodblock prints of heroes and heroines such as the female samurai warrior Tomoe Gozen (1157?–1247) sold well too. Plays performed by either puppets (*bunraku*) or live actors (*kabuki*) about courtesans and their patrons were especially popular and are still performed today. The most respected playwright of the Edo period (1600–1868) was Chikamatsu Monzaemon (1653–1724), whose most enduring plays portray the plight of courtesans and their lovers who choose suicide over familial obligations.[5] As peace prevailed and the ruling samurai class turned from violence to governing, plays that reminded samurai who had become bureaucrats of their glory days as brave warriors emphasized loyalty no matter the personal cost.[6] Partly because all feudal lords were required to spend alternate years in Edo, travel became safe and convenient. Even common people took to the roads in great numbers, enjoying new sights and sounds, usually on religious pilgrimages. The adventures of two penniless but clever rascals from Edo capture the spirit of such a road trip in *Tokaidōchū Hizakurige* by Jippensha Ikku (1765–1831).[7]

Fearing the destabilizing effect of Christianity, the Tokugawa shogun ordered Japan sealed off from the West in 1633. Only a trickle of trade was permitted with the Dutch in the port of Nagasaki in the extreme southwestern part of the country; meanwhile, the Japanese were forbidden to travel overseas. Japan nonetheless was influenced by the outside world, as seen in a more empirical style of painting that developed at this time, exemplified by "Insect Quire: Summer Version" by Masuyama Sessai (1754–1819).

Commodore Perry arrived in Japan from the United States in 1853 and demanded that Japan open itself to international trade. The national debate about how to respond to this demand led to the overthrow of the Tokugawa regime and the establishment of a new government under the nominal leadership of the sixteen-year-old Emperor Meiji. The actual decision makers were young samurai from domains in the southwest who had long been excluded from political power. Their first priority was to bring the military might of Japan to parity with the Western nations, which were then expanding their colonial empires all over the world. Japan modernized rapidly, choosing to model its navy on that of the British, its army on that of France, and its educational system on Germany's. The new government abolished the samurai class and, believing that Western wealth and power were in part based on constitutional democracy, created a national assembly and wrote a constitution. Political parties were formed, but the ruling elite was reluctant to relinquish power and the national assembly was designed to do little more than provide a site for debate. The constitution kept power in the hands of the emperor, but it was his advisers who actually made decisions. In the Taishō period (1912–1926), people demanded the expansion of political rights and the franchise was gradually extended until all men gained the right to vote in 1925, but the government simultaneously restricted freedom of assembly, of speech, and of the press. Socialist, Communist, and feminist ideas were welcomed by some, but ultranationalism ultimately drowned out those voices. The growth of Japanese military power can be traced through its victories over China in 1895 and over Russia in 1905, the colonization of Korea in 1910, the occupation of Manchuria in 1931, and the assaults on China in 1937 and on the United States of America at Pearl Harbor in 1941. This period of imperialism ended with the atomic bombing of Japan, which would be graphically depicted in Nakazawa Keiji's *Barefoot Gen* series of manga beginning in 1973.

In the Meiji period (1868–1912), translations of Western novels became widely available and Japanese authors began to address contemporary issues, such as how to balance tradition with modernization. A recurring theme for Natsume Soseki was the tension between the independence and isolation that he felt modernization had brought. Modern self-consciousness led to an intense focus on one's own experiences and feelings in a genre called the I-novel. An early example is Toson Shimazaki's *Broken Commandment* (1906), about a man who decides to reveal his identity as a member of the despised class of people known as *burakumin*. Ryūnosuke Akutagawa (1892–1927) became famous for successfully combining the techniques of the modern short story with traditional Japanese themes in works such as *In a Grove* (1922), which Akira Kurosawa made into the movie *Rashomon* (1950).

There was a lull in literary output during the Pacific War: dissent was severely suppressed and paper shortages curtailed publication of even innocuous works. Jun'ichirō Tanizaki (1886–1965) made a name for himself with *Naomi* (1924–1925), a novel that explored issues of Westernization, but during the war he devoted himself to translating *The Tale of Genji* into modern Japanese. Yasunari Kawabata (1899–1972) became a reporter during the war, but resumed writing evocative stories about difficult emotional relationships that won him the Nobel Prize in 1968. In the postwar period, Yukio Mishima (1925–1970) used his literary skills to write stories about various obsessions until he disemboweled himself in the manner of a traditional samurai in 1970 to draw attention to the weaknesses he saw in modern Japan. Kenzaburo Ōe (1935–) won the Nobel Prize in 1994 and is especially known for *A Personal Matter* (1964) and other novels about the emotional issues faced by a man like himself, who has a brain-damaged son. Currently internationally popular writers include Banana Yoshimoto (1964–), known for magical realism, and Haruki Murakami (1949–), whose work is often surreal. Japanese literature—sometimes in the formats of manga and anime now—has found favor with readers all over the world.

Notes

1. *The Ise Stories: Ise monogatari*, translated by Joshua S. Mostow and Royall Tyler (Honolulu: University of Hawaii Press, 2010).

2. "The Tosa Diary" in Earl Roy Miner, *Japanese Poetic Diaries* (Berkeley: University of California Press, 1969), pp. 57–91.

3. Michitsuna no Haha *The Kagerō Diary: A Woman's Autobiographical Text from Tenth-Century Japan*, translated by Sonja Arntzen (Ann Arbor: Center for Japanese Studies, University of Michigan, 1997).

4. "The Little Man" and "Lazy Tarō" from Virginia S. Skord, *Tales of Tears and Laughter: Short Fiction of Medieval Japan* (Honolulu: University of Hawaii Press, 1991), pp. 115–127, 185–204.

5. Chikamatsu, *Four Major Plays*, translated by Donald Keene (New York: Columbia University Press, 1961).

6. Izumo Takeda, Shōraku Miyoshi, and Senryū Namiki, *Chūshingura* (The Treasury of Loyal Retainers), translated by Donald Keene (New York: Columbia University Press, 1971).

7. Ikku Jippensha and Hiroshige Andō, *Shanks' Mare, Being a Translation of the Tokaido Volumes of Hizakurige, Japan's Great Comic Novel of Travel and Ribaldry*, translated by Thomas Satchell (Tokyo: C.E. Tuttle, 1960).

16

Japanese Poetry

As in China, a good education in Japan always included memorizing large numbers of poems and learning to compose poetry. Japanese poetry is overwhelmingly lyrical, but some poems metaphorically express philosophical or spiritual ideas. Rhyme is so easy in the Japanese language that it is not used in Japanese poetry. Instead, we find rhythm created by alternating lines of five and seven syllables, and word play based on homonyms, alliteration, and allusions. The vast majority of *waka* (Japanese poems) are *tanka* (short poems) of just thirty-one syllables in five lines, although there are some impressive *chōka* (long poems), which may be of any length. Linked verse, which is composed by multiple authors contributing two or three lines each to a poem that constantly evolves, became popular in the twelfth century. Poetry contests, in which poems were presented in pairs and judged, were important social events in the premodern era. Poetic talent was a valuable asset in both private and public life. A well-phrased poem could affect the course of a love affair or a political career. A great many people kept personal collections of their best poetry, and memoirs and fictional tales of the premodern era invariably included poems.

The first great collection of Japanese poetry, the *Man'yōshū* (Collection of Ten Thousand Leaves, ca. 785), contains about 4,500 poems on a wide range of topics by a wide variety of authors. It is unique in that it contains 265 long poems on such subjects as mourning for deceased imperial personages and lamenting poverty. Beginning with the *Kokinshū* (ca. 905,

1,111 poems), emperors commissioned twenty-one official anthologies (the last in 1433). In these anthologies, poetic topics are predominantly elegant (close observation of natural phenomena, the anxieties and disappointments of love, congratulations, travel, grief, and wordplay), and poetic diction is refined. Poetry anthologies were carefully organized according to various principles, such as temporal progression—say, from the beginning to the end of a year for the seasonal poems or the typical development of a love affair from first awareness through deep longing to loss of interest. Another principle is based on association, in which case poems that share a particular motif such as the cry of a cicada or red autumn leaves are grouped together. The *Shūishū* is the third imperial collection (compiled between 1005 and 1011).

The *Shinkokinshū* (1205, 1,978 poems) is one of the most highly admired anthologies. Especially prominent in the *Shinkokinshū* is the technique of using simple concrete images evocatively and a tone of poignancy, which may reflect the drastic political changes of the late eleventh century when the warrior class challenged the long-held authority of the imperial aristocracy. Humorous and vulgar poetry became quite popular in the sixteenth century. The best-known Japanese poet, Bashō (1644–1694), infused new seriousness into common topics. He traveled widely, visiting places of religious and poetic importance and then edited his travel diaries for publication. For him poetry became virtually a spiritual practice by means of which he might express ideas traceable to Zen Buddhism, such as radical compassion and embracing the here and now. He composed linked verse and what we now call haiku, brief poems of only seventeen syllables, which usually include a seasonal reference and provocatively juxtapose two images.

Continued interest in poetry is evident in newspapers that routinely publish contemporary poems and the public television broadcast on New Years Day of the *First Poetry Reading*, which presents poems by members of the imperial family and the general public. After the earthquake, tsunami, and meltdown of the nuclear power plant in Fukushima in March 2011, the Asahi newspaper published many poems by survivors expressing their trauma, grief, and will to endure.

Questions

1. In what ways are different aspects of nature personified?
2. Try answering the rhetorical questions, usually by assuming the poet is projecting a feeling of his or her own onto a natural object.
3. What are the most common themes in these poems? What is the predominant tone?

Japanese Poetry

> Man'yōshū poems based on W.G. Aston, *A History of Japanese Literature* (New York: D. Appleton, 1899), pp. 36–38, 42.
> Kokinshū, Shūishū, Shinkokinshū, and haiku poems translated by Margaret Helen Childs from *Kokinwakashū, Shinkoten Nihon bungaku taikei 5*, edited by Noriyuki Kojima and Eizō Arai (Tokyo: Iwanami shoten, 1989); *Shūiwakashū, Shinkoten Nihon bungaku taikei 7*, edited by Teruhiko Komachi (Tokyo: Iwanami shoten, 1990); *Shinkokinwakashū, Shinkoten Nihon bungaku taikei 11*, edited by Yutaka Tanaka and Shingo Akase (Tokyo: Iwanami shoten, 1992); *Matsuo Bashōshū 1–2, Nihon Koten Bungaku Zenshū*, edited by Imoto Nōichi and Nobuo Hori (Tokyo: Shōgakukan 1995); *Ryōkan no haiku*, edited by Seitei Kawaguchi (Osaka: Yukawa shobo, 1977).
> Poems composed in the aftermath of the earthquake and tsunami on March 11, 2011, translated by Laurel R. Rodd, Amy V. Heinrich, and Joan E. Ericson from *The Sky Unchanged: Tears and Smiles* [Kawaranai sora nakinagara, warainagara] by 55 Japanese Affected by the Triple Disaster of March 2011 (Tokyo: Kōdansha, 2014), #5, 24, 36, 39, 71.

Man'yōshū Poems

1. "In Praise of Japan" by Emperor Jomei (r. 629–641)
The land of Yamato
Has many mountains,
But peerless among them
Is high Kaguyama.
When I stand on its summit

And view my realm,
Above the spacious land
Smoke rises through the air,[1]
Above the spacious lakes
Gulls soar through the air.
O land of Yamato!
Fair Akitsushima![2]
How fine a land you are!

2. An excerpt from a poem lamenting the death of Prince Hinami by Kakinomoto Hitomaro (fl. ca. 689–710)

Mighty Prince, if you had deigned
To rule this world beneath the wide skies,
You would have been to all your people
Beloved as the flowers in spring,
Reassuring as the full moon,
Trusted as a great ship,
Welcome as the rain from heaven.
Thus did all your people await you.

3. An excerpt from a poem lamenting poverty by Yamanoue no Okura (660?–733?)

Heaven and earth are wide, but for me they have become narrow;
The sun and moon are bright, but for me they yield no radiance.
Is it so with all men, or with me alone?
Born a man by the rarest of chances,
I am made in human shape like any other,
Yet on my shoulders I wear a cloak without padding,
Which hangs down in tatters like seaweed—
A mere mass of rags.
Under a sagging roof, within tilting walls
Straw is strewn on a bare earthen floor.
Father and mother at my pillow,
Wife and children at my feet,
Gather round me weeping and wailing.
For no smoke rises from the kitchen stove,
In the pot spiders have spun their webs,
The very art of cooking is forgotten.
Still worse—cutting off the end, as the proverb has it,
Of a thing that is too short already—
The village headman comes with his stick,

Summoning me from my bed [to forced labor].
Such hopelessness is but the way of the world.

Kokinshū poems

A preface to the *Kokinshū* by Ki no Tsurayuki (ca. 872–945) concisely
explains the Japanese view of poetry:

"Japanese poetry grows from seeds within the human heart into myriad
leaves of words. People experience all kinds of things and express their
feelings by describing what they see and hear. The voices of the warblers
among the blossoms and of the frogs in the water tell us that every living
thing sings its own songs.

It is poetry that effortlessly sways heaven and earth, inspires pity in
unseen demons and gods, softens the relations between men and women,
and soothes the hearts of fierce warriors . . ."

Spring

1. Ki no Tsurayuki
On this night in spring
the darkness is quite silly.
It may hide from us
the plum blossoms' coloring
but it cannot hide its scent. [#41]

2. Anonymous
Now scattered and gone
though all your petals may be,
plum blossom, please leave
a trace of your scent so I
may recall my love for you. [#48]

3. Ariwara no Narihira (825–880)
If only our world
contained no cherry blossoms
then how peacefully
our hearts might savor the
pleasures of the days of spring. [#53]

4. Sosei
Who knows where the wind
that blew away the blossoms

"Woman Seated Under Cherry Blossoms" by Kuniyoshi Utagawa (1797–1861), ink and color on paper. *Ukiyo-e* (pictures of the floating world) such as these featured renowned courtesans of the day in fashionable attire. *(Wikimedia Commons)*

is lodging tonight?
If you tell me I will go
and speak of my resentment. [#76]

5. Ki no Tomonori (fl. ca. 850–904)

Diffuse rays of sunlight
softly warm the peaceful air
on this springtime day:

Why, then, do cherry
blossoms scatter restlessly? [#84]

Autumn

6. Anonymous
Though not yet fallen,
I mourn for autumn's red leaves.
I recognize that
having now achieved their peak,
they have also reached their end. [#264]

Winter

7. Anonymous
Only at year's end,
when all is covered with snow,
then and only then,

"Maple Tree in Autumn" by Tosa Mitsuoki (1617–1691), cover for collection of cal-
ligraphic writings by famous poets, including Saigyō, titled Poems on the Chapters
of the Lotus Sutra ("Ipponkyō kaishi"), color on paper. *(Wikimedia Commons, Kyoto
National Museum)*

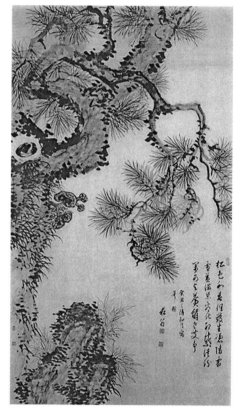

"Old Pine Tree" (1841) by Nukina Sūō (1778 – 1863), hanging scroll, ink and light color on paper. *(Wikimedia Commons, Lake Biwa Cultural Center, Shiga)*

do we take notice of the
steadfastly evergreen pine. [#340]

Parting

8. Henjō (816–890?)
You cherry blossoms!
Let the mountain winds swirl you
up and into clouds
that obscure the path and thus
detain our Prince here with us. [#394]

9. Anonymous
He insists he'll leave
but I hope to make him stay.

You cherry blossoms!
scatter so profusely that
he cannot discern the way. [#403]

Love

10. Anonymous
Within every
raging river there are some
quiet pools and yet
in the torrents of my love
there is no eddy or shoal. [#493]

11. Anonymous
If a seed takes root
even on bare cliffs of rock
it may dare to grow.
If I go on loving him,
why shouldn't we someday meet? [#512]

12. Anonymous
Like mist that rises
from a river and hovers
in the air above,
my heart drifts away from me
to search for you. Such is love. [#513]

13. Anonymous
If seaweed could grow
in a river's swift currents,
I would plant it in
the stream of tears on my sleeves.
Such is my hope to see you. [#531]

14. Ono no Komachi (fl. ca. 833–857)
Lost in longing for you
I fell fast asleep.
That is why I dreamt of you.
If I known it was a dream
I would have refused to wake. [#552]

"Ono no Komachi" (1648) by Kano Tanyu (1602–1674), ink, color, and gold leaf on wood. Komachi was considered one of the six best waka poets of the early Heian period and one of the few females counted among the Thirty-Six Immortal Poets of Japan. Her works express anxiety, solitude, and passionate love. *(Wikimedia Commons, Kotohira-gu Shrine, Shikoku)*

15. *Mibu no Tadamine (fl. 898–920)*
Were it possible,
I would turn myself into
the light of the moon.
Then my hard-hearted lover
might look upon me fondly. [#602]

16. Anonymous
A world without lies.
If only that were the case.
Then with so much joy
would I listen to the words
of a man pledging his love! [#712]

17. Ariwara no Narihira wrote this poem while visiting the place where he had previously engaged in a romance.
Isn't this that moon?
and isn't this the same spring
as it was last year?
Only I am left unchanged
from the way I used to be. [#747]

18. Henjō (816–890?)
I will be back soon
he said as he left my side.
But since that morning
the cicadas' piercing whine
echoes my own misery. [#771]

"Insect Quire: Summer Version" (nineteenth century) by Masuyama Sessai (1754–1819), ink and color on paper. Sessai was the art-name of Masuyama Masakata, the daimyo (military lord) of the Nagashima fief in Ise province. Art was a way for the daimyo to prove their legitimacy, their right to rule. *(Wikimedia Commons, Tokyo National Museum)*

19. Anonymous
That he won't show up
Is something I know full well.
And yet, as night falls,
Cicadas whine piercingly
While I wait uselessly. [#772]

20. Anonymous
With the moon above
Shining so beautifully
How can I not wait?
If it would cloud up and rain
I could at least try to sleep. [#775]

Shūishū poem by Ki no Tsurayuki

Moonlight reflecting
in the tiny pool that I
hold cupped in my hands.
Is it there or is it not?
Such is the world we live in. [#1011]

Shinkokinshū poems

Autumn

1. Saigyō (a monk, 1118–1190)
The heart even of
one who has renounced all things
of this mundane world
is stirred to deep emotion
by the first winds of autumn. [#299]

2. Fujiwara no Teika (1162–1241)
Wherever I look
there are no cherry blossoms
nor autumn leaves.
Just a small hut by the bay
as the autumn twilight fades. [#363]

Winter

3. Saigyō
If only there were
another who could bear such
solitude as this!
our simple huts, side by side:
mountain hamlet in winter. [#627]

Love

4. Fujiwara no Teika
Perhaps he sees it
as he returns from a tryst.
I look up at it
after a night of waiting:
The moon in the dawning sky. [#1206]

Haiku

1. Matsuo Bashō
The old pond is still,
Until a small frog jumps in.
Then, kerplunk, and splash!

2. Matsuo Bashō
On a naked branch
A crow alights, settles down:
Twilight in autumn.

3. Matsuo Bashō
Composed while visiting Hiraizumi where famed general Minamoto no Yoshitsune met an ignominious end:
In summer grasses
Linger the only remnants
of warriors' dreams.

4. Attributed to Ryōkan (a monk, 1758–1831)
There was just one thing

"Portrait of the Poet Bashō with His Most Famous Poem 'An Old Pond—A Frog Jumps In' (ca. 1820) by Kinkoku Yokoi (1761–1832), ink and color on paper. East Asian art often mixes text and images. *(Wikimedia Commons, British Library)*

"Crow on a Snowy Plum Branch" (ca. 1880) by Kawanabe Kyōsai (1831-1889). *(Wikimedia Commons)*

the thief could not steal from me:
Moon in my window.

***Poems composed in the aftermath of the earthquake and
tsunami on March 11, 2011, and resulting disaster at the
Fukushima nuclear power plant:***

1. Yo Kikuchi, March 2011
after seismic tremors greater than six
at my parents' place,
I call my father and mother;
it rings ten times . . . eleven times . . .
terror at no response [#5]

2. Yo Kikuchi, April 2011
a solitary survivor
said
I was left behind
just so I
would weep [#24]

3. Itsu Kato, May 2011
standing behind the children
lined up at the school's
    entrance ceremony,
two mothers, holding
    photos of the deceased [#36]

4. Miyoko Shiraishi, May 2011
embracing
a corpse still shouldering
its book bag—
a member of the Self Defense Force
in the muddy bog [#39]

5. Saburo Shinohara, October 2011
the full moon
climbs up over
the mountain of rubble
like a silent
requiem [#71]

Notes

1. Smoke refers to hearth fires where people are cooking, implying prosperity.
2. Yamato and Akitsushima, literally meaning dragon-fly island, are alternative names for Japan.

17

The Pillow Book

SEI SHŌNAGON

Sei Shōnagon (ca. 966–1017) wrote this collection of lists, reflections, and anecdotes while in service at court to Empress Teishi (977–1000). It reflects the interests and values of a well-educated, witty, and sensitive member of the aristocracy during the golden age of premodern Japanese culture. While the entries may seem to reflect a rather carefree and pampered existence, the fact is that one aspect of the keen competition among an emperor's consorts was the employment of ladies-in-waiting who were expected to make the imperial lady's quarters a place where the emperor might want to spend all his time. There are later collections of essays and anecdotes, but none that includes the kinds of lists found here.

Questions

1. Which observations are still relevant today and which are antiquated?
2. Try making up your own lists on these topics.

The Pillow Book

The Pillow Book selections, translated by Margaret Helen Childs from Sei Shōnagon, *Makura no sōshi, Nihon koten bungaku taikei*, vol. 11 (Tokyo: Shōgakukan, 1974), #1, 25, 60, 74–75, 254. See also #1, 25, 44, 69, 148 in Sei Shōnagon, *The Pillow Book*, translated by Meredith McKinney (London:

Penguin, 2006), and #1, 14, 38, 45, 148 in Sei Shōnagon, *The Pillow Book of Sei Shōnagon*, translated by Ivan I. Morris (Baltimore: Penguin, 1971).

#1. In the Spring: Dawn

In the spring: dawn. The gradually whitening mountain ridges brighten a little and wisps of purplish clouds drift along.

In the summer: night. A moon in the sky is beyond words. When it's a pitch black night, the random flashes of fireflies flitting about is lovely. On such a night even a rain shower is delightful.

In autumn: dusk. The mountain ridges, illuminated by the red setting sun, seem closer than they are. As the crows fly off to their nests in threes and fours or pairs, even they are touching. Still more moving is the sight of a line of geese winging their way to a resting place, growing smaller as they go. Once the sun has set, there is the sound of the breeze and buzzing of insects.

In winter: early morning. I need not describe the beauty of a freshly fallen blanket of snow. At times the frost paints everything white. But even when such is not the case and it's just very cold, someone stirs the coals, reviving them, and another carries fresh charcoal along the corridor, how fitting it is. It's disappointing when at midday the cold has loosened its grip and the burning charcoal in the braziers has all turned to white ashes.

#25 Irritating Things

A guest who arrives and talks on and on when you have something urgent to attend to. When it's someone ordinary you can brush them off with a promise to see them later, but when it's someone important whom you can't offend, how irritating!

Finding a hair in your inkwell while you're grinding ink. The grating noise when there is grit lodged in your ink stick. . . .

People who are jealous, complain about their lot in life, and who criticize others. People who want to know every little thing and complain when you don't tell them what they want to know. People who talk as if they've known every detail all along when they've only just heard a scrap of news. Really irritating!

. . . When you're lying down, trying to sleep, a mosquito announces itself with a sharp, faint buzzing. It flies around your face and you can feel the fluttering of its tiny wings. It's extremely irritating.

. . . When someone with whom you're involved starts reminiscing about a previous lover, saying how wonderful she was. Even though it's a thing of the past and quite a bit of time has gone by, it's still irritating. If it's a current girlfriend it's unbearable. And yet, sometimes it doesn't bother you that much. . . .

#60 Children and Babies

Children and babies should be chubby. Provincial governors and other mature men should be portly. If they're gaunt it makes you imagine that they're anxious and fretful.

#74–75 For a Lovers' Tryst

For a lovers' tryst, summer is delightful. On short nights dawn comes so soon that you haven't slept a wink. Since every aperture has been left wide open you can get a cool feeling by looking out over the garden. While you're sharing your remaining unspoken thoughts, a bird suddenly sings out from right in front of you as if declaring itself a witness to your tryst. How amusing!

On a freezing cold winter morning, while you're still curled up under the quilts with your lover, you hear the muffled echo of a temple bell. How appealing! The first rooster to crow sounds as if he has his beak tucked up under his wing and he seems far away, but as others join in, their crowing grows louder, as if they are coming closer. How charming!

#254 Things that Make You Happy

Getting hold of lots of stories that you haven't read yet. Finding the sequel of a story that was really good. But sometimes the sequel can be disappointing.

Finding enough pieces of a torn up letter to be able to put it back together.

Having a nightmare but being told by a dream interpreter that it doesn't mean anything. That makes me extremely happy.

When a person of high rank is telling a story of something that happened long ago or of something recent that everyone is gossiping about and he looks at you while he's talking. That makes me very happy.

When you hear that someone you care about, whether they're far away or living here in the city, has fallen ill and you're worried about them but then you get news that they are on the mend. That makes me happy.

Hearing someone you love being praised by another or mentioned approvingly by someone of high rank.

Having people take notice of and praising a poem you wrote for a certain occasion or in response to someone else's poem. Having people copy it down in their notebooks. That has never happened to me but I can imagine how happy I would be. . . .

When you're urgently looking for something and someone tells you where it is. And when you're searching for something you need right away but you've misplaced it, you're turning everything upside down, looking everywhere, and then you find it. That makes me happy.

18

The Tale of Genji

MURASAKI SHIKIBU

The Tale of Genji is the story of a man blessed with nearly super-natural beauty, charm, and talent who enjoys a number of love affairs but finds happiness elusive. Although his mother was the emperor's favorite concubine, she was of relatively low status and died young, leaving Genji without the connections neces-sary to compete for the throne. Genji's father makes his son a commoner, but this does not entirely insulate Genji from political jealousies. The story follows the rise, fall, and ultimate success of Genji's career but primarily focuses on his love life and the pageantry and elegant pastimes of the aristocracy. Then the story turns to the lives of Genji's putative son Kaoru, a devout young man who is unlucky in love, and his rival, Prince Niou, Genji's grandson, who seems to have inherited much of Genji's charm, if not his thoughtfulness.

The author is known as Murasaki Shikibu (ca. 973–1014?), a nickname derived from the name of the most central of the female characters in the tale and a government position that her father once held. She became a lady-in-waiting in the service of an empress around 1006, probably because of the popularity of this tale that circulated as she wrote successive chapters. Her talent as a writer was certainly enhanced by her knowledge of Chinese literature, gained from her father, who was a scholar of Chinese literature and a provincial governor.

This lengthy novel—over 1,000 pages long—is considered by many to be the first novel in the world, and it immediately became and has remained extremely popular. In the twelfth and thirteenth centuries, the greatest poets of the time declared that to be a good poet one needed to be familiar with it. In the fifteenth century it was the source of descriptive language and characters in Noh plays by the great playwright Zeami (ca. 1364–1443), and in the eighteenth century it was appreciated as an expression of an especially Japanese sensibility, *mono no aware*, which refers to anticipatory regret for the transience of things. In modern times it has been made into plays, films, manga, and anime.

"Illustration of *The Tale of Genji*, Chapter 5," attributed to Tosa Mitsuoki (1617–1691), ink, color, and gold flake on paper. Prince Genji glimpses the young lady Murasaki and falls in love. *(Wikimedia Commons, Mary Griggs Burke Collection)*

In the portion of a chapter given here, Genji is eighteen years old and his love life is already very complicated. He has an official wife thanks to an arranged marriage, but she is older than he and cool toward him. Polygamy was common for the aristocracy and, like most young couples, Genji has his own residence while his wife lives in her parents' household. Genji is in love with his young stepmother, Fujitsubo, who is pregnant with his child but trying to keep Genji at arm's length due to the impropriety of their relationship. It was Myōbu, a lady-in-waiting in Fujitsubo's service, who engineered the encounter that resulted in Fujitsubo's pregnancy. Also, Genji has kidnapped the ten-year-old Murasaki, who resembles Fujitsubo, with the intention of marrying her when she reaches the appropriate age, usually fourteen, although others think their relationship is already a sexual one.

It is probably Genji's emotionality that endeared him to readers. The antihero of the novel is the mother of the crown prince, the Kokiden lady who is coldhearted and ambitious. Love was seen as virtually uncontrollable and unreliable and therefore inevitably causing heartbreak. Also, there were no religious beliefs to restrain sexual intimacy, so although infidelity might cause social discomfort, it was not considered immoral. It is also useful to know that men and women lived quite segregated lives, with women keeping themselves behind screens and communicating with visitors mostly through intermediaries.

Characters (in order of appearance):

- the emperor: Genji's father
- Genji: son of the emperor and a lower-ranking imperial concubine, the hero
- Tō-no-Chūjō: Genji's brother-in-law and best friend
- mother of the crown prince, also known as the Kokiden lady: hostile to Genji
- Genji's primary wife, daughter of the Minister of the Left, age 22
- Fujitsubo: Genji's stepmother, age 23
- Koremitsu: a male servant of Genji's
- bishop: brother of Murasaki's deceased grandmother
- Murasaki, age 10: daughter of Prince Hyōbukyō by a woman of rather low status; Fujitsubo's niece. Like Genji's

mother, Murasaki's mother died when Murasaki was very young. Genji kidnapped her to prevent her father from taking custody of her when her grandmother died.

- Shōnagon: Murasaki's nursemaid
- Genji's father-in-law, Minister of the Left

Questions

1. How do the many various observers react to the dances performed by Genji and his brother-in-law Tō-no-Chūjō? Why does the emperor prefer the dancing of amateurs to that of professionals?
2. What kind of relationship does Genji have with Murasaki at this point?
3. Why are Genji and his official wife alienated from each other?
4. Near the end of the selection, Genji and Fujitsubo exchange poems about the wild pink flower, which serves as a metaphor for their infant son. To what extent do these poems sum up the complexity of their feelings at this time?

The Tale of Genji

Excerpts from *Genji and Heike: Selections from the 'The Tale of Genji' and 'The Tale of the Heike,'* translated by Helen McCullough (Stanford, CA: Stanford University Press, 1994), pp. 113–123 (footnotes amended for clarity and simplicity). Copyright © 1994 by the Board of Trustees of the Leland Stanford Jr. University. All rights reserved. Used with the permission of Stanford University Press, www.sup.org.

Chapter 7: A Celebration Amid Autumn Leaves [Momiji no ga]

The emperor's visit to the Suzakuin was to take place soon after the tenth of the tenth month.[1] Since it promised to be much more interesting than the usual imperial excursion, the consorts were upset about missing the spectacle. The emperor himself felt that something would be lacking if the Fujitsubo lady were not able to see the dances, and he arranged for a rehearsal in the courtyard outside his private residence.

Genji danced "The Waves of the Blue Sea." His partner, Tō-no-Chūjō, was extraordinarily handsome and confident, but he was like a nondescript mountain tree alongside a blossoming cherry. It was a moment of absorbing interest, the music especially beautiful in the glittering rays of the setting sun; and Genji's dancing and demeanor seemed to belong to another realm of existence, familiar though the piece was. When he chanted the Chinese lines, it was like hearing the voice of a *kalavinka* bird in paradise. The emperor wiped away tears of admiration, and all the senior nobles and princes wept.

When Genji straightened his sleeves at the end of the chant, the waiting musicians resumed in a tempo so spirited that he flushed and looked even more radiant than usual. "His is the kind of face a heavenly spirit might take a notion to carry off. I call it creepy," said the crown prince's mother, ill-pleased by the brilliance of the performance. Her young attendants considered the remark distasteful.

The Fujitsubo lady thought that she might have enjoyed his dancing more if her mind had not been tormented by the heinous impropriety of their relationship, which seemed more dream than reality. She spent the night with the emperor.

"It seemed to me that 'The Waves of the Blue Sea' swept the board in the rehearsal today," the emperor said to her. "What did you think of it?"

Conscious of a strange awkwardness, she replied merely, "It was remarkable."

"Tō-no-Chūjō wasn't at all bad, either," he said. "There's something distinctive about the way the son of a good house moves and gestures. Our famous professionals are highly accomplished, of course, but they can't create the same effect of fresh, youthful charm. After such a dazzling rehearsal, I'm afraid the real event under the autumn foliage may be an anticlimax, but I arranged this because I wanted you to see it."

Early the next morning, the lady received a letter from Genji. "How did the performance strike you? I've never felt as agitated as I did during my dance." [His poem:]

monoomou ni	Did you understand
tachimaubeki mo	the sentiments of the one
aranu mi no	who fluttered his sleeves,
sode uchifurishi	all but unable to dance
kokoro shiriki ya	for the burden of grief he bore?

"But I ought not to write this way."

She sent an answer, apparently unable to let the message pass in silence while the beauty of his face and figure was still vivid in her mind:

karabito no	Though I know not why
sode furu koto wa	a man of Cathay might have wished
tōkeredo	to flutter his sleeves,
tachii ni tsukete	I watched every movement
aware to wa miki	with the deepest feeling.

"I was exceptionally impressed."

For Genji, it was the most precious of gifts. "She's even a connoisseur of dance, and she's already talking like an empress with that reference to ancient China," he thought, an unconscious smile on his lips. He sat gazing at the letter, which he had spread with as much care as if it had been his special sutra.

The emperor was attended on his excursion by the entire court, princes and all. The crown prince also made the journey. The musicians' boats moved across the lake as usual, and there were innumerable dances, both Chinese and Korean. The sounds of instruments and the throbbing of drums filled the air. After having watched Genji in the late sunlight on the day of the rehearsal, the emperor had felt uneasy enough to commission sutra recitations at various temples, a precaution that received sympathetic approval from all who heard of it—all, that is, except the crown prince's disapproving mother, who considered it excessive. Nobody who was not a recognized expert had been selected for the flutists' circle, which included both courtiers and men of lower rank.[2] The two groups of dances, those of the left and those of the right, were under the supervision of two consultants, Saemon-no-kami and Uemon-no-kami.[3] The performers had been rehearsing in the seclusion of their homes, with the finest dancing masters as coaches.

The wind in the pines, a veritable mountain gale, gusted in concert with the strains of the flutes, which were played with indescribable beauty by forty men standing in a circle under the tall maple trees; and the spectacle was almost frightening to behold when Genji emerged from among the swirling colored leaves, dancing "The Waves of the Blue Sea" with dazzling brilliance. Upon observing that most of the leaves had fallen from the maple twig in his headdress, making it a poor match for his glowing face, the major captain of the left picked some chrysanthemums from the garden as a substitute. A few scattered raindrops fell in the waning light, as though the very heavens had been moved to admiration. Genji danced that day as never before, his beauty enhanced by the delightful hues of the fading chrysanthemums,[4] and his performance of the withdrawal was chilling in its perfection, a thing not of this world. Even among the menials who watched from behind trees, rocks, and piles of leaves—people who could scarcely have been expected to appreciate what they saw—those who possessed a modicum of taste were moved to tears.

Second only to "The Waves of the Blue Sea" was "The Song of the Autumn Wind," danced by the emperor's fourth son (the offspring of the Shokyōden lady), who was still a child. The two performances exhausted the spectators' capacity for enjoyment. The other numbers attracted little attention, and actually seemed to detract from the occasion.

That night, Genji was granted senior third rank, and Tō-no-Chūjō received senior fourth lower rank. All the eligible senior nobles also enjoyed suitable promotions, thanks to their association with Genji's triumph. One wondered what deed in a previous life might have enabled him to both astonish people's eyes and delight their hearts.

The Fujitsubo lady retired from the palace around that time, and Genji began to frequent her premises as usual, hoping against hope for a meeting. His neglect gave rise to complaints at his father-in-law's mansion, and his wife grew even unhappier when one of her ladies-in-waiting caught word of young Murasaki's discovery and abduction, and proceeded to inform her that he had brought a mistress to live in the Nijō Mansion. Her feelings were natural for someone ignorant of the facts. If she had spoken out about her discontent like an ordinary woman, he would have explained it all and set her mind at rest, but her habitual mistrustfulness made her put the worst construction on his behavior, and that was why he sometimes indulged in unfortunate frivolities. Still, she was a woman of flawless appearance and demeanor, impossible to fault. She was also the first one with whom he had been intimate, and his feeling for her was special. "She acts that way now because she doesn't realize how much love and respect I feel for her. She'll change some day. She's reasonable; she's not flighty; she's bound to come around," he thought hopefully.

Sweet, pretty, and innocent, young Murasaki grew ever more attached to Genji as she came to know him better. For the time being, he resolved to let nobody know who she was, not even the members of his household. He kept her in the isolated wing, which he had furnished with incomparable splendor, and devoted much of his time to her education. As he prepared calligraphy models and set her to writing, it seemed to him quite as though he had welcomed home a daughter who had lived elsewhere. To the bafflement of everyone but Koremitsu, he safeguarded her position by providing her with an independent administrative office, stewards, and other functionaries. Meanwhile, her father had been unable to find out anything about her.

There were still many times when the child remembered the past and missed her grandmother. She had other things to distract her while Genji was there, and he spent an occasional night at home. But more often, he would prepare to leave at dusk, bound for one of his usual destinations, and then she would sometimes protest his departure in a manner that he found tremendously appealing. Whenever he spent two or three days on duty and went straight from the palace to his father-in-law's house, she would lapse into deep gloom, and he would feel like a man with a pathetic motherless child. He no longer found it possible to pursue casual amours in a carefree spirit.

The bishop heard and rejoiced, even though it was hard for him to understand. When he performed memorial services for the nun [Murasaki's grandmother], Genji sent impressively generous condolatory offerings.

Eager for news of the Fujitsubo lady, Genji went to her house on Sanjō Avenue one day. He was received by Myōbu, Chūnagon, Nakatsukasa, and others of the ladies-in-waiting. It galled him to be categorized so obviously as an ordinary visitor, but he concealed his displeasure and chatted about general subjects.[5] Meanwhile, Prince Hyōbukyō arrived, learned of his presence, and came to greet him. The prince was elegant, romantically inclined, and mild-mannered—someone who would be of more than passing interest if he were a woman, Genji thought to himself. Attracted to him also because of his relationship to Murasaki and the Fujitsubo lady, he addressed him with quiet seriousness. The prince, for his part, admired the beauty of the companion who seemed so much more friendly and relaxed than usual. Always on the alert for a conquest, he thought, "What a pity he's not a woman!" Genji's desirability as a son-in-law failed to occur to him.

Genji watched with envy as the prince went inside his sister's blinds at nightfall. In the old days, thanks to his father, he had seen her close at hand and talked to her without an intermediary, and he took it rather unreasonably amiss that she should be intent on keeping him at a distance now. He ended his visit with a brusque speech. "I ought to have called more frequently, but the time slipped by because there seemed to be nothing I could do for you. Should there be anything, I will be delighted to put myself at your disposal."

Myōbu could find no way to help him. She felt both intimidated and moved to pity by the unyielding attitude of her mistress, who was more than ever convinced that the meetings with Genji were fated to cause her misery. So the empty days went by, with the two of them agonizing endlessly over the relationship that had proved so brief.

When the nurse Shōnagon thought about her charge's unexpected good fortune, she could not help seeing it as a buddha's response to the prayers the anxious nun had offered for Murasaki during her religious exercises. With a most imposing lady at the minister of the left's house, to say nothing of numerous attachments in other places, difficulties seemed all too likely to arise after the child grew up, but Genji's remarkable devotion was surely a portent of good things to come.

Genji arranged for Murasaki to discard her dark robes at the end of the twelfth month, three months being the prescribed period of mourning for a maternal grandparent. But the nun had been like a mother to her, and she wore no ostentatious colors—only semiformal outer robes in unfigured reds, purples, and yellows, in which she looked very smart and attractive.

Genji peeped into her room as he was leaving for the congratulations.[6] "Did you turn into a grown-up today?" He smiled, handsome and charming. She had already marshaled her dolls and was absorbed in play. He had provided her with accessories, kept on the shelves of a pair of three-foot cabinets, and with a group of tiny buildings, all of which now littered the floor.

"Inu said she was chasing demons and she broke this.[7] I'm fixing it," she said with a serious face.

"That was careless of her. We'll get it mended right away. This is a day for avoiding inauspicious things; you mustn't cry." His departure with a throng of attendants was a marvelous spectacle. The ladies-in-waiting went to the veranda to watch. Murasaki also went out and looked, after which she dressed a doll as Genji and dispatched him to the palace. Shōnagon tried to make her feel embarrassed about her addiction to play. "You must act a little more grown up this year," she said. "Someone who's past ten isn't supposed to play with dolls. Now that you have a husband, you need to be quiet and gentle when you're with him, like a proper wife. As it is, you even fret when someone does your hair."

Her speech was a revelation. "So I have a husband!" Murasaki mused. "My ladies' 'husbands' are ugly, but mine is young and handsome." Despite her love of dolls, such reflections suggested that she had indeed grown a year older. The members of the household puzzled over her childishness, which was apparent on innumerable occasions, but it did not occur to any of them that she and Genji might not be sleeping together as man and wife.

Genji went from the palace to his father-in-law's mansion. His wife was her usual self, elegant and correct, with a guarded air that made him feel awkward. "I can't tell you how happy I'd be if you could at least decide to let this year mark a turning point for us, the beginning of something a little closer to a normal marriage," he said. But it was only to have been expected that she would seem even more distant and constrained than in the past, for she had heard that he was lavishing attentions on someone whom he had installed in his house, and she must have been worrying ever since about the seriousness of the relationship. Forcing herself to act as though there was nothing on her mind, she unbent and responded to his sallies in a manner distinctively her own. She was four years his senior, enough older to be in her prime, and to make him feel callow. He realized that she was a woman who left nothing to be desired, and that his own philandering was to blame for her coldness. The true cause of their estrangement was probably that they viewed their relationship in different ways. As the cosseted only daughter of the nation's preeminent minister, her mother an imperial princess, she possessed an unparalleled appreciation of her own importance and reacted with shocked indignation to any lapse on Genji's part, whereas he considered her unreasonably proud and tried to mold her into conformity with his notion of what a wife should be.

The minister was also disturbed by Genji's unreliability, but the mere sight of him was enough to make him forget his resentment and shower him with attentions. Dropping by early the next morning, as Genji was preparing to leave, he personally brought in a famous belt to go with his ceremonial robes, straightened the rear of his costume, and all but put on his shoes for him in a moving display of solicitude.

"The palace banquet will be coming up; I'll use the belt then," Genji said.[8] But the minister insisted that he wear it. "You'll have a better one for the banquet; I just brought this because it looks a little unusual," he told him. It was in fact only when he was fussing over Genji and admiring his beauty that his life seemed worth living. Infrequent though the visits were, there could be no greater pleasure than seeing such a man come and go as his daughter's husband.

Although Genji had announced that he intended to pay New Year calls, he visited only a few places: the imperial palace, the residences of the crown prince and the retired emperor, and the Fujitsubo lady's house on Sanjō Avenue.

"His Lordship looks remarkably handsome today. The more he matures, the more beautiful he seems; it makes one quite nervous," said the Fujitsubo lady's admiring attendants. Many thoughts crowded into their mistress's mind as she peeped at him through a gap in her curtains.

It was cause for some concern that the twelfth month had passed with no sign of the Fujitsubo lady's delivery. Her people continued to wait—the child was bound to arrive in the first month, they said—but the first month also went by, disappointing their expectations. To the lady's dismay, the gossips began to speculate. Might a malicious spirit be impeding the birth? It would surely be the death of her, she lamented. Sunk in misery, she fell ill. Genji made quiet arrangements for esoteric rites at numerous temples, more convinced than ever that the child must be his. He mulled over the situation with a sinking heart. Was her death to mark the end of a fleeting moment in a world of impermanence? But she gave birth to a son toward the middle of the second month, and the emperor and her household rejoiced, their worries forgotten. She felt now that she must cling to life. It was a painful decision, but she began a gradual recovery, spurred by the thought that news of her demise would produce a gleeful response from the Kokiden lady, who was said to have referred to her in language that amounted to a curse.

The emperor could hardly wait for his son to arrive in the palace. Burdened with his secret and consumed with worry, Genji went to the Sanjō house at a time when no other visitors were present. "His Majesty says he is eager to see his son. I wonder if I might see him; then I can tell him what he looks like," he said.

"I'm afraid he's still at the ugly newborn stage," the lady demurred.

Her refusal sounded not unreasonable, but the truth of the matter was that nobody could mistake the child's astonishing, almost uncanny resemblance to Genji. Her conscience nagged. "Once people see him, everyone will know I've committed a transgression so terrible I can hardly believe it myself. People are always ready to find fault, even when it's nothing of importance—nothing like this. What will happen to my reputation?" Beset by such thoughts, she seemed to herself the victim of a uniquely bitter fate.

From time to time, Genji saw Lady Myōbu. Making use of every conceivable argument, he implored her to arrange a meeting with her mistress, but it need hardly be said that his efforts were futile. He badgered her with pleas to let him see the baby. "Why be so unreasonable? You'll see him soon enough in the natural course of events," she said. Inwardly, she was as distressed as he. Too embarrassed to come to the point, he said, "I wonder if there will ever be a time when I can talk to her without an intermediary." He was a pathetic figure, his eyes brimming with tears. [His poem:]

ikasama ni	What was the nature
mukashi musuberu	of the karma we fashioned
chigiri nite	in a time gone by,
kono yo ni kakaru	that in this world we suffer
naka no hedate zo	separation such as this?

"I just don't understand this kind of thing," he said.

Myōbu, a witness to the lady's anguish, could not bring herself to rebuff him. She murmured a soft reply:

mite mo omou	The one who sees grieves.
minu hata ika ni	And what must be the sorrow
nagekuran	of the one who sees not?
ko ya yo no hito no	Might this be the darkness
madou chō yami	where humans are said to stray?

"It distresses me that neither of you should know a moment's peace."

Since he could find no way to send in a message, Genji left. The Fujitsubo lady, worried about gossip, told Myōbu not to dream of helping him. She no longer admitted her attendant to the trustful intimacy of old, and there must have been times when she showed displeasure with her, even though she treated her well enough to avoid comment. Myōbu must have felt very forlorn and disappointed.

The baby was taken to the imperial palace in the fourth month. He was large for his age and precocious, already showing signs of wanting to sit up. The emperor was not at all suspicious of his amazing resemblance to Genji. "It's just as they say; two supremely handsome individuals do tend to look very much alike," he thought. He was enchanted. His affection for the infant Genji had been equally warm, and he still much regretted that fear of public disapproval had kept him from naming the boy crown prince. It had been a sorrow to watch him develop into someone whose bearing and appearance were far too distinguished for a subject. But now he possessed a son with the same radiant beauty, born of a mother whose status was irreproachable; and he treated him as a flawless gem. Meanwhile, the Fujitsubo lady existed in perpetual apprehension and gloom, worried as much by the emperor's joy as by the child's appearance.

One day, when Genji was participating as usual in a musical gathering at the Fujitsubo pavilion, the emperor came out with the baby in his arms. "Of all my sons, you were the only one I saw constantly, beginning with the days when you were just this young. Perhaps it's the association of ideas, but I seem to notice a close resemblance. I wonder if all babies look alike when they're tiny." He gazed at the child with deep affection.

Genji was sure he was changing color. Trepidation, shame, joy, tenderness—one emotion seemed to follow another, and his eyes brimmed with tears. The baby looked almost ominously appealing as it cooed and smiled. Though he said it himself, it was no small thing to resemble such a paragon, he thought rather egotistically. The Fujitsubo lady perspired in an agony of embarrassment.

Despite the eagerness with which he had looked forward to seeing the child, Genji found the experience so unsettling that he left the palace. Back in his own apartments, he lay down to rest. He would go on to his father-in-law's house after he regained his composure.

Wild pinks were blooming in the garden outside, a splash of color against a green background. He picked one and sent it to Lady Myōbu, with a letter that probably ran on at considerable length. [His poem:]

yosoetsutsu	Small consolation
miru ni kokoro wa	to gaze at the pink in bloom,
nagusamade	mindful of another:
tsuyukesa masaru	the tears I shed outnumber
nadeshiko no hana	the dewdrops on its petals.

"I had looked forward to the flower's bloom, but ours is a hopeless situation."

A suitable opportunity must have arisen, for Myōbu showed the letter to her mistress. "Please do send him an answer on a petal, even if it's no more than a speck of dust," she said.

The Fujitsubo lady herself was wrestling with painful emotions. She produced what seemed half an answer, a single poem written in faint characters:

sode nururu	Though I tell myself
tsuyu no yukari to	it is the source of dewdrops
omou ni mo	dampening sleeves,
nao utomarenu	I cannot look with dislike
yamatonadeshiko	on the wild pink of Yamato.

Myōbu sent it on, happy even with so little. Genji had been lying down in wretched spirits, staring into space, with no expectation of anything but the usual silence. The poem made his heart beat wildly, and he shed tears of joy.

No matter how long he might lie there moping, he thought, his spirits would be unlikely to revive. He went to seek diversion in the west wing, as was his custom at such times. Blowing a pleasant air on his flute, he peeped into Murasaki's room, his hair untidy and his robes rumpled. She reminded him of the dewy pinks as she leaned against an armrest, looking bewitchingly sweet and pretty. Apparently piqued by his failure to come as soon as he reached home, she kept her face averted in uncharacteristic fashion. He knelt at the threshold. "Come here," he said. As though she had not heard, she murmured a line from a poem: "A rock when the swelling tide rolls in."[9] She raised a sleeve to her mouth in a delightfully coquettish gesture. "You're not being nice at all. When did you learn to talk that way? I don't want you to get a surfeit of seaweed."[10] He told someone to bring a koto for her. "The second string on the thirteen-stringed instrument doesn't stand up very well to high notes. It would be a nuisance to have it break," he said. He took it down to the *hyōjō* mode, played a few notes to tune it, and pushed it away. She stopped pouting and began to play with childish grace, looking very sweet as she bent her tiny body to twang the strings with her left hand. Charmed, he coached her while he played the flute. She was so bright that a single hearing was all she needed to master a difficult melody. Her lively intelligence and delightful disposition were exactly what he had hoped for. He gave "Hosoroguseri" a spirited rendition that made its ugly name seem acceptable, and she accompanied him in perfect time, her touch immature but rich with promise.

The servants lighted the lamps, and the two of them looked at pictures.

Since Genji had announced that he would be going out, his attendants began to clear their throats. "It looks like rain," a voice said. As usual, Murasaki's spirits sank. She turned away from the pictures and lay face down, a pathetic sight. He stroked the abundant hair tumbling over her shoulders. "Do you miss me when I'm away?" he asked. She bobbed her head.

"It's very hard for me, too, if I have to go without seeing you for a day. But I feel I can be at ease with you while you're still a little girl, and there are some jealous ladies whom I don't want to offend. They're being rather difficult, so I'm going to have to go out like this for a while. I'll never go anywhere after you grow up. The reason I don't want anyone to hate me is that I hope to live a long life and spend it happily with you." His long explanation left her abashed and speechless. She put her head on his lap and promptly fell asleep. Overcome with compassion, he told the ladies-in-waiting that he had decided not to go out that evening, and they all went off to bring his dinner to the west wing.

He woke Murasaki up. "I've decided not to go out," he said. She sat up, her good humor restored, and they dined together. She toyed with her food. "Well, then, please go to bed," she said, as though afraid he might change his mind. How could he ever leave such a one, even to set off on the Shide Mountain road itself?

There were many times when Genji was detained in the same way. People naturally heard about what was happening, and the stories were passed along to the household of the minister of the left. "Who can she be?" the ladies-in-waiting at the mansion asked one another. "It passes belief! Still not a word about her identity, and look at the way she hangs onto him like a spoiled child! She can't have much to recommend her in the way of birth or refinement; she's probably someone he met at the palace or some place, fell in love with, and hid for fear of criticism. Maybe that's why they say she's childish and unreasonable."

The emperor heard that Genji was keeping a woman at home. "It's pitiful that the minister of the left should feel so unhappy," he told his son. "He's been doing everything imaginable for you ever since you were a child, and it's not as though you weren't old enough now to understand what you owe him. What makes you so heartless?" Genji preserved a respectful silence. "Poor lad," the emperor thought. "He doesn't seem to care much for his wife." He continued, "And yet I don't see or hear anything to suggest that you're promiscuous or infatuated with one of the ladies-in-waiting here or the women you see elsewhere. What kind of hole-in-the-corner affair is it that's causing so much resentment?"

Notes

1. The Suzakuin was a residence used by retired emperors. Judging from the title of this chapter, "A [Longevity] Celebration Amid Autumn Leaves," the purpose of the visit was to honor a former sovereign, but we are not given a full account of the occasion. Longevity celebrations (*ga*) usually took the form of decennial observances, held from a man's or woman's fortieth year on. They were sponsored by relatives, or occasionally by friends or patrons, and always included a banquet, dances, and the recitation of suitable poems.

2. A feature of "The Waves of the Blue Sea" was that the dancers put on their costumes inside a ring of musicians behind the stage. Old commentaries surmise that there may have been forty men in the ring because the retired emperor's fortieth year was being celebrated.

3. An indication of the importance of the occasion. Lesser officials usually oversaw such events.

4. Most of the chrysanthemums in Heian gardens were white. Contemporary taste admired the reddish, brownish, and purplish tinges they acquired as they faded.

5. The attendants act as intermediaries in the conversation.

6. The congratulations (kojōhai) was a ceremony honoring the emperor, held at the imperial palace on New Year's Day.

7. Demon-chasing (tsuina) was a vigorous ritual performed on the last night of the year. Its purpose was to rid the premises of pestilence demons.

8. The palace banquet (naien) was a Chinese poetry gathering, held annually in the first month of the year.

9. An allusion to an anonymous poem (Man'yōshū 1398): "Seldom do I see you, often do I yearn for you. Yet you are not seaweed on a rock that vanishes when the swelling tide rolls in."

10. Genji uses aku to mean "surfeit" instead of "one's fill," twisting the meaning of the anonymous poem he quotes (Kokinshū 683): "I long for a means of seeing my fill of you—seeing like the weed, the 'see weed' Ise fishers harvest morning and evening." There is a pun on mirume ("seeing," "seeing eye"; a type of seaweed).

19

Tales of Times Now Past

Among the more than 1,200 stories in this collection from the twelfth century are Buddhist tales from India, China, and Japan plus secular tales set in Japan. They are all brief, vivid, and tend to conclude with advice inspired by the tale. They include specific names, dates, and places, as if to imply that these are true stories— although many of them are obviously too fantastic to be true. The first tale included here represents a large category of stories of miracles brought about by faith in Buddhist teachings. The second reveals the value placed on music, and the third is an early expression of the samurai ethic of extreme stoicism.

Questions

1. Re 12.28: How are our expectations of the two *oni* (demons) radically altered as the story proceeds?
2. Re 24.23: Why does not Hiromasa just knock on Semimaro's door and ask the blind man to play the tunes Hiromasa wants to hear?
3. Re 25.11: What is the difference between Chikataka's reaction to the kidnapping and that of Yorinobu? Why do they also have different ideas about how to treat the kidnapper when the incident is resolved?

Tales of Times Now Past

> *Tales of Times Now Past* excerpts from Marian Ury, *Tales
> of Times Now Past: Sixty-Two Stories from a Medieval
> Japanese Collection* (Berkeley: University of California
> Press, 1979), pp. 87–89, 143–145, 150–152. Used with
> permission.

12.28: How a Government Clerk of Higo Province Escaped a Rakshasa[1]

At a time now past, in Higo Province, there was a government clerk. He went each day to the government office where he performed his duties; he had been doing this for some years. On one occasion an urgent matter arose and he set out from his home early in the morning. He was on horseback and without a single attendant. The office was scarcely a mile from his home, so that as a rule he arrived there after a short time, but today the farther he went the farther away it became. Unable to get there, he lost his way entirely and came out upon a broad plain. Where he was, he did not know. He had ridden all day, and now the sun had set. There was nowhere to spend the night all was open plain.

In his distress he kept hoping to come upon some human habitation; and then, from an outcropping of the foothills, he caught a faint glimpse of the corner of a prosperous-looking dwelling. "I must have come near a settlement," he thought, and hurried joyfully toward it. When he examined the house from close by, however, there was no sign of human beings. He went all around it. "Is anyone there? Come out, please. What is the name of this place?" From within a woman answered, "Who are you, sir? Come right in, sir!" At the sound of her voice the clerk was terrified, but he said, "I've lost my way. I've urgent business, so I can't come in. Just tell me how to find the road." "Wait a moment," said the woman, "I'll come out and show you." His fear mounted, and he wheeled his horse about and began to flee. Hearing the hoofbeats, the woman cried "Wait, wait!" Looking back, he saw her come out; she stood as high as the eaves of the house and her eyes glowed light. "So it was, indeed! I came to the house of an oni," he thought, and applied the whip. "Why are you trying to run away?" said the woman. "Stop this instant, you!" To say that he was terrified would scarcely suffice. His head swam; he felt as though his guts would split. He saw a being ten feet tall; fire issued from its eyes and mouth, brilliant as lightning; its mouth was wide open, and it was striking its hands together as it pursued him. His senses all but failed him at the sight, and he would have fallen from his horse; but he whipped it onward and onward again, praying: "[Bodhisattva] Kannon save me! Save my life, even for just one day!" The horse stumbled and fell. The clerk was thrown free in front of it. Now surely the creature would catch him and devour him, he thought. There was a cave close by, and he ran in, beside himself with fear.

The oni came hot on his tracks. "Hey, where'd he go? He was here a moment ago," it said, but instead of going to look for him, it first ate his horse. The clerk heard everything, and he had not the slightest doubt that as soon as it had finished with the horse it would eat him. Was there a chance that it did not know he was in the cave? All he could do was pray. "Kannon save me!"

Now, when the oni was through eating the horse it came up to the mouth of the cave and said, "This man is supposed to be my supper today. Why won't you give him back? You're always doing things like that. It's not fair. You're mean to me." "I thought I'd found a place to hide, but it knows I'm here," thought the clerk. From within the cave came a voice: "He'll be my supper today. You can't have him. You've had the horse and that's enough." "There's no way I can survive now," thought the clerk. "The oni that chased me was dreadful enough, but there is one in this cave who is even more terrible. It is certain to eat me," and his distress was boundless. "Even though I pray to Kannon, my life will soon be over. This must be because of the sins of my previous lives."

The oni outside the cave earnestly repeated its pleas, but the one within would not yield, and the clerk heard the one outside return home, whining. Now, surely, the other would drag him off and devour him, he thought. But just then the voice in the cave said, "Today you would have been eaten by an oni, but by virtue of your fervent prayers to Kannon you have escaped harm. Hereafter you must devote yourself to the Buddha with all your heart and recite the Lotus Sutra. Now then, do you know who it is that speaks to you?" The clerk replied that he did not. The voice said, "I am no oni. Once, long ago, a holy man lived in this cave. On a peak to the west he built a reliquary mound, burying under it a copy of the Lotus Sutra. Year upon year has passed since then, and mound and sutra both have crumbled away. All that remains is the first character of the title, Myō. That first character is none other than I, myself. During my time here I have rescued nine hundred and ninety-nine persons who would have been eaten by the oni. You are the thousandth. Leave this place at once and go home. Strive always to worship the Buddha and recite the Lotus Sutra." The clerk was sent home, with a beautiful boy to escort him.[2]

Weeping and performing reverent salutations, the clerk followed the boy and regained his home. The boy saw him to the gate and said, "Have single-minded faith; recite the Lotus Sutra"—and then the boy vanished. The clerk wept and made obeisance; it was midnight when he returned home. He told his parents and his wife and children everything, and they were profoundly moved. Thereafter, arousing earnest faith, the clerk recited the Lotus Sutra and was all the more fervent in worshiping Kannon.

Now think: though only one character of the Lotus Sutra remained, it saved a man's life. You can imagine, then, the merit that will come from copying the Lotus Sutra in the prescribed form and with true faith. If such is the benefit in this present life, do not doubt that you will escape all torments in the life to come. So the tale's been told, and so it's been handed down.

24.23: *How Minamoto no Hiromasa Ason Went to the Blind Man's House at Ōsaka*

At a time now past, there was a man named Minamoto no Hiromasa Ason. He was son of a prince who was Minister of War and himself a son of the Engi emperor. He was a master of all the arts and sciences, but among them, especially, the Way of musical instruments. His skill at the lute was amazing, the beauty of his flute-playing indescribable. He was a courtier of middle rank during the reign of Emperor Murakami.[3]

At this time there was a blind man who had built himself a hut to live in at the barrier of Ōsaka. His name was Semimaro.[4] He had once been no more than a menial attendant in the household of Prince Atsumi, the Minister of Ceremonial. That Prince was a son of the cloistered emperor Uda and had mastered the Way of musical instruments. Year after year Semimaro had constantly heard him play the lute, until he himself grew amazingly skillful at it.

Now Hiromasa was passionately fond of the Way of music and passionately eager to learn everything related to it, so that when he heard that the blind man who lived at the Ōsaka barrier was a proficient musician he decided that he simply had to hear him. But the blind man's house was so singular that, instead of going there, he sent a servant to speak to Semimaro in private. "Why do you live in such a strange place? Suppose you were to come to the capital to live?"

The blind man heard this and made no reply, only speaking this verse:

> *In this world*
> *No matter how*
> *We pass our days—*
> *Neither palace nor hovel*
> *Is our final dwelling.*

The messenger returned and recounted this. Hiromasa was impressed with the blind man's gentility. He thought to himself, "It is because of my devotion to this Way that I am profoundly convinced that I must meet him. Furthermore, it's hard to tell how much longer the blind man may live; nor do I know how long my own life will last. There are two tunes for lute called 'Flowing Spring' and 'Woodpecker' that are likely to become extinct with this generation. They say that only this blind man knows them. Somehow or other I'll contrive to hear him play them."

With this in view, he journeyed one night to the barrier at Ōsaka. Semimaro, however, never once played those tunes. And so, thereafter, night after night for three long years, he journeyed to the hut at Ōsaka. He hid himself and waited, listening: would he play tonight? Would he play tonight? But the blind man never played at all.

In the third year, on the night of the fifteenth day of the eighth month, a fine mist lay over the face of the moon and a gentle breeze was blowing. "What a charming evening it is!" thought Hiromasa. "Surely this night the blind man of Ōsaka will play 'Flowing Spring' and 'Woodpecker.'" He went to Ōsaka, and as he waited, listening, the blind man plucked the strings, with the expression of one who is deeply moved. Hiromasa listened with mounting joy as the blind man, to cheer his loneliness, chanted this poem:

> *The storm winds*
> *At Ōsaka barrier*
> *Are wild;*
> *Yet here I spend my days*
> *Stubbornly, blind.*

As he made the lute sound, Hiromasa felt the tears stream down his face. The blind man was speaking to himself. "Ah, it is a charming night. I wonder if somewhere there is someone besides myself who appreciates it. If only a visitor would come who understood my art. We should talk together."

Hiromasa heard this and spoke up: "A man named Hiromasa who lives in the capital has in fact come here." "By whom have I the honor to be addressed?" said the blind man. Hiromasa told his name and origin. "Because I am devoted to this Way, for the past three years I have come to your hut. Tonight, to my great good fortune, I have met you." The blind man heard this and rejoiced. Thereupon, Hiromasa, in the midst of his own rejoicing, entered the hut. Together they talked. Hiromasa said, "I should like to hear 'Flowing Spring' and 'Woodpecker.'" "His late lordship played them this way," said the blind man, and transmitted the knowledge of the pieces in question to Hiromasa. Hiromasa had not brought his lute with him, and so he learned them orally. Over and over again he gave thanks. At dawn he returned home.

Now think: this is the sort of devotion that should be shown toward each of the many Ways. In this Latter Age, men who have achieved mastery in the various Ways are few. Truly this is a deplorable state of affairs.[5]

Though Semimaro was a base-born fellow, through hearing the Prince play the lute year after year he acquired consummate skill. It was because he had gone blind that he was living at Ōsaka. The tradition of blind lute-players begins from that time. So the tale's been told, and so it's been handed down.

25.11: How Fujiwara no Chikataka's Son Was Taken Hostage by a Robber and Freed Through Yorinobu's Persuasion

At a time now past, when Minamoto no Yorinobu Ason, Governor of Kōchi, was Governor of Kōzuke[6] and residing in that province, there was in his retinue a man named Fujiwara no Chikataka, Lieutenant of the Middle Palace Guards, who was the son of Yorinobu's old nurse. Chikataka too was everything that a warrior should be. During the time that he was in Kōzuke with Yorinobu, he caught a thief and placed him under guard in his own house. Somehow or other the man managed to slip his shackles and get away. Chikataka's son, a pretty child of no more than five or six years, was running about. Perhaps because the thief saw no means of completing his escape, he seized the child

as a hostage and took him into a storage shed. There he forced him
down between his knees. He drew a knife and sat there with the tip
pressed to the child's belly.

Someone ran to the government office where Chikataka was. "A thief
has taken the young master hostage," was the report. Chikataka hurried
back in alarm. He saw it: it was true. The thief was sitting in the shed
with a knife at the little boy's belly. The father grew faint at the sight.
But what was he to do? It occurred to him that he might just go up and
snatch the boy away—but there in full view was the knife, large and
glittering, pressed to his boy's belly.

"Keep away! One step closer and I'll run him through," the thief said.
"He'll kill him, just as he says," thought Chikataka. "I could hack the
scoundrel to bits—but what good would it do?" To his followers he said,
"Keep your wits about you. Don't get near. Surround him, but from a
distance." And he ran to Yorinobu's office to inform him.

It was not far to go. The Governor was astonished to see Chikataka rush
in, in evident consternation. "Is something the matter?" he asked. "My
little boy, my only son, has been taken hostage by a robber," Chikataka
said in tears.

The Governor laughed. "Not that you haven't cause," he said, "but
what are you doing here weeping? You should want to put up a fight,
even if it were with a god or a demon. You're weeping like a child! Isn't
that ridiculous. You should think, 'Let him be killed if need be. He's only
one little boy.' If that's how you can feel, you will fulfill your duty as a
warrior. If you worry about your own safety, if you worry about your wife
and child, you'll be beaten at every turn. Fearlessness means to have no
thought for yourself or your family. All the same, though, I'll go have
a look." And carrying only his long sword for a weapon, the Governor
went to Chikataka's house.

The Governor stood at the entrance to the shed and peered inside. The
thief saw that it was the Governor who was there, and instead of flaring
up, as he had when he spoke to Chikataka, he lowered his eyes, gripping
his knife all the harder to show that he was ready to run the boy through
at the first attempt to come near. All the while the child was howling.
The Governor addressed the thief: "You've taken this boy hostage. Was
it in the hope of saving your life? Or did you simply want to kill him?
Which is it? Speak up, scoundrel."

In a pitiful, thin voice the thief replied: "How could I think of killing
a child, sir! It's only that I don't want to die. I wanted to stay alive, and
I thought that taking a hostage might give me a chance."

"Then throw that knife away," said the Governor. "It is I who command you, I, Yorinobu. I don't intend to look on while you kill a child. I mean what I say, you know that: my reputation gets around. Just throw it away, thief!"

The thief considered a while. "Thank you, sir, I will. I wouldn't dare disobey you. I'll throw my knife away," and he flung it far away, jerked the boy to his feet, and released him. Once on his feet, the boy scampered off as fast as he could go.

The Governor withdrew a short distance and summoned his retainers. "Get that man over here," he said. The retainers took the thief by the collar and dragged him into the courtyard in front of the house. Chikataka wanted to cut him down with his sword, but the Governor said, "This fellow let his hostage go—now that's a fine thing to have done! He became a thief because he was poor and he took a hostage in order to save his life. There's no need to hate him. After all, he did as I told him: that shows there's some sense in the scoundrel. Let him go at once." Turning to the thief, he said, "What do you need? Tell me," but the thief only wept speechlessly.

"Give him a few provisions," the Governor said. "He's done other bad deeds, and he's likely to end up killing someone. Look among the draft horses in the stable for one that's strong. Put a cheap saddle on it and bring it here." He sent men to fetch them. He also sent for a crude bow and quiver. When all had been brought out, he had the robber put the quiver on his back and mount the horse in the front courtyard. The men put ten days' worth of dried rice in a bag, wrapped it in a coarse sack, and fastened it to his waist.

"Now then, ride right out of here and begone!" Obedient to the Governor's command, the thief galloped away and was lost from sight.

It must have been the dread he felt at a single word from Yorinobu that made the thief release his hostage. Now think: never was there a more fearsome warrior than Yorinobu.

When the boy who had been taken hostage grew up, he abandoned secular life on Mount Mitake[7] and ultimately attained the office of acharya [Buddhist teacher]. His religious name was Myōshū. So the tale's been told, and so it's been handed down.

Notes

1. *Rakshasa* are man-eating demons in Hindu and Buddhist lore.
2. This refers to a special kind of supernatural being, the "divine boy who protects the Dharma." These beings are the messengers of the divinities who uphold

the Buddha's teaching; they also make themselves servants of religious adepts, and in *setsuwa* [ancient Japanese stories] they are often given the task of escorting home persons who have strayed into fairyland.

3. The Engi emperor was Emperor Daigo (r. 897–930). Emperor Murakami (r. 946–967).

4. Ōsaka, not to be confused with the modern city of the same name, was a mountain pass a few miles east of modern Kyoto which was the site, during various eras, of a military checkpoint. Nothing is known of the historical Semimaro, or Semimaru.

5. Anecdotes of this nature suggest some of the parallels between art and religion in Japanese tradition. Both art and religion demand total devotion. To acquire a secret tradition or become the disciple of a great man, the aspirant must demonstrate almost superhuman persistence; yet a great master's influence is such that it may transform those who have come into contact with him simply through living in his household. The word translated as "Way" is the same as that for religious path. And the Latter Age was the time of decline not only of the Buddha's Dharma but of the arts as well. It might be added that mastery of the arts can confer supernatural powers that resemble, though in lesser degree, those enjoyed by the religious adept.

6. This celebrated warrior (968–1048) is recorded as having been Governor of Kōzuke (modern Gunma prefecture) in 999. He came to be called Governor of Kōchi (also read as Kawachi) because this was his final official post.

7. Mount Mitake is another name for Kinpusan in Yoshino, center of the esoteric school of Buddhism known as Shugendō.

20

The Tale of the Heike

This tale of the twelfth-century conflict between the Taira (or Heike) and Minamoto (or Genji) clans is historical fiction that first circulated as vocal literature with the purpose, at least in part, of pacifying the angry spirits of the defeated Taira warriors. It became extremely popular as a performing art thanks to the innovative *biwa* (Japanese lute) player and singer Kakuichi (d. 1371). It has remained popular and its characters appear in Noh plays and many other genres.

The Tale of the Heike covers the years 1131–1192, beginning with the Taira clan chieftain Tadamori (1096–1153), who allied himself with the powerful retired emperor Toba (r. 1107–1123) and was able to raise his clan above its provincial warrior origins and gain entry to the aristocracy. Then succession disputes within the imperial family led to armed clashes that created the opportunity for Taira clan chieftain Kiyomori (1118–1181) to win the patronage of retired emperor Go-Shirakawa (r. 1155–1158). Kiyomori rose quickly through the ranks of government to the topmost post of chancellor and was even able to have his grandson Antoku named emperor when he was just a toddler. However, the Taira made many enemies because they wielded their power arrogantly and finally alienated their patron. *The Tale of the Heike* focuses on resistance to Taira rule in the 1170s and the armed conflict against them that lasted from 1180 to 1185. It concludes with the peaceful death of Kiyomori's daughter, who spent her final years mourning her young son, Emperor Antoku, who had drowned during the final rout of the Taira forces by the Minamoto. One of the major motifs in the tale is that the Taira had taken up aristocratic pastimes such as poetry and music while the Minamoto were rough and tough, closer to their military roots. The narrator's voice is not that of the victor, who might have demonized the enemy, but of an observer who sees the Taira warriors as individual human beings.

Questions

1. Re 7.16: Identify the several points that indicate just how important poetry was to Tadanori. The poem that Shunzei chose to include in the *Collection for a Thousand Years (Senzaiwakashū)* refers to Shiga, the site of the capital from 667 until it was destroyed in a war between rivals for the imperial throne in 672. What are the parallels between the poem and Tadanori's situation?
2. Re 9.4: Compare Kanehira and Yoshinaka's attitudes toward impending death.
3. Re 9.16: Why does Kumagae hesitate to kill Atsumori? What discovery makes him regret killing the youth?

The Tale of the Heike

Excerpts from *Genji and Heike: Selections from the 'The Tale of Genji' and 'The Tale of the Heike,'* translated by Helen McCullough (Stanford, CA: Stanford University Press, 1994), pp. 358–359, 378–381, 394–396 (footnotes amended for clarity and simplicity). Copyright © 1994 by the Board of Trustees of the Leland Stanford Jr. University. All rights reserved. Used with the permission of Stanford University Press, www.sup.org.

In 1183 the Taira fled the capital as the forces of Kiso no Yoshinaka, a Minamoto general, approached. Among them was Taira no Tadanori (1144–1184), a younger brother of the Taira clan chieftain, Kiyomori. His poetry teacher was Shunzei (1144–1204), the most respected poet of his generation.

7.16 Tadamori's Flight from the Capital

Somewhere along the way, Satsuma Governor Tadanori turned back to Shunzei's house on Gojō Avenue, attended by five samurai and a page. The gate was locked.

"It's Tadanori," he announced.

There was agitation inside. "One of the fugitives is back!" voices said.

Tadanori dismounted. "It's nothing special, Shunzei," he shouted. "I've just come back to speak to you. Come out here if you'd rather not open the gate."

"I think I know what he wants," Shunzei said. "He won't make any trouble. Let him in." They opened the gate and Shunzei received him. It was a moving scene.

"I haven't meant to be neglectful since you accepted me as a pupil several years ago," Tadanori said, "but my clan has had to bear the brunt of the unrest in the city and the rebellions in the provinces. During the last two or three years, I haven't been able to pay you regular visits, even though poetry is still very close to my heart. Now the emperor has left the capital, and my clan's good luck has come to an end. I had heard people say there was to be a new imperial anthology, and I had thought it would be the greatest honor of my life if you might include even one of my poems. What with all this turmoil, no commission has been handed down, but there's sure to be one after peace is restored. If this scroll contains one suitable poem, and if you should see fit to include it, I'd rejoice in my grave and act as your guardian spirit."

When he was about to leave home, he had snatched up a scroll in which he had recorded more than a hundred poems—to his mind the best of the many he had composed and saved over the years. Now he withdrew it from the armhole in his armor and gave it to Shunzei. Shunzei opened it and looked inside. "I couldn't possibly consider this a keepsake of no importance. Please don't have any fears about that. Your coming here at a time like this shows how much the art of poetry means to you; it moves me to tears," he said.

Tadanori was delighted. "Now I won't mind drowning in the western waves or leaving my bones to bleach in the wilds. Nothing remains to bind me to this transitory existence. Goodbye!" he said. He mounted his horse, tied his helmet cords, and rode off toward the west. Shunzai watched until his figure receded far into the distance. Someone was chanting a *rōei* in a resonant voice that sounded like this:

Distant lies the way ahead;
My thoughts run on the evening clouds at Yanshan.[1]

Moved again by the sorrow of parting, Shunzei had to restrain tears as he went inside. Later, after the restoration of peace, he compiled the *Collection for a Thousand Years*; and then, with a full heart, he remembered how Tadanori had looked and what he had said. There were many eligible poems in the scroll, but he limited his choice to one, taking cognizance of the fact that the author was someone who had suffered imperial censure. Its topic was "Blossoms at the Old Capital." He labeled it "Anonymous."

sazanami ya	It lies in ruins now—
shiga no miyako wa	the old capital at Shiga
arenishi o	of rippling wavelets—
mukashi nagara no	but the cherries at Nagara
yamazakura ka na	bloom as they bloomed long ago.

Tadanori was an enemy of the throne, so there's nothing more to be said. Still, the story is a pathetic one.

9.4. The Death of Kiso

Kiso no Yoshinaka had brought two female attendants, Tomoe and Yamabuki, with him from Shinano Province. Yamabuki had fallen ill and stayed in the capital. Tomoe was the more beautiful of the two, with white skin, long hair, and charming features. She was also a remarkably strong archer, and with a sword she was a warrior equal to a thousand, ready to confront demon or god on horseback or on foot. She handled unbroken horses with superb skill; she rode unscathed down perilous descents. When there was a battle to be fought, Yoshinaka sent her out to act as his first captain, equipped with stout armor, an especially long sword, and a strong bow, and she performed more deeds of valor than any of his other warriors. Now she was one of seven who remained after all their comrades had either fled or perished.

There were rumors that Yoshinaka was making for the Tanba Road by way of Nagasaka, and also that he was heading north through the Ryūge Pass. As a matter of fact, though, he was retreating toward Seta in the hope of finding Imai Kanehira. Kanehira had lost all but fifty of his eight hundred defenders at Seta, and had started back toward the capital with

"Tomoe Gozen with Uchida Ieyoshi and Hatakeyama no Shigetada" (1899) by Toyo-hara Chikanobu (1838–1912), color woodblock print. During the Battle of Awazu (1184), Uchida Ieyoshi *(on left)* and Hatakeyama Shigetada *(on right)* tried to cap-ture Tomoe Gozen, but she slew Uchida and escaped. *(Wikimedia Commons)*

his banner furled, worried about his master. The two arrived simultane-ously at Uchide Beach in Ōtsu, recognized each other from a distance of three hundred and fifty feet, and galloped together.

Lord Kiso took Kanehira's hand. "By rights, I ought to have died on the riverbed beyond Rokujō Avenue, but I broke through an enemy host and retreated because I wanted to find you," he said.

"It's a great honor to hear you talk like that," Kanehira said. "I ought to have died at Seta, but I've come this far because I was worried about you."

"I see that our karmic bond still holds. My warriors scattered into the mountains and woods after the enemy broke our ranks, but some of them must be near here. Tell your man to raise that furled banner!" Yoshinaka said.

When Imai's banner was unfurled, more than three hundred riders responded—men who had fled from the capital or Seta, or who had come from some other place. Yoshinaka's spirits rose. "We have enough for one last battle. Who's the leader of that band I see over there?" he said.

"They say it's Ichijō Tadayori from Kai Province," someone answered.

"What's his strength?"

"He's supposed to have six thousand riders."

"Then it's just the right match! If we have to die, let's do it by attack-ing good men and going down because we're outnumbered," Yoshinaka said. He rode forward in the lead.

That day, Lord Kiso wore a tunic of red brocade, a suit of armor laced with thick Chinese damask, and a horned helmet. At his side, he had strapped a magnificent long sword; high on his back, there was a quiver holding the few arrows that remained from his earlier battles, all fledged with the tail feathers of eagles. He grasped a bow wrapped with rattan and sat in a gold-edged saddle astride his famous horse Oniashige [Roan Demon], a very stout and brawny animal. Standing in the stirrups, he announced his name in a mighty shout. "You must have heard of Kiso no Kanja; take a look at him now! I am the Morning Sun Commander, Minamoto no Yoshinaka, director of the imperial stables of the left and governor of Iyo Province. They tell me you're Ichijō no Tadayori from Kai. We're a good match! Cut off my head and show it to Yoritomo!" He galloped forward, yelling.

"That fellow who's just named himself is their commander-in-chief," Tadayori said. "Wipe out the whole force, men! Get all of them, boys! Kill them!"

The easterners moved to surround Yoshinaka with their superior numbers, each hoping to be the one to take his head. Yoshinaka's three hundred horsemen galloped lengthwise, sidewise, zigzag, and crosswise in the middle of the six thousand, and finally burst through to the rear. Only fifty were left.

As the fifty went on their way after breaking free, they came to a defensive position manned by two thousand horsemen under the command of Toi Sanehira. Again, they broke through and went on. Again, they galloped through enemy bands—here four or five hundred, there two or three hundred, or a hundred and forty or fifty, or a hundred—until only five of them were left. Even then, Tomoe remained alive.

"Hurry up, now!" Lord Kiso said to Tomoe. "You're a woman, so go on off. Go wherever you please. I've made up my mind to die fighting, or else to kill myself if I get wounded, and it wouldn't be right to let people say I kept a woman with me during my last battle."

At first, Tomoe refused to leave. When she could resist no longer, she pulled up. "If I could find somebody worth bothering with, I'd fight one last battle—give His Lordship something to look at," she thought.

As she sat there, thirty horsemen came into view, led by Onda Moroshige, a man famous in Musashi Province for his prodigious strength. Tomoe galloped in among them. She rode up alongside Moroshige, seized him in a powerful grip, and pulled him down against the pommel of her saddle. Holding him motionless, she twisted off his head and threw it away. Then she abandoned her armor and helmet and fled toward the eastern provinces.

Tezuka Mitsumori died fighting and Tezuka no Bettō fled. Only two riders were left, Kanehira and Lord Kiso.

"I've never noticed it before, but my armor feels heavy today," Lord Kiso said.

"You aren't tired yet, your horse is still fresh. Why should the weight of a suit of armor bother you? You're discouraged because there's nobody left on our side. But don't forget—I'm worth a thousand ordinary warriors. I'll hold off the enemy awhile with my last seven or eight arrows. That place over there is the Awazu Pinewoods. Kill yourself among the trees," Kanehira said.

As the two rode on, whipping their horses, a new band of fifty warriors appeared. "Get into the pinewoods! I'll hold these fellows off," Kanehira said.

"By rights, I ought to have died in the capital. The only reason I ran off here was because I wanted to die with you. Let's not be killed in different places; let's go down together," Lord Kiso said. He brought his horse alongside Kanehira's, ready to gallop forward.

Kanehira jumped down and took Lord Kiso's horse by the bit. "No matter how glorious a warrior's earlier reputation may have been, a shameful death is an eternal disgrace. You're tired; you haven't got any followers. If you get isolated, and if somebody's no-account retainer drags you down to your death, people will say, 'So-and-so's retainer killed the famous Lord Kiso, the man known throughout Japan.' I'd hate to see that happen. Please, please, go into the pinewoods," he said.

"Well, then ..." Lord Kiso galloped toward the woods.

Kanehira dashed into the fifty riders alone. He stood in his stirrups and announced his name in a mighty shout. "You must have heard of me long ago; take a look at me now with your own eyes! I am Imai no Shirō Kanehira, aged thirty-three, foster-brother to Lord Kiso. The Kamakura Lord Yoritomo himself must know that I exist. Kill me and show him my head!" He fired off his remaining eight arrows in a fast and furious barrage, felling eight men on the spot. (It's hard to say whether or not they were killed.) Then he galloped around, brandishing his drawn sword, without finding anyone willing to face him. Many were the trophies he amassed! The surrounding easterners released a hail of arrows, hoping to shoot him down, but none of their shafts found a chink in his armor or penetrated the stout plates, and he remained uninjured.

Lord Kiso galloped toward the pinewoods, a lone rider. It was the twenty-first of the first month. The evening shadows were gathering, and a thin film of ice had formed. Unaware that a deep paddy field lay in front of him, he sent his horse plunging into the mire. The horse sank, head and all, and stayed motionless, despite furious flogging with stirrups and whip. Lord Kiso glanced back, worried about Kanehira. As he did so, Ishida Tamehisa, who was hard on his heels, drew his bow to the full and sent an arrow thudding into his face. Mortally wounded, he sagged forward, with the bowl of his helmet against the horse's neck.

Two of Tamehisa's retainers went up and took Lord Kiso's head. Tamehisa impaled it on the tip of his sword, raised it high, and announced in a mighty shout, "Miura no Ishida no Jirō Tamehisa has slain Lord Kiso, the man known throughout Japan!"

Kanehira heard the shout as he fought. "I don't need to protect anybody now. Take a look, easterners! This is how the bravest man in Japan commits suicide!" he said. He put the tip of his sword in his mouth, jumped headlong from his horse, and perished, run through. Thus, it turned out that there was no fighting worth mentioning at Awazu.

9.16. The Death of Atsumori

After the defeat of the Heike, Kumagae no Naozane walked his horse toward the beach. "The Taira nobles will be fleeing to the shore to get on board the rescue vessels," he thought. "I wish I could wrestle with one of their high-ranking commanders-in-chief!" Just then, he saw a lone rider splash into the sea, bound for a vessel offshore. The enemy was wearing a silk tunic embroidered with cranes, a suit of armor with shaded green lacing, and a horned helmet. At his waist, there was a sword with gilt bronze fittings; on his back, he carried a quiver containing arrows fledged with black-banded white eagle feathers. He held a rattan-wrapped bow and rode a white-dappled reddish horse, with a saddle trimmed in gold. When the horse had swum out a hundred and fifty or two hundred feet, Naozane beckoned with his fan.

"I see that you're a commander-in-chief! It's dishonorable to show your back to an enemy! Come on back!" he shouted.

The warrior came back. As he left the water, Naozane rode up beside him, gripped him as hard as he could, and crashed with him to the ground. Holding him motionless, he pushed aside his helmet, intending to cut off his head, and saw that he was only sixteen or seventeen years old, with a lightly powdered face and blackened teeth,[2] a boy just the age of Naozane's own son Naoie, and so handsome that he could find no place to strike.

"Who are you? Announce your name. I'll spare you," Naozane said.

"Who are you?" the youth asked.

"Nobody of any special importance: Kumagae no Jirō Naozane of Musashi Province."

"Then I don't need to give you my name. I'm the kind of opponent you want. Ask about me after you take my head. Somebody will recognize me, even if I don't tell you."

"He's bound to be a commander-in-chief," Naozane thought. "Killing this one person won't change defeat into victory, and sparing him won't change victory into defeat. When I think of how I grieved when Naoie got just a little wound, it's easy to imagine how this young lord's father would feel if he heard that he'd been killed. I have a notion to let him go." Casting a swift glance to the rear, he discovered Sanehira and Kagetoki coming along with fifty riders.

"I'd like to spare you," he said, restraining tears, "but there are Genji warriors everywhere. You can't possibly escape. It will be better if I'm the one to kill you, because I'll offer prayers for you."

"Just take my head; don't waste time," the boy said.

Overwhelmed by compassion, Naozane could find no place to strike. His senses reeled, his brain seemed paralyzed, and he was scarcely conscious of his surroundings. But matters could not go on like that forever. In tears, he took the head.

"No life is as miserable as a warrior's. It's only because I was born into a military house that I've had this terrible experience. What a cruel thing I've done!" He pressed his sleeve to his face and wept.

But matters could not go on like that forever. He started to remove the youth's tunic, preparatory to wrapping the head in it, and found a flute in a brocade bag tucked in at the waist. "Poor fellow! He must have been one of the people I heard playing inside the stronghold just before dawn. There are tens of thousands of riders in our eastern armies, but I'd be willing to bet not one of them carried a flute to the battlefield. Those court nobles are men of refinement," he thought.

When Naozane's trophies were presented to Yoshitsune for inspection, they brought tears to everyone's eyes. It was learned later that the slain youth was Atsumori, aged seventeen, a son of Tsunemori, the head of the Palace Repairs Office.

After that Naozane thought increasingly of becoming a monk.

The flute in question is supposed to have been a present from Retired Emperor Toba to Atsumori's grandfather Tadamori, who was an excellent musician. I believe I have heard that Tsunemori inherited it, and that he turned it over to Atsumori because the boy played so well. Saeda [Little Branch] was its name. It is deeply moving that music, a profane entertainment, should have led a warrior to a life of religion.

"Ushiwaka Playing a Flute" (ca. 1830) by Toyoya Hokkei (1780–1850), surimono, color woodblock print. Samurai like Ushiwaka—another name for Minamoto no Yoshitsune—were urged to master both martial arts and fine arts hence his depiction with both swords and a flute in this surimono, a privately commissioned print. (Los Angeles County Museum of Art)

Notes

1. Lines from a poem in Chinese by the literatus Ōe no Asatsuna (886–957).
2. Court nobles began to blacken their teeth early in the twelfth century.

21

Essays in Idleness

Yoshida Kenkō

Yoshida Kenkō (1283–1350) was a poet-monk of distinction who lived in a time of political turmoil. (In 1331 Emperor Go-Daigo challenged the power of the samurai regime based in Kamakura and reinstituted imperial rule, but soon was overthrown by his samurai ally, Ashikaga Takauji, who reestablished military rule with himself as shogun.) Despite the inherent contradiction, Kenkō embraced both the Buddhist teachings of transience and was nostalgic for the elegance of life during the aristocratic rule of the Heian period (794–1185). His random collection of 243 brief essays presents values, insights into human nature, and aesthetic principles that became fundamental in Japanese culture.

Questions

1. What contradictions are there in the passages below?
2. List some of the values that are explicit and implicit in the passages below. Are they still relevant today?
3. Analyze the logic of the aesthetic principles outlined below.

Essays in Idleness

> Based on G.B. Sansom, *The Tsuredzure Gusa of Yoshida no Kaneyoshi*, in *Transactions of the Asiatic Society of Japan* 39 (1911), pp. 13–14, 15–16, 17, 26–27, 32, 42, 85–86.

7

Were we to live on forever—were the dews of Adashino never to vanish, the smoke on Toribeno[1] never to fade away—then indeed would men not feel the pathos of things.

Truly the beauty of life is its uncertainty. Of all living things, none lives so long as man. Consider how the dragonfly awaits the fall of evening, and the summer cicada knows neither spring nor autumn. Even a year of life lived peacefully seems long and happy beyond compare; but for those who never weary of this world and are loath to die, a thousand years would pass away like the dream of a single night.

What shall it avail a man to drag out till he becomes decrepit and unsightly a life which some day must end. Long life brings many shames. At most before his fortieth year is full it is seemly for a man to die.

After that age it is pitiful to see how, unashamed of his looks, he loves to thrust himself into the society of others, and, cherishing his offspring in the evening of his days, craves to live on and on that he may watch them grow and prosper. So he continues, his heart set on naught but worldliness, and hardening to the pathos of things.

10

There is a charm about a neat and proper dwelling house, although this world is but a temporary abode. Even the moonshine seems to gain in friendly brilliancy, shining into the house where a good man lives in peaceful ease

The man is to be envied who lives in a house, not of the modern, garish kind, but set among venerable trees, with a garden where plants grow wild and yet seem to have been disposed with care, verandas and fences tastefully arranged, and all its furnishings simple but antique.

A house which multitudes of workmen have devoted all their ingenuity to decorate, where rare and strange things from home and abroad are set out in array, and where even the trees and shrubs are trained unnaturally—such is an unpleasant sight, depressing to look at, to say nothing of spending one's days therein. Nor, gazing on it, can one but reflect how easily it might vanish in a moment of time.

The appearance of a house is to some extent an index to the character of its inhabitant.

"Landscape" (1445) by Tenshō Shūbun (flourished 1414–1463). During the Muro-machi period, Japanese art and culture was heavily influenced by China as seen in the style of this ink painting. *(Wikimedia Commons, Nara National Museum)*

There is a story that Saigyō,[2] when he saw that the Minister Go-Tokudaiji had stretched ropes across the roof of his residence in order to keep the kites from settling here, exclaimed, "And if the kites do settle there, what harm can they do? This then is the sort of man his Lordship is!" and ever after refused to visit him.

So, when I once saw ropes stretched on the palace roof of His Highness Prince Aya-no-Kōji, I remembered this story, but then I heard people say that the truth was, His Highness could not bear to see the frogs in his pond caught by crows that settled there in flocks,[3] and I thought this is a very praise-worthy action, and, after all, perhaps Go-Tokudaiji had some good reason for what he did.

13

To sit alone in the lamplight with a book spread out before you, and hold intimate converse with men of unseen generations—such is a pleasure beyond compare.

25

This world is as mutable as the pools and shallows of the river Asuka! Time passes, things vanish. Joy and grief go and come. What once was a gay and crowded spot becomes a deserted moor: or, if the dwelling rests unchanged, yet those within are not the same. "The peach and the pear tree cannot speak. With whom then shall I talk of bygone days?" How much more fleeting, then, the traces of the great that lived in ages we have never seen.

Looking on the remains of Kyōgoku-den or Hōjōji,[4] one stands amazed to see how a man's ambition can come to naught, and to note the changes wrought by time. . . .

It is useless for a man to plan for a time he will not live to see.

31

One morning, after a fine fall of snow, I had to write to a friend, but in my letter I said not a word about the snow. Whereupon the answer came, "How can I do what is asked of me by a man of such poor taste as not to write, 'What do you think of this snowfall?' or a line of that sort? I am truly disappointed in you." I thought this an amusing reply. The writer is now dead, so that I do not readily forget even such a trifle as this.

37

Although some will say, 'After all this time, why stand on ceremony?,' I myself feel that it is a sign of genuine and proper feeling when even the most inseparable of friends treat one another, if the occasion demands, with due reserve and decorum. On the other hand, it is sometimes well for people who are not intimate to speak freely.

55

A house should be built with the summer in view. In winter one can live anywhere, but a poor dwelling in summer is unbearable. Deep water does not give a cool sensation. Far cooler is a shallow running stream. Coming to details, a room with sliding doors is lighter than one with those on hinges. When the ceiling is high the room is cold in winter and difficult to light. In construction people agree in admiring a place with plenty of spare room, as being pleasing to the eye and at the same time useful for all sorts of purposes.

82

"It is a pity that thin cloth covers soon wear out," said someone to Ton'a[5] who replied, "It is only when the covers are torn top and bottom and the mother-of-pearl has fallen out of the ends of the roller that a volume looks well." By this one perceives him to be a man of excellent taste.

Some people dislike seeing a complete set of writings—sketches and so on—of which all the volumes are not alike. But the Bishop Kōyū said (it seems to me very admirably), "It is only a person of poor understanding who wishes to arrange things in complete sets. It is incompleteness that is desirable." In everything regularity is bad. To leave a thing unfinished gives interest, and makes for lengthened life. They say that even in building the palace an unfinished place is always left. In the writings of the ancients there are many missing chapters and parts.

137

Are we only to look at flowers in full bloom, at the moon when clear?

Nay, to look out on the rain and long for the moon, to draw the blinds and not to know the passing of spring—these arouse even deeper feelings. There is much to be seen in young boughs about to flower, in gardens strewn with withered blossoms. Where, in the titles of verses, it is written, "On going to see the blossoms, but they had too quickly fallen and passed away," or "On being prevented from going to see the blossoms," are the verses inferior to those written, "On seeing the blossoms"?

Men tend to regret that the moon has waned or that the blossoms have fallen, and this must be so; but they must be perverse indeed who will say, 'This branch, that bough is withered, now there is naught to see.'

In all things, it is the beginning and end that are interesting. The love of men and women, is it only when they meet face to face? To feel sorrow at an unaccomplished meeting, to grieve over empty vows, to spend the long night sleepless and alone, to yearn for distant skies, in a neglected home to think fondly of the past—this is what love is.

Rather than to see the moon shining over a thousand leagues, it sinks deeper into the heart of man to watch it when at last it appears towards the dawn. It never moves one so much as when seen, pale green over the tops of the cedars on distant hills, in gaps between the trees, or behind the clustering clouds after showers of rain. When it shines bright on the leaves of oak and evergreen, and they look wet, the sight sinks deep into one's being, and one feels, 'Oh! for a friend with a heart,' and longs for the capital.

And must we always look on the moon and the blossoms with the eye alone? Nay, in the very thought thereof, in the spring though we do not go out, on moonlit nights though we keep to our chamber, there is great comfort and delight.

A well-bred man does not show strong likings. His enjoyment appears careless. It is rustic boors who take all pleasures grossly. They squirm and struggle to get under the blossoms, they stare intently, they drink wine, they link verses, and at last they heartlessly break off great branches. They dip their hands and feet in springs; they get down and step on the snow, leaving footmarks; there is nothing they do not regard as their own.

Notes

1. Adashino and Toribeyama are cremation sites.
2. Saigyō (1118–1190) was an eminent poet-monk; see poems on pages 152 and 153.
3. Ropes on the roof discouraged birds from perching there and feeding from ponds which traditionally were constructed in front of mansions.
4. Both of these buildings were residences of Fujiwara no Michinaga (966–1027), the most powerful man of his era.
5. Ton'a (1289–1372) was an eminent poet-monk.

22

Nakamitsu

The highly ritualized art of Noh drama dates from the fourteenth century. Performances involve only a few actors who both sing and speak their lines, a chorus that often takes over for the characters, musical accompaniment from flute and drums, plots that focus on feelings rather than events, poetic descriptions, and stately dances. Realism is not a feature of Noh drama. Time is often sped up or slowed down, and only the most minimal props are used. The most famous plays explore emotional extremes. *Nakamitsu* realistically depicts a man who takes his loyalty to his lord to an excruciating extreme. Other plays tell the story of someone who died harboring unrequited love or who was a murder victim and has therefore become a ghost obsessed with revenge.

Questions

1. What other themes besides the conflict between love and duty can be found in this play?
2. What is the effect of having a chorus speak for the characters and of having characters speak of themselves in the third person and utter some of the stage directions? (Italicized text in brackets represents unspoken stage directions.)

From *Yōkyoku taikan* by Kentarō Sanrai, translated by Margaret Helen Childs (Tokyo: Meiji shoin, 1963), vol. 4, pp. 2307–2324. See also Mae J. Smethurst in *Dramatic*

Representations of Filial Piety: Five Noh in Translation,
Cornell East Asia Series 97 (Ithaca, NY: Cornell University,
East Asian Program, 1998.)

Nakamitsu (also known as Manjū)

List of Characters:

Nakamitsu (*shite* or main actor), retainer of Manjū
Manjū (*tsure* or actor who complements the main actor), Governor
 of Settsu
Bijō (child actor), son of Manjū, and still a boy
Kōju (child actor), son of Nakamitsu, and foster-brother of Bijō
Servant
Eshin (secondary actor), a priest at the great monastery on Mount
 Hiei near the capital
The Chorus
Scene: Lord Manjū's residence in Settsu
Time: tenth century

Part I

[Nakamitsu enters.]
 Nakamitsu.—I am Fujiwara no Nakamitsu, a retainer of Tada no
Manjū, Governor of Settsu. Bijō, my lord's son, was sent to a temple,
Nakayamadera to get an education. I, too, have a son called Kōju, who
accompanied the young lord as a page. But the young lord has no interest
in studying. He has spent all his time practicing martial arts. My lord has
just found this out and is furious. He has ordered me to bring his son home.
 [Nakamitsu, Bijō and Kōju arrive at Manjū's residence.]
 Nakamitsu.—My lord, I have brought the young lord Bijō home.
 Manjū.—Well, Bijō! The reason I left you up at the monastery for so
long was to have you make good progress in your studies. Let me see
how well you've done. Please read aloud from the scriptures. He places
a sacred text, written in letters of gold, on a rosewood desk.
 Bijō.—Although Bijō knew what his father expected of him, he had
never copied out even the most elementary writing assignment. How
might he be able to read even a single word of scripture? Bijō can only
weep.

Manjū.—Ah! Of course! As a child of mine everyone in the temple engaged you in elegant pastimes. You had no time for scripture. How about some poetry?

Bijō.—I cannot compose poetry.

Manjū.—And music? Though I ask, you have no answer.

Chorus.—Your father sent you to study for nobody's benefit but your own. You have ignored my strict instructions. Like the poet who hoped to show off the beauty of the unblemished blanket of snow in his garden, I had hoped to take pride in presenting you to the world. But there is no point in introducing you to anyone as my son. He takes hold of his sword, but Nakamitsu intervenes and clutches Manjū's sleeve. Bijō is in danger! How pitiable!

[Nakamitsu signals with his eyes for Bijō to retreat.]

Manjū.—Nakamitsu! What are you doing? Listen to me. I sent Bijō to the temple to study but he did nothing but fool around with martial arts. What was the point?

Nakamitsu.—It's quite reasonable for you to be upset and certainly appropriate to scold your son, but this? Please relinquish your sword to me.

Manjū.—Fine. In that case, I order you to kill him! If you don't, as our clan god is my witness, you will not escape punishment even if Bijō does.

[Manjū hands his sword to Nakamitsu.]

Nakamitsu.—I will not fail to comply with your orders. Please retire to an inner room.

[Manjū withdraws.]

Nakamitsu.—This is incredible! He is in a furious rage. I expected Bijō to get a scolding, but I never dreamed it would come to this. Whatever Manjū may say later, for the time being I will have Bijō go into hiding. *[Nakamitsu addresses Bijō.]* Let me have a word with you. Your father is so furious that now I'm in trouble too.

Bijō.—That I am still alive is thanks to you. I overheard my father tell you to kill me. Hurry up! Take my head and show it to my father.

Nakamitsu.—You speak so bravely! Whatever Manjū may say later, I intend to save your life. What's that? Manjū has sent another messenger? This is ridiculous. What do I do now? Alas! Every deed, whether for good or ill, brings retribution or reward in this sad world. Didn't Crown Prince Ajatashatru murder his father Bimbisara?[1] Everything is a matter of destiny.

Bijō.—What was done in the past,

Nakamitsu.—inevitably, in the present,

Chorus.—brings retribution! There is no one to blame. It would be foolish to resent what you yourself have wrought and hate the world. Nakamitsu! Time is passing as we speak of our sorrows. Just take my head. How moving to see him weep as he speaks!

Nakamitsu.—Ah! My young lord, if I were your age, I would trade places with you. How I regret that this life I do not cherish is not mine to discard.

Kōju.—Father, I heard what you just said. We must hurry! Strike off *my* head, say it is Bijō's, and show it to our lord.

Nakamitsu.—What's that? You would trade your life for Bijō's? You are indeed worthy of being my son. I will take your head, wrap it in gauze, and show it to our lord from a distance in the dim light of evening. His eyes will be clouded by fatherly love. He will not realize the truth. It is a good plan. You shall give your life for Bijō!

[*Nakamitsu prepares to wield his sword.*]

Nakamitsu.—We must not wait any longer. Nakamitsu grasps his sword, stands behind his son, and …

Bijō.—Bijō cannot bear it! He catches Nakamitsu's sleeve. If Kōju dies I will kill myself. He weeps but stays Nakamitsu's hand.

Nakamitsu.—But it is the duty of a warrior to lay down his life for his lord.

Bijō.—How sad! We are competing with each other to die!

Nakamitsu.—Alas! Alas! They both want to die!

Kōju.—Kōju approaches.

Bijō.—Bijō comes closer.

Kōju.—There stands our lord!

Nakamitsu.—Here stands my dear child!

Bijō.—In between the two,

Nakamitsu.—is Nakamitsu.

Chorus.—I would freely give my own life, but I don't know what to do now. He is a brave man, but he looks helpless now.

Bijō.—My own father does not value my life, why do you care? Your pity only makes me feel more wretched.

Kōju.—It is not a matter of pity. If I do not die in your stead, I will be unable to bear the dishonor that would bring to a warrior's house.

Chorus.—They are both young, but they are speaking the truth.

Nakamitsu.—One of these is my lord, the other my son. They are both precious, yet how can I raise my hand against my lord? His resolve weakens, but he knows his son is standing to his left. He steels his heart, and despite the anguish that threatened to swallow him up in darkness, he turned his son into only a dream.

Servant.—Nakamitsu, I see the anguish in your heart. I can only weep along with you.

Nakamitsu.—It is as you say. Please bear witness to my anguish! Now, go with Bijō. Take him somewhere where he'll be safe.

Servant.—As you wish. Bijō, come with me. Well, well. You were in danger but you have been saved, thanks to the trustworthy Nakamitsu and his son. Kōju died in your place. You must never forget your debt of gratitude. Lowly servant though I am, I have been asked to escort you and will remain in your service wherever we go. Ah! I have an idea. We should consult Abbot Eshin. Let's go as quickly as we can.

[*The servant and Bijō leave the stage.*]

Nakamitsu. [*He approaches Manjū.*] My lord, I must make my report. I have slain young lord Bijō.

Manjū.—Well done. He met his end as a coward, didn't he?

Nakamitsu.—No, my lord. As I hesitated with my sword in my hand, your son spoke up. "Nakamitsu, have you lost your nerve?" Those were his final words.

Manjū.—Nakamitsu, as you know, Bijō was my only child. I will adopt Kōju as my heir. Have him come here right away.

Nakamitsu.—If only I could. In his sorrow at parting from the young lord, Kōju decided to become a monk. He has cut his hair and disappeared into the night. I too would like to commit myself to a religious life. I request your permission to retire from your service.

Manjū.—He speaks with composure, but he treated my son like his own and now both boys are gone.

Chorus.—This is the way of our world. No one can ignore his lord's commands. He tried to console Nakamitsu, but his words had no effect. Truly, because of the bond between parent and child, because of the love between father and son, I mourn my dear son. Now I must conduct funeral rites. Oh, the grief! The grief of conducting my son's funeral!

Part II

Eshin.—I am the Abbot Eshin of Mount Hiei, and am hurrying to lord Manjū's residence, since I have a certain matter to attend to. [*Addressing Bijō.*] Come over here, young lord.

Eshin.—Hello!

Nakamitsu.—Who is it? Oh, Abbot Eshin has graced us with a visit.

Eshin.—Nakamitsu, regarding Kōju, my condolences. But first, please announce my arrival.

Nakamitsu.—Of course. I would like to report that Abbot Eshin is here.

Manjū.—This is a surprise. Show him in.

Nakamitsu.—As you wish. [*Addressing Eshin.*] Please come this way.

Eshin.—Thank you.

Manjū.—What is it that brings you here today?

Eshin.—It is just this: I have come to speak with you about Bijō.

Manjū.—As far as Bijō is concerned, he was an unforgivable disgrace, so I ordered Nakamitsu to kill him.

Eshin.—That's the thing! Please stay calm and listen. You did indeed command Nakamitsu to kill Bijō, but how could Nakamitsu bring himself to raise his hand against his lord with whom he shares a bond that encompasses three lifetimes?[2] He cut off the head of his own son Kōju and told you it was Bijō's. Nakamitsu sacrificed his own son in Bijō's place. Please forgive the flaws of someone who was loved as much as that. I have brought Bijō with me. Bijō, step forward.

Manjū.—If Bijō still lives, he is indeed a failure. He should have killed himself when Kōju was killed.

Eshin.—No, no. Put such thoughts aside. Forgive your son and dedicate the merit of that compassionate act to the repose of Kōju's soul. He wept as he spoke.

Chorus.—Manjū's hard heart softened and he consented. Nakamitsu, overjoyed, brought out cups and wine to celebrate. The joy of the hermit who got lost in time and met his descendants in the seventh generation was no greater than this.[3] It was as if the bond of a single lifetime had been extended to two.

Nakamitsu.—Cups of wine exchanged by father and son

Chorus.—to celebrate their enduring bond!

Eshin.—Nakamitsu, please dance for us to mark this happy occasion

Chorus.—to celebrate their enduring bond.

[*During the following song Nakamitsu dances.*]

Nakamitsu.—A single mandarin duck bobs up and down in the waves

Chorus.—harboring tumultuous feelings.

[*Nakamitsu finishes his dance.*]

Nakamitsu.—How sad! If my son Kōju were here, I would have him dance with Bijō. I would clap my hand to mark the beat. If only my tears were tears of joy, how glad I would be.

Chorus.—He hides his tears of sorrow behind waving hands as he dances. He wipes away his tears with his fluttering sleeves. Like drops of dew clinging to leaves and dew dripping down from them, the way of this unreliable world is that one or the other must go first. Yesterday Bijō grieved, today he is back in the capital, rejoicing. Eshin says goodbye and departs with Bijō. Nakamitsu accompanies their palanquin for quite a distance.

Nakamitsu.—Your father's anger was your own fault. You must commit yourself to studying diligently. I will turn back here. [*Bijō leaves the stage.*] Ah, the agony! If only Kōju were with him. He watched until the palanquin disappeared from view. But still he stood there, his shoulders suddenly drooping.

Notes

1. King Bimbisara ruled part of the Magadha empire (now part of India) from 543 to 491 BCE.

2. According to Buddhist teachings, the relationship between a parent and child lasts for one lifetime; that between a husband and wife continues for two lifetimes; and the relationship of a servant with his lord or of a disciple with his master is repeated over the course of three lives.

3. This is an allusion to a Rip Van Winkle type of story.

23

Lord Kikui's Wife

The Seven Nuns is an example of a religious awakening story, a common topic of the many short narratives of the fourteenth through early seventeenth centuries. In the story, seven women including one who had been married to Lord Kikui spend one whole night telling each other why they became nuns. In several cases the reason was the heart-rending death of a child or husband. Lord Kikui's wife suffers the loss of her husband's affections when he takes a mistress. *The Seven Nuns* may have been inspired by an earlier religious awakening story, *The Three Monks*, in which a monk who took religious vows after his wife was murdered meets the murderer, who had also become a monk after that crime. In most religious awakening tales the storytellers give credit to the bodhisattva Kannon or some other deity for causing the sorrowful circumstances that led them to faith, and they commit themselves to praying for the salvation of their deceased loved one. In the case of Lord Kikui's wife, a wandering ascetic helped her let go of resentment and attain serenity.

Questions

1. What are the several different reactions of the wife to her husband's infidelity?
2. Why is the end surprising?

Lord Kikui's Wife, from *The Seven Nuns*

Lord Kikui's Wife

Then the elderly nun told her story. "Since all of my companions have told their tales, if I don't tell mine, I would seem to have encouraged you insincerely. Please forgive my lack of modesty in talking about myself, but I have a strange and wonderful tale to tell.

"I was born in Awa Province. When I reached a marriageable age, I wed a man called Kikui no Ukon. When he went off to the capital on business, I waited impatiently for him. I asked, 'Is the capital this way?' and day and night I did nothing but gaze in that direction. I would call together my attendants and chat through the night, speaking of nothing but him. I was still obsessed with thoughts of him and burning with love when my husband came home three years later. I was so happy that, ignoring people's stares, I ran out of the front gate crying: 'You've been so long in coming home.'

"'So I have,' he replied, not looking particularly happy to be back.

"'That's an unexpected attitude,' I thought, and for two or three months I wondered what might have happened in the capital to upset him. Then I heard a rumor on the wind: 'Lord Kikui has brought a beautiful woman back with him. She's young and has the elegant and aristocratic diction of someone from the capital, a woman with the grace of a willow in a spring breeze. He has established her in a house that he found for her.'

"Now I understood. Judging from the expression on his face when I ran out to meet him at the gate, this rumor was quite true. Well, if there was another woman, I would have to do something about it. Being from the distant capital, she wouldn't have any friends here, while I had many relatives. Since others would certainly take my side in this matter, I decided to teach this woman a lesson. I would make an example of this degenerate, husband-stealing female and wrest her away from my husband. But then, on second thought, I reasoned, 'No, my husband is not an irresponsible man [he isn't likely to abandon me]'; besides, I was approaching thirty, and I couldn't look forward to very many more years. And it certainly wasn't unusual for a man to be fickle. As long as he didn't shun me, I'd let things be. And so I slept alone on a pillow dampened by my tears, and the bells at dawn echoed my desolation.

"I had spent several months being patient and understanding, when one day my husband said listlessly: 'I can't hide this from you indefinitely. I brought a wonderful woman home with me from the capital. I can't send her all the way back now. There's no point in your getting angry. I don't intend to replace you. You mustn't hold this against me.'

"What he said seemed reasonable. 'It's a very common thing,' I replied graciously. 'Why should I be upset? It's not a question of this one woman from the capital, there certainly have been plenty of other cases of this kind of thing. That's how men are.'

"'I'm so glad [to hear you say that],' he replied happily. 'You are indeed a well-bred woman.'

"Some months went by, but things were not as my husband had said. The number of days he spent with his mistress increased, and I was brushed aside. No matter what I said, he was cold toward me. At first I worried about what people might think and about my future. 'Well,' I thought, 'even if that's how it is, as long as he will provide for me ...' But I felt he was very cruel, and although I did not show it outwardly, inside I resented him terribly. Night after night, day upon day, I brooded about the two of them, and then I developed a strange condition on my back. I had it examined and learned it was something like scales. I was horrified. Another day, looking at myself in a mirror, I noticed that my hair was tangled and my eyes gleamed brightly. My mouth had broadened and two horn-like lumps had risen on my forehead. Until then I had thought that this kind of thing only happened in old tales to other people, but now I was in more and more pain. I began to feel as though my body were on fire. Everyone who noticed these changes in me was frightened, and after a while all my attendants left me. Well, the world would soon know, I thought, sighing deeply. I spent months just gazing off into space.

"There was, however, one attendant who had served me for years and who still kept me company at times. One day when an ascetic came begging, this attendant said to him: 'This woman's jealousy is causing physical changes in her. Won't you instruct her in the sacred teachings and save her?'

"'Of course,' he replied.

"Then my attendant said to me: 'This ascetic is a rare and wonderful man, let him guide you to faith.'

"I was furious. 'I'll do no such thing! I'm not going to listen to a word about Buddhas or Buddhist doctrine. All I want is to turn this place into a swamp and cover it with black clouds. I'll spout flames like those of the Red Lotus and Deep Red Lotus hells and drive that hateful woman away from my husband. If I could just swallow her up in a gulp, I'd be satisfied. After that my husband and I will live together in the Three Evil Realms[1] and wreak havoc for the rest of eternity. I want only to become a great villain.' I gave a great angry shout that shook the mountains and valleys and made the earth tremble. My attendant was frightened out of her wits. Then I remarked, 'If he is an ascetic who has been wandering throughout the provinces, he must know everything. I'll see him.'

"Tenkeisei, the God of Heavenly Punishment" (twelfth century), detail of a hanging scroll, ink and color on paper, a National Treasure of Japan. Images such as these were meant to scare the viewer into better behavior. *(Wikimedia Commons, Nara National Museum)*

"'What can I do for you?' the ascetic inquired.

"'I'm ashamed,' I answered, 'to have you see me looking like this and embarrassed to ask you about this, but a hateful woman has been making me miserable. There must be a way to kill her. Teach me.'

'That's easy,' the ascetic replied.

"I was delighted and explained, 'I have hated that woman for years. I can't begin to tell you what my days and nights have been like. I haven't even been able to sleep. I have harbored a fire in my breast; three times a night and three times a day, I feel as though flames are shooting out from my body. Look at this. When I put water in this tub and hold it in my arms, it comes to a boil, and I suffer all the more. If I could kill that woman, my suffering would come to an end, so [please tell me how to do it].'

"'It's very simple,' said the ascetic. 'To kill someone you must take a certain attitude. If you do as I teach you, it may at most take fourteen or fifteen days, but surely not so long as sixteen or seventeen.'

"'Whatever it is, I'll do as you say,' I agreed.

"'Think of nothing,' the ascetic told me. 'Let no thoughts arise. Forget good and bad. Don't think about the person you care for, and don't think about the one you hate. Abandon all thoughts. Let your mind be as empty as if your head had been cut off. If you do this, your original fundamental self will emerge. This is said to be the way most favored by the Buddhas to do away with hated people. If you still have an occasional thought that suddenly occurs to you, don't abandon it, but think hard where it came from, and what kind of thought it is. Think well, think and think. Devote your mind to the question of the four origins of all things.[2] You will see there will be no source for your evil thoughts. There will be the ultimate reality of the *Lotus Sutra*, the single truth behind all things. At that time all those you hate will be slain at once,' he explained.

"I put my faith in his words and quieted my mind. I made myself oblivious to the passing of time, and when, whether walking, standing, sitting, or lying down, I had an evil or wrong thought, I meditated, practiced religious rites, or confined myself to a quiet place. I sought in various ways to accomplish what I had been taught. But none of this had any effect at all.

"After fourteen or fifteen days, the ascetic summoned me. 'What has become of the woman you hate?' he inquired.

"'I am not aware of her at all,' I replied.

"'Then what is most noble in your true self has appeared. When you conquer the thoughts that arise, love and hate are destroyed like snowflakes falling into a fire, and evil and goodness are indistinguishable.

There is no you and there is no other. The other is you and you are the other. This is the true way to do away with those you hate. This is vanquishing the source and annihilating life and death.'

"No sooner had he finished speaking than I clapped my hands and said that truly, truly, the awful woman was gone, that my dear husband was gone. I heaved a great sigh of relief. My chest felt unbound. I awoke from my dream. The traces of snake scales were gone. Physically I was back to normal. I suddenly understood. I realized that past, present, and future are like an illusion, and immediately I became the ascetic's disciple."

Notes

1. The Three Evil Realms are the various hells, or life as a hungry ghost or as an animal.

2. Living things are categorized into four groups according to how they are born: creatures born from a womb, from eggs, from moisture, that is, insects, and by self-transformation, that is, heavenly beings, the inhabitants of hell, and so on.

24

Short Stories

IHARA SAIKAKU

In 1600, peace and a unified central government were restored after a century of widespread conflict. As commerce flourished and cities grew, prosperity led to the development of an urban culture in which licensed prostitution and theaters played a prominent role. In the medieval period, literature had tended to take a Buddhist perspective, focusing on how the sorrows of this life might lead one to seek salvation in the next, but in early modern times (Edo period, 1600–1868), literature came to focus on life's pleasures and the conflict between what one's duty required and what the heart desired. The development of printing made it possible for professional writers to earn a living by writing fiction. The first of these writers was Ihara Saikaku (1642–1693). Saikaku was born and raised in a merchant family, but became a master of *haikai* (popular poetry) in 1673 and then turned to prose fiction after 1682. He began with *The Life of an Amorous Man*, a parody of *The Tale of Genji*, and went on to write dozens of books about romantic passion, samurai courage and honor, and financially astute townsmen. Some tales are simply vividly told accounts of remarkable events, but he often adds a comic touch that lessens the pathos of tragic stories. *Tales of Samurai Honor* was written in 1688 and *Great Mirror of Male Love* in 1687.

Tales of Samurai Honor Questions

1. II: 4. Do you think that justice was achieved by the heir's killer replacing him?
2. III: 1. What qualities does the older samurai display?
3. V: 2. Why did Lord Tango decide to let the wife of an enemy escape? Did this action really show "compassion"?
4. V: 2. Identify both the comic and tragic aspects of this story.
5. V: 2. What is presented realistically and what seems idealistic in this story?

Great Mirror of Male Love Questions

1. Identify both the comic and tragic aspects of this story.
2. What is presented realistically and what seems idealistic in this story?

Short Stories

"A Surprise Move—The Heir's Killer Replaces Him," "Inspiration from a Gourd," and "The Mother Kept One Child and Abandoned the Other," by Ihara Saikaku, translated by Caryn A. Callahan in *Tales of Samurai Honor: Buke Giri Monogatari* (Tokyo: *Monumenta Nipponica*, Sophia University, 1981), pp. 65–67, 71–74, 115–117. Used with permission.
"Fireflies Also Work Their Asses Off at Night" from *The Great Mirror of Male Love* by Ihara Saikaku, translated by Paul G. Schalow (Stanford, CA: Stanford University Press, 1990), pp. 247–253. Copyright © 1990 by the Board of Trustees of the Leland Stanford Jr. University. All rights reserved. Used with the permission of Sanford University Press, ww.sup.org.

Selections from Tales of Samurai Honor

II: 4 A Surprise Move—The Heir's Killer Replaces Him

> *He skillfully killed his man at Monju Temple in Kireto.*
> *How a most incongruous successor is chosen.*

Every year at dawn on the 25th day of the sixth month, the people of Tango begin to arrive at Kireto to pay their respects to the deity Monju on his festival day.[1] In one particular year, among the worshippers was Ōshiro Densaburō's fifteen-year-old son, Dennosuke, who came with a servant. On pilgrimage at the same time was the son of a fellow retainer, a samurai named Nanao Kyūhachirō, who had recently entered the lord's service. His thirteen-year-old son, Hachijūro, was attended by a sandal-bearer. This was Hachijūro's first visit to the area, and the lovely shoreline so fascinated him that he went around looking at this and that until the moon and the twilight glow were visible through the pines on the Ama no Hashidate Bridge.[2]

Just as Hachijūro was about to leave, his sleeve brushed against Dennosuke's. Each boy accused the other of insulting him by jostling his sword sheath, and they drew their swords and dueled heroically. Hachijūro emerged the victor by killing Dennosuke, and then, since no witness was in sight, he left the scene. The two servants had killed each other with their swords.

Dennosuke's father heard the dreadful news and rushed to the spot. He tried to find his son's opponent, but there was not a single clue to his whereabouts; it was also too dark to identify the dead servant and thus trace his master. So the father could do nothing for the time being but carry Dennosuke's body home.

"View of Ama-no-Hashidate" by Sesshū Tōyō (1420–1506), hanging scroll, ink on paper. One of the three most famous scenic spots in Japan, it is still a popular tourist destination today. *(Wikimedia Commons, Kyoto National Museum)*

Hachijūro reached home and told his father the whole story.

'What do you mean by slinking home at a time like this?' his father said. 'Resign yourself to your fate!'[3] He then sent him off in a palanquin to Dennosuke's home with the following note: 'I entrust his fate to your decision. Do as you will with him.'

Densaburō received Hachijūro and the letter, and for the time being he put the boy in the best room. His wife was delighted to have Dennosuke's slayer at her mercy and went at him with a halberd, but Densaburō restrained her, saying, 'You cannot just kill this boy in cold blood when his father acted so honorably by sending him here. As a matter of fact, although he is only thirteen, he is much better at the military arts than our own fifteen-year-old son was. So I am going to ask that Hachijūro be made my heir and successor. If you don't agree, I will divorce you.'

A woman's lot is to obey her husband's will. Densaburō was pleased by her acquiescence and submitted his request for adoption to the lord. Such an extraordinary request was quite unprecedented, but the lord acceded and let him have Hachijūro as his son. After the adoption, the boy did his best to be a filial and dutiful son, even to his new mother. Never again did he permit himself to see his natural parents. He changed his name to Dennosuke and spent every day practicing the martial arts. When he came of age, he married Densaburō's daughter. The old grudges were forgiven, and even the mother gave him her love. He succeeded to the headship of the Ōshiro family, and his name was remembered in later ages.

III: 1 Inspiration from a Gourd

> *Give a monk a hand and he will take an arm.*
> *How a quarrel was resolved by proof on the waves.*

Our present age has witnessed a drastic change in the behavior and attitude of samurai. In bygone days, proving his mettle was the samurai's paramount consideration and life was held cheap. If the sword sheaths of two samurai accidentally brushed against each other, the men would rail at each other and then begin a profitless duel; as a result, either they would both be killed, or else the victor would stride away from his slain opponent. Such behavior was praised for it was said to reflect the true samurai spirit, but in fact this kind of bravado is completely contrary to the Way of a samurai. In order to be prepared for the worst eventuality, a lord bestows a considerable stipend upon each of his retainers. Any man who ignores the obligation thus incurred and selfishly throws his life away in a personal quarrel is a villain, deaf to righteousness. And so, no matter how outstanding a samurai's feats may be in his personal battles, his lord will fail, understandably enough, to be impressed by such exploits.

A daimyo from the western regions was in Edo—how peaceful is the realm!—fulfilling the requirement to spend every other year there in attendance.[4] Among his retainers were two samurai whose names were Takeshima and Takitsu. These two men had completed identical tours of

"Portrait of Masuda Motoyoshi" by Kanō Shōei (1519–1592), hanging scroll, ink and color on silk. *(Wikimedia Commons, Iwami Art Museum)*

duty in Edo and were now returning home. They had arranged to travel back together and had already spent many happy days on the road.

One night they stayed at an inn in Okazaki. After they had taken their baths in a tub which had been especially prepared for them, they enjoyed some relief from the hot weather by sitting on the edge of a narrow porch, each dressed in a thin robe. Takitsu, who had just torn up some pieces of paper with his teeth to use as dressings for the open sores left by his moxa treatment,[5] now made a request of Takeshima. 'I'm sorry to trouble you,' he said, 'but would you mind putting one of these on my lower back?'

As Takeshima was applying the dressing, he noticed a small scar and remarked carelessly, 'Did you get this running away?' No matter how beautiful the friendship between them, no samurai can say such a thing to another with impunity.

Takitsu took the remark very seriously and thought to himself, 'I got this wound some time ago on the hunting field when I was attending my lord, but I have no proof of this with me. When we reach our fief, I will send for the surgeon who treated me then and have him tell exactly what happened. After that, I will kill Takeshima in a duel and that will be the end of that.' Thus Takitsu made his decision, but he hid what was in his heart.

The two men hurried on their way, and presently arrived at the shore of Fushimi; here they applied at the Boat Office and rented a fifty-*koku* boat.[6] They made sure that all their luggage was on board, and were just about to give the order to cast off when a samurai around sixty years old, accompanied by a beautiful samurai boy of twelve or thirteen, came up and said that he wished to board. The boatman replied that the boat had already been engaged, whereupon the man, disappointment written on his face, turned back, leading the boy by the hand. The two travelers could not remain indifferent to the sight and said, 'We aren't using the forecabin anyway, so let them come on board.' Pleased at the prospect of a tip, the boatman prepared the cabin and brought the newcomers aboard.

Just then, a monk in his early thirties came running toward the boat, carrying a bundle of his possessions wrapped in oilcloth, and out of charity, they let him get on too. The two samurai and the monk thanked their hosts repeatedly and seemed to be delighted to be spending the night in such spacious accommodations.

At length the boat passed under the Yodo no Kobashi Bridge, and the travelers enjoyed the enchanting view of the setting sun dancing on the waves churned up by the waterwheels outside the castle.[7] Inspired by this visual aperitif, Takeshima and Takitsu brought out a bamboo canteen of *sake* and proceeded to take turns filling and refilling each other's cups. They called to the two men whom they had invited on board and invited them to have a drink, and the party became quite boisterous. The boy chanted an excerpt from a noh play, while the monk amused the company by singing a popular ditty. Everyone vastly enjoyed the entertainment.

As the night drew on, the men continued to drink together under the oil lamps. At some point or other, a large cup was produced and drained by each in turn: When it reached Takitsu, he exclaimed, 'Impossible! Impossible! I just can't drink it.' He started to move away, but Takeshima grabbed him by the sleeve and said, 'What! Trying to escape again?'

Takitsu took deep offense at the words and retorted, 'You asked me at Okazaki if I had been wounded running away, and now this—I can't take any more!' He rose to his feet, holding his sheathed sword ready. Takeshima accepted the challenge, but when he reached for his sword that had been next to him, he found that it was gone. Takitsu waited briefly and then said, 'It is very odd that your sword has disappeared. Set your mind at rest and look for it—I will wait for you.'

The sword was still missing after an exhaustive search. Takeshima resigned himself to his fate, saying, 'Fortune has turned against me. There is no way I can meet your challenge and I am completely disgraced.' He tried to kill himself, but the elderly samurai restrained him, saying, 'I have a very good idea where the sword is. If you promise to grant me what I wish, I will produce it for you.' Takeshima naturally agreed, and so did Takitsu.

The old samurai then said, 'The sword was stolen by that monk.' The accused man changed expression and said, 'Are you accusing me because I am a man of religion?' The old man replied calmly, 'While we were drinking, you reached for a gourd fastened by a long cord to your sash. From the gourd, you took some peppers which you ate. Where is that gourd now? If it is missing, then you are the culprit.' The monk was completely trapped by this question and committed suicide by jumping into the river.

Dawn had already come, and the boat was poled back along its route. Looking out over into the shallows, they spotted a small gourd floating motionlessly in the withered reeds of Udono.[8] When they pulled it from the water, they saw that it was attached to the sword as a float. Apparently the monk had submerged the sword here during the revelry.

The two men were deeply impressed by the old man's solution. 'You're a man with an uncanny intuition,' they declared. 'You notice the small things that the average person misses.'

The samurai replied, 'You promised to grant my request if the sword was recovered. Well, my wish is that you reach a reconciliation.' In this way, he patched up their quarrel before he left them.

V: 2 The Mother Kept One Child and Abandoned the Other

What a woman of noble purpose attempted.
How the samurai code is no stranger to compassion.

This incident happened during the battle at the Ane River in Ōmi.[9] On the 29th day of the sixth month of Eiroku 12,[10] the opposing forces briefly ceased hostilities in order to rest and regain strength. During this truce a figure crept out from behind the camp and stole away in the dying light of the sun. A man from Mokuta Tango's lookout squad spotted the fugitive and gave chase with other soldiers through the thick bamboo grass, trying to intercept the person fleeing down a path in the fields.

When they closed in, they saw that their prey was a spirited and valiant woman who wore a single sword. At her side ran a boy about seven years old, who was keeping up as best he could. She rushed ahead, holding tightly in her arms an infant whose lips were even then fastened to her breast. But when she saw the pursuers about to overtake her, she tossed the infant aside, hoisted the bigger child on to her shoulders, and fled on more than two *chō* [about 200 yards] further.

The wailing of the abandoned baby drew pity even in the heat of the chase, and a soldier picked up the infant and discovered that it was a beautiful girl. Some stayed with the child while the others raced after the mother. At last, the woman was cornered, and putting the boy down under a willow tree, she drew her sword. Her gallantry would have put many a man to shame for she fought bravely, but she was soon surrounded by a large number of soldiers and escape was out of the question. Among the soldiers was a wise old hand who shouted for all to hear, 'Don't kill her!' Although no one escaped uninjured in the struggle, the woman was finally captured alive.

Convinced that she had a story to tell, the soldiers handled her gently as they brought her back to Lord Tango's camp. Tango listened to the full report and was careful not to let the news spread to hostile ears. He turned to the woman and asked, 'Who is the father of these children? Tell me the truth.'

But the woman told him nothing, only hanging her head, weeping, and muttering, 'I've failed, I've failed. How humiliating.'

The whole affair seemed increasingly mysterious and Tango began to suspect that the boy might even be the son of an enemy general. He tried for quite a while to get at the truth, when suddenly the seven-year-old pulled at his mother's sleeve and said in quite unaristocratic language, 'I wanna go to pa.'[11]

Relieved that the child was one of the common people, Tango said, 'Tell me who your husband is. I will overlook your actions and spare your life because your determination sprang from love. But I want to hear how you decided which child to abandon. Parents usually love all their children equally, yet you did not hesitate to desert the babe at your breast in order to save the older child. Was it because you thought that the older one would be grown up sooner and so would be more useful to you?'

At this point the woman raised her head and spoke frankly of what was in her heart.

'My husband is named Takebashi Jinkurō,' she said. 'He once, I am proud to say, drew a modest samurai stipend, but after he became a *rōnin*,[12] he made himself a new life as a farmer in this village. He exchanged his war horse for a plow ox and made his spear into a hoe handle, and he has since spent his time cultivating the fields. But the farmers of this fief were all conscripted for this battle.'

'Last night,' she continued, 'my husband said to me, "There is no hope of winning. I am certain that I will be killed, but there is no point in your dying with me. So hurry up and make your escape. Bring up the two children and let them take my place in your heart. When they are grown up, have the boy succeed to my name and property." He begged me over and over to carry out his wishes, and I had no choice but to part tearfully from him. In this way I became your prisoner. I abandoned the girl and saved the boy because neither of the children is our own. The years passed after our marriage and yet we remained childless. Feeling that we lacked something in our lives, we adopted these children from our relatives. The boy is my husband's nephew, and the girl is my own niece. Even though I am only a woman, I could not bear to have people say after my death that I gave preference to my own flesh and blood.'

Tango was deeply moved by her fidelity to duty and secretly arranged for a servant to guide her and the children to safety by a side road so that her life would be saved.

Selection from Great Mirror of Male Love

7.1 Fireflies Also Work Their Asses Off at Night

> *The capital's moon and blossoms: Yoshida Iori and Fujimura Handayū.*
> *A stealthy visitor questioned on a rainy night makes no reply.*
> *Someone places new flowers at the altar of Buddha.*

There is nothing in this world more painful than making a living. To do any job well requires hard work, but the most difficult I have ever seen (and I have seen many) is that of the drum-holder[13] in the pleasure quarter, for his success depends on patience and forbearance in the face of impossible provocation.

One time I had the opportunity to see the actors Yoshida Iori and Fujimura Handayū of Murayama Matabei's troupe together side by side at a party at Otsuruya in Ishigaki-machi.[14] My immediate reaction was that they are unequaled in the present-day world of theater. Their figures were just like those of famous beauties of ancient times preserved for us in paintings. All those who saw them dance in the latest style went mad with desire.

The skill of these two in entertaining patrons was especially remarkable. Playful and affectionate, they were pliant without being weak. Even while seeming to follow the patron's lead they continued to make sure that everything was going smoothly. Once in bed, Iori would say all sorts of pleasing things to his adversary,[15] and before long the gentleman on the pillow would forget both life and fortune in his frenzied excitement. Handayū used a different approach, however. He said not a word after getting into bed and refused to snuggle up close, always making the gentleman wonder uncomfortably what he had done wrong. Just when the man's discomfort began to turn to annoyance, Handayū would whisper a single happy suggestion, one the man would remember for the rest of his life. If you were to teach this method to any other boy he could never learn to do it right. These two could flatter and seduce even the pros with their lies, they were so utterly convincing.

"There are 31 boy actors in the capital today and they all go for the same price, so you'd be a fool not to ask for these two."

"If you have any gold or silver saved up, you should spend it on a boy. Leave it to your son and he may prove to be a thrifty dolt who would live his whole life without ever buying a kabuki actor. Imagine your hard-earned money lying in the corner of a safe, never to experience life's pleasures. Why, even money itself would regret being left to rot away like that."

"Why is it that men like us who have the proper perspective on things and know how to use money are always without it? Life is certainly unfair."

Thus, entertainers from Gion-machi could be heard complaining among themselves.

Before long, Kagura Shōzaemon[16] began whistling a melody from night *kagura*.[17] To this accompaniment, each of the other drum-holders performed in turn whatever feat of skill struck his fancy. Their antics surpassed even those of actors onstage. Our laughter could not wait until later; we held our sides and howled uproariously.

One of the drum-holders at this party was Muraoka Tannyū, once the respected son of a certain man of importance. He was talented, lived well, and was liked for his generous nature, but as so often happens in this floating world he squandered the family fortune and was reduced to selling calligraphy manuals in the Ōhashi style near the intersection of Shita-tachi-uri and Horikawa. The business failed to prosper, however. Next, he put out a sign advertising himself as an acupuncturist, but no one called for his services. In dire straits and desperate for money, he took to entertaining wealthy patrons in the pleasure quarter. On that day, he had been summoned to this party.

Tannyū was annoyed that the table for his meal was the last to be brought out. To compound the offense, the gentleman hosting the party shed his outer robe and kicked it into the next room, ordering him to fold it. Tannyū was in no position to refuse, so he did as he was told. Then the man sent him to empty an ashtray. Having no other recourse, he was about to oblige when suddenly other drum-holders jumped on him and tied him up. They pretended he was the "thief from Narutaki" and dragged him around the room. Tannyū knew that they were doing it to entertain the gentleman, but he could not control his anger. He swore that when they untied the rope he would kill two or three of them and then show how nobly he could die.

Just then, the gentleman took four or five Chōtoku-ji coins[18] from his packet of tissues and scattered them on the floor. This was Tannyū's reward for the teasing he had just suffered. When he saw the glittering objects thrown at him, his mood changed completely.

"Really, sir, you are too generous!" he said shamelessly, his greed making him forget the humiliation he had just experienced. From that moment he hid his talent and intelligence and simply played the idiot, slavishly pandering to the foolish gentleman's every whim. He exhausted every word of flattery in the language until he himself could hardly bear it anymore. Even the young actor who had been bought to be Tannyū's bed-fellow for the night made his contempt for him obvious. No one knew it, but later poor Tannyū had to all but worship the boy before he was allowed to untie the youngster's sash.

Because Tannyū was without influential friends at the party, he had been treated brusquely when he checked his sandals at the entrance. Later, on his way out, he found one sandal here, one sandal over there, and had to rush on foot to keep up with the gentleman in his fast palanquin. It is strange that even among residents of the capital there should be such a variety of ways to make a living.

Though the wares he sold were different, a working boy like Handayū was in an equally painful occupation. The previous day, for example, he was forced to drink from sunset to late at night with a stubborn country samurai who took a liking to him, and today he had to work again, this time bought by a group of seven or eight pilgrims on their way to Ise. Sleeping partners were decided in secret by drawing straws, and as luck would have it he was assigned to a repulsive old man, even though there were others among them he actually found attractive.

From the start, the old man was leaning all over him and stroking him with his long fingernails without a thought for how it messed up his hair. He brought his mouth close to Handayū's for a kiss. Obviously, the man had never used a toothbrush in his life. The boy cowered from the coarse touch of the man's cotton under-robe and tried to plug his nose against the musty stench of deerskin socks that clung to the man's feet. Then, without any sense of the finer aspects of boy love, the man began to fumble with his own loincloth. For the sake of money, the boy had no recourse but to let the old man have his way, though he satisfied him with the secret thigh technique.[19] Between nightfall and when they got up and parted, the boy must have aged years with worry that his deception would be discovered.

And none of this effort brought him any financial gain; it all went into his proprietor's coffers, which made the work even less agreeable. What made it possible for him to forget the agony of the job were those moments when he saw the love-lorn faces of men and women gazing after him on his way home and could hear their countless cries of admiration. It filled him with a sense of pleasure and pride in his own beauty, and this alone made him willing to bear his bone-grinding regimen. When you think of it, he resembled a beautiful woman. His wares were different, but otherwise he was exactly like a courtesan.

One night, the faint sound of an early summer rain echoed on the shingled roof overhead where Handayū was entertaining a familiar group of patrons until dawn. They had downed a vast quantity of chilled sake in their second-floor room at the Ōtsuruya and were presently arguing among themselves whether the bell just now had tolled eight times or seven.[20]

"Well, shall we make an attempt to leave?" someone finally suggested.

Just then, two or three fireflies entered through a lattice-work window, rekindling excitement in the room. They seemed accustomed to people and flew around the room, their glow rivaling the lamplight. One of them came to rest on Handayū's sleeve.

"'I am just like the firefly,'" Handayū said, quoting from the *michiyuki*[21] scene in the play "Heianjō." The roomful of patrons was somewhat taken aback and laughed awkwardly.

"You may be right. This firefly's work also involves using its ass," someone said rudely.

"But it shines only at night and rests during daylight hours. I am envious. Here I am, working until dawn, and yet I must be on the stage all day again tomorrow. It's not fair." Handayū was blunt with his complaint.

More and more fireflies appeared in a frenzied tumult. Curious as to where they were coming from, someone went out to take a look. In cover of darkness, a priest wearing a sedge hat was releasing fireflies one by one from a thin paper package hidden inside the sleeve of his black-dyed robe. It was apparently meant to please someone there in the room. They were reminded of that incident long ago when fireflies were slipped into a certain lady's carriage.[22] It seemed suspiciously like a confession of love (done, I might add, with unusual refinement).

When the man came back and reported what he had seen, Handayū began to weep even as he listened.

"The same thing has happened before," he said. "A man of religion was coming in secret every night to my proprietor's house to release fireflies, or so I was told. Everyone wondered who they were intended for, and now I realize that they were meant for me. I am overjoyed. Please, allow me at least to share a cup of sake with him."

When the priest heard this, he fled. They could hear the clatter of his clogs on the stone wall as he rushed away; then, it seemed he lost his footing, for he fell with a splash into the normally shallow river. Swollen now with constant rains, it was a raging torrent. By the time they rushed out to the spot, he was gone without a trace. The men were left standing there, desolate and grief-stricken.

From that time on, Handayū suffered with thoughts of the priest he had never met. He lived each day in sorrow.

Some time later a certain gentleman fell deeply in love with Handayū and ransomed him from his contract at the theater. He set up residence in Kamisuki-chō near the Great Buddha, but Handayū still found it impossible to forget the love of that priest. Finally, he went into seclusion at Makino-o and took the tonsure.

His piety was admirable. Morning and evening he faithfully recited the sutras and purified his inner soul. He stayed up all night to build religious discipline in himself, but whenever he quietly drifted into a slumber the priest would appear to him and converse affectionately. It gave him the greatest joy. When he awoke, the figure faded, but as soon as he fell asleep it appeared again vividly, albeit in his dreams. To comfort the boy, the priest brought new flowers every day that he had plucked from among those that bloomed in each of the four seasons on the mountain paths, and placed them as an offering on the altar before the figure of the Buddha. Handayū told someone about this, but the man refused to believe him and insisted on spending a night in his bed at the temple.

Later, the man reported that although he had seen no priest, the flowers were indeed changed in the morning.

Notes

1. Kireto is located in Miyazu City in Kyoto prefecture; the temple in which Monju is enshrined there is Chionji, popularly called Kireto no Monju in former days.

2. One of the three famous beauty spots of Japan, Ama no Hashidate, "The Bridge of Heaven," is a narrow strip of land, about two miles long and lined with pine trees, projecting into Miyazu Bay like a bridge. In fact, on the twenty-fifth day of the lunar calendar the moon rose late, so Saikaku's lyrical description, alluding to the play *Utsubozaru*, is added merely for effect.

3. The penalty for an unauthorized duel, especially when a high-ranking retainer of the same lord is killed, was often death by obligatory ritual suicide.

4. A reference to the *sankin kōtai* system, introduced in 1635, by which daimyo were obliged to reside alternately in Edo and their domains, usually for one-year periods.

5. Moxa cauterization left small open wounds, which were protected by little pieces of paper smeared with ointment.

6. The Boat Office was located at Kyobashi in Fushimi (Fushimi Ward in present-day Kyoto). This government office handled the rental of boats with permits

to carry passengers up the Yodo River from Kyoto to Osaka; the boat hired on this occasion could carry fifty *koku* [about 250 bushels] of rice.

7. Two large waterwheels outside Yodo Castle; they drew water for the castle's needs.

8. The reeds growing at Udono, located in the present-day city of Takatsuki, had been used from ancient times for making wind instruments.

9. The Ane River, which flows into Lake Biwa, was the scene of a victory of Oda Nobunaga and Tokugawa Ieyasu against Asai Nagamasa and Asakura Yoshikage in 1570.

10. A mistaken date, as Eiroku 12 corresponds to 1569. The battle took place on the twenty-eighth day (not twenty-ninth) of the sixth month of Genki 1 (1570).

11. *Totosama no tokoro e initai.* A samurai child would have used *o-chichi-ue* for 'father' and perhaps *omomukitai* for 'I want to go.'

12. An anachronism, for although in Saikaku's peaceful time there were many *rōnin* [masterless samurai] unable to find posts, 100 years earlier soldiers had been in great demand. As is seen in this tale, even farmers were conscripted for battle, so there was no need for a warrior to remain a *rōnin* for long.

13. A drum-holder was a professional male entertainer who helped manage parties.

14. These two actors worked in the same theater in 1660. The Otsuruya was a restaurant/hotel. Ishigaki-machi was near the Kamo River.

15. "Adversary" means a prostitute's client.

16. A popular drum-holder between 1673 and 1687.

17. *Kagura* are dances performed at Shinto shrines to entertain gods.

18. Gold coins named for the price of a room at Chōtoku-ji.

19. This technique gives the sensation of sexual intercourse without penetration.

20. Eight bells signals 2 a.m.; seven bells signals 4 a.m.

21. *Michiyuki* refers to travel scenes. In love suicide plays it is the final, sad scene.

22. A reference to trying to illuminate a woman's face in the dark in order to catch a glimpse of her.

25

Jusan'ya. The Thirteenth Night

HIGUCHI ICHIYŌ

Higuchi Ichiyō (1872–1896) was born just a few years after the fall of the Tokugawa regime and the establishment of a new government, nominally under the leadership of the sixteen-year-old Emperor Meiji. Having seen the weak central government of China succumb to pressure for economic concessions by the European colonial powers in the nineteenth century, Japan's leaders decided to modernize in hopes of avoiding that fate. At the time, Japan was a well-organized society with a highly literate population. In a very short time, Japan was able to adopt a great deal of Western technology and many useful Western practices, such as the telegraph, railroad, solar calendar, and widespread compulsory education. Higuchi's family struggled financially, but she was able to study classical poetry. She turned to fiction in hopes of helping support her family. She achieved popularity but died of tuberculosis after writing only twenty-one short stories. Her stories evoke the lyricism of *The Tale of Genji*, but, like Saikaku, she writes about ordinary people's struggles.

Questions

1. Compare the reactions of Oseki's mother and father to their daughter's dilemma.
2. How do you explain the change in Oseki's husband from ardent suitor to bullying husband?
3. What is Oseki's theory as to why Rokunosuke ended up as he did? What is his own attitude about his situation?

4. What social conditions contribute to the problems experienced by the characters?

Jusan'ya. The Thirteenth Night

> Excerpt translated by Hisako Tanaka from Higuchi Ichiyō,
> *Jusan'ya. The Thirteenth Night* in *Monumenta Nipponica*
> 16, no. 3/4 (October 1960–January 1961), pp. 377–394.

I

Customarily Oseki rode a stunning black-lacquered ricksha to her parents' home, and at the sound of its halting in front of their gate, they used to rush out to meet her. But tonight she had sent back a ricksha, which she had caught on a street corner, and there she stood, dispirited, in front of their lattice door.

It must be her father talking to her mother, she thought, as she heard his usual loud voice from within:

"I am, so to speak, one of the fortunate fellows. All of our children are obedient and they have been easy to bring up. Besides, they have been the object of praise. I do not wish for anything more, unless I become excessively greedy. Really, I am thankful!"

"They seem to be in such a happy mood without knowing what I am here for," Oseki said to herself. "How can I tell them to get a divorce for me? I am positive that they are going to rebuke me. Since I am the mother of little Tarō, I have given all possible thought to this matter before running away and leaving him behind. But still it is painful to me to shock the old people, to shatter the joy which has been theirs till this moment. Ought I to return without telling them anything? If I do, I would be looked upon as the mother of Tarō and forever, the wife of Harada. Then my parents would still be able to boast that their son-in-law is a government official appointed by imperial approval. As long as I am thrifty, I would be able to give them good things to eat and some spending money from time to time. But if I have my own way and am divorced, I would have to let Tarō go through the hardship of a step-mother, and wreck my parents' pride. Moreover, what would people think of me? What about my younger brother's future? As the result of such a decision, his budding success might be nipped. Should I return? Should I return to that fiendish husband's side? To that devil? To that devil who is my husband? Oh! No, no!"

She shuddered as she uttered these words and staggered accidentally against the lattice door.

Hearing the noise, her father said in a loud voice, "Who is that?"

He must have mistaken the noise for some mischievous urchin passing by.

Smiling softly, she replied, "Father, it is I!" Her voice sounded very sweet outside the door.

"What? Who? Who is that?" he asked as he opened the paper sliding-door. "Oh! It's you, Oseki! What ails you, standing in a place like that? And why are you here so late? You didn't come in your ricksha and your maid didn't come with you, either! Well, well!" he continued. "Come right in, anyway, come on in. You've shocked me and I am confused. You don't have to shut the lattice door. I'll shut it. Well, well, the inner room will be more comfortable. Sit farther in where the moon shines in. Sit on a cushion, on the cushion! The *tatami* are really badly worn and I've told the landlord about it; but for one reason or another concerned with his workers, he said he wouldn't be able to fix them right away. Don't be so formal! The old *tatami* are hard on your kimono, so sit on the cushion. Now, why did you come so late? Is everyone well in your family?"

As she was being honored profusely as usual, she felt uneasy. She even felt resentful at being treated as the wife of someone important. Swallowing her tears she said, "Yes, they are all right in spite of the weather. I am sorry for my long silence. Have you and Mother been well?"

"Naturally," he replied, "I am feeling fine. But Mother, as you know, is afflicted by those dizzy-spells occasionally. It isn't anything to cause alarm because she recovers very quickly. All she has to do is to stay in bed for half a day or so." He laughed loudly.

"Has Ino (short for Inosuke) gone somewhere tonight?" Oseki then inquired about her younger brother. "I don't see him around. Is he keeping up his studies as before?"

With a contented look on her face, her mother served some tea and said, "Just a while ago Ino left for night school. With your help, you know, he had a promotion just the other day, and he is well liked by the chief of his section. It is all quite encouraging. Everything has been made possible through your husband Mr. Harada's connections, and we talk about it every day. There is no question about your tact, and I want you to try your best to please your husband. As you know, reticent as Ino is, I am afraid he wouldn't be able to say anything more than a few awkward words, when he has a chance to see Mr. Harada. So, I want you to represent us to Mr. Harada and convey our thanks to him, and at the same time ask him to continue to help Ino along. In spite of the change in the season and disagreeable weather, is Tarō all right? Does he get into mischief as usual? Why didn't you bring him along tonight? Grandfather and I have been longing to see him."

Being spoken to in this manner, Oseki became all the more sad. "I had thought of bringing him along," she said, "but he has a habit of going to sleep early. He was already asleep, so I left him at home. Really he gets into all sorts of mischief and he is as unreasonable as he can be. When I go out he wants to follow me, and when I am in he always clings to me. He is really a handful. I wonder how he happens to be so. . . ."

As she spoke, suddenly she recalled her son and she was overwhelmed by tears. She had left him with determination but she could not help thinking about him. She thought, "He must be awake by now and longing for me. Perhaps the maids wouldn't know what to do with him. No rice-cracker nor millet cookie would stop him from crying. They must be pulling him by the arms and threatening to feed him to the devil. Oh! The poor little fellow!" She felt like crying out loud, but seeing her parents in such good humor she could hardly begin to tell them what was on her mind. She repeatedly puffed at her tobacco to camouflage her sorrow and she coughed delicately into the edge of her under sleeve to hide her tears.

"Today is the Thirteenth day of the Ninth month in the old calendar," Oseki's mother said. "You may think it old fashioned of me, but I've made some sweet dumplings to offer to the moon. As they are your favorite, I had thought of having Ino take some of them to you, but he seemed unwilling, saying that they were not good enough for your family. Besides, since we didn't give you any on the Fifteenth [of the Eighth month] I figured, too, that it wouldn't be proper to bring you some this time. I've kept on wishing to let you taste them, even though I found no way to send them over. It's like a dream to have you here tonight. Somehow my heart's intention must have found its way to you. No doubt you have all sorts of delicacies at your place, but what your mother has made is something special. Just for tonight, do away with your lady-like manners, and be like the Oseki I used to know. Eat some of the green beans or chestnuts or whatever you like! Don't mind what you look like; just let me watch you eat. You know, your father and I talk about you all the time. There is no doubt about your marriage being a success. You associate with men of rank and ladies of distinction. I can see it must be quite a strain on you at times to keep up as the wife of Harada among those fine people. Whether it be managing your maids or attending to those who come and go, when you are in a position to supervise others, you are bound to have difficulty. Besides, when the status of your former home is as low as it is, you have to be all the more on guard so as not to be slighted. Naturally, both your father and I wish to see our daughter and our grandchild, but as we think about these things, we hesitate to go to your place too often. Occasionally I pass in front of your gate; but when I am dressed in my cotton kimono and carry only a satinet umbrella, I walk by, keeping my eyes on your bamboo blinds upstairs. All I can do is to imagine what you might be doing at the moment. If your former home were somewhat better off than it is, you wouldn't feel quite so humiliated; and other things being equal, you could perhaps feel a bit more at ease. But what can we do? Even if we were to send over some dumplings, wouldn't our set of lacquered boxes we would send them in be too shabby? Really, I can sympathize with your feelings!"

No doubt she was happy about her daughter's marriage, but realizing the wide gap which separated them, she had to throw in a handful of complaints as she greeted her daughter.

Hearing her mother grieve over her lowly status, Oseki had this to say: "I really think I am an undutiful daughter. Of course I may look grand when I go out dressed in silk in our own private ricksha; but I am not able to help you as much as I wish. Actually, my happiness is only on the surface. I would much rather live with you even if I would have to do needlework or something else."

"How stupid! How stupid you are!" Her father interrupted her, "Don't ever say such a thing! You are a married woman. To support your parents is the last thing you should think of. While you were home, you were the daughter of Saito; once married, you are the wife of Harada, aren't you? Everything will be fine, just so long as you try your best to suit Isamu Harada and manage your household. Although your circumstances may be exacting, if this is your fortune, you should be able to carry through to the end. Women folks tend to complain. What's wrong with you, Mother, starting all this talk? Your mother has been very much out of sorts all day, just because she couldn't have you eat her dumplings. She has put all her efforts into making them; so eat plenty of them to make her satisfied. Aren't they good?"

Hearing her father joke, she still couldn't begin to tell what was really on her mind. She began to eat the chestnuts and boiled green beans which her mother had served.

During the seven years she had been married, she had never called on them at night; it was utterly unprecedented for her to come alone and without a present. Even her kimono did not seem quite so gorgeous as usual. Happy over seeing their daughter after a long silence, her parents had not thought anything of it at first; but now they realized she had not offered a word of greeting from her husband. Although Oseki had a forced smile on her face, she could not conceal her gloomy spirits. Certainly there must be some reason behind it!

Looking at a clock on his desk, her father said, "It's close to ten o'clock, Oseki. Is it all right for you to stay overnight? If you are going home, it's about time to get started." His face turned serious as he tried to discern what was on his daughter's mind.

Suddenly Oseki looked up resolutely and said, "Father, I am here because I have a request to make of you. Please listen to me!" As she placed her hands firmly on the *tatami* in front of her, a tear slipped down her face. Little by little she began to reveal her many sorrows for the first time.

With an uneasy air her father hitched forward and said, "What are you so formal about?"

"I am here tonight with the decision never to return to Harada," she began. "I've come without his permission. After putting Tarō—my dear Tarō—to sleep, I left home never to see his face again. He is so attached to me that he won't go to anyone else. I had to fool him into going to sleep. Making myself heartless as a demon, I left him while he was dreaming. Father! Mother! Please try to understand how I feel! I have never spoken to you before about my husband, nor have I told anyone about what has been going on between us. Hundreds of thousands of times I have hesitated about this, and in the last two or three years I have wept myself out. Finally, today I have made up my mind to seek a divorce. Please! I beg of you, please get me a decree of divorce from my husband. From now on I will try my best and do any kind of work to help Inosuke. Please let me be single for the rest of my life."

Suddenly she burst into tears, and bit the edge of her sleeve to hold back her sobs. Poor girl! Her tears seemed to empurple the black and white bamboo patterns on her garment!

"Tell us all about this," exclaimed her mother and father as they drew closer to her.

"I have kept silent till now; but if you could see the two of us together for half a day, you would be able to realize what kind of couple we are. The only time he speaks to me is when he wants me to do something for him; and when he speaks, it is only to give me orders harshly. In the morning when I ask him how he feels, he abruptly turns away from me and says something unnatural, such as praising the flowering plants in our garden. This, of course, provokes me; but I bear with it, thinking that, after all, he is my husband. And so I have never argued with him either. His fault-finding starts at our breakfast table and he mercilessly points out before our maids that my manners are coarse. If it were just that, I could endure it, but whenever he opens his mouth he slights me by repeatedly saying, 'A woman without education.' Of course, I wasn't brought up as a student in the Peeresses' school. There is no doubt about this. I haven't taken lessons in the art of flower arranging, the ceremony of tea making, singing, or painting, as the wives of his associates have. And so I can't very well carry on conversation with them on an equal footing. But still, if he is not satisfied, he could let me study these subjects secretly. He doesn't have to make public that I come from a poor family, thus causing our maids to stare. For about half a year after our wedding, he used to treat me gently, calling me by my name, but since Tarō came, he has changed completely. It is dreadful when I recall how much worse things have grown. I feel as if I have been pushed into a dark ravine. For a long time, I have never seen or felt the warmth of the sun's rays. At first I thought he was joking, but I was wrong. He must have grown tired of me. He does all sorts of things to torture me, with the hope that I may run away or ask for a divorce. As you know, I am not the type to get jealous even if my husband were to get infatuated with a geisha girl or to keep a mistress. I hear such rumors from my maids, but he is such an active man; and such diversions are rather common among men. When he goes out, I lay his garments out for him and try my best not to do anything to annoy him. But still every single thing I do upsets him. He says that the reason he does not thoroughly enjoy being at home and dining with his family is that I am not doing things properly for him. If he would only tell me exactly what is wrong or what particular thing is displeasing, it would be better; but all he says is that I am no good, I am good for nothing. He mocks me by saying that I am too stupid to confide in, and that he is keeping me in his house merely as wet nurse for Tarō. Certainly that man is not my husband! A devil, that's what he is! He does not openly tell me to go away. I am a coward and my affection for Tarō is such that I listen to his grumblings and obey every word he speaks. Then he calls me a weak-spirited good-for-nothing without any will-power, and he hates me on this account. On the other hand, if I should get my spirit up and talk back to him, I am certain that he would tell me to go away, making an issue out of what I say. Mother, it means nothing to me to leave him! I would never regret being divorced by Isamu Harada, who is good only in name. But as I think of my innocent little Tarō left without his mother, I am disheartened and give in. So I have been apologetic and eager to please my husband; I've endured everything till this day without saying a word. Father! Mother! I am utterly miserable!" Oseki thus poured out her vexation and sorrow.

Her story was something her parents had never even dreamed of. They looked into each other's faces, dumbfounded at learning about Oseki's sad relations with her husband.

It is natural that mothers are indulgent with their children. The more Oseki's mother listened, the more mortified she felt.

"I don't know what you think about this, Father," she began, "but, in the first place, we did not beg that man to marry our daughter. How in the world could he have made such rude remarks about her low birth or poor schooling? He may have forgotten, but I even remember the exact date on which he first saw Oseki. It was at New Year when Oseki became seventeen, in the morning of the Seventh; we hadn't even taken down our pine-tree decorations at the gate. Oseki was playing at battledore with the neighbor's little girl in front of our house on Sarugaku-chō. Her white shuttlecock fell into Mr. Harada's ricksha which happened to be passing by, and she went up to him to get it. After that he started sending people over, asking for Oseki as his bride, saying that he first saw her on that day in New Year. I don't know how many times we refused. We told him, first of all, that our social standing was not quite on a par with his. We said that she was still a child and hadn't taken any lessons in various accomplishments, and that due to our circumstances we would not be able to do anything to prepare her for the marriage. He pressed his suit very urgently and said that since there would be no parents-in-law to fuss and he was taking her as his bride from his own wish, there was no need for talking about social standing or anything of the sort. He further assured us that as far as lessons in various arts were concerned, he could let her study them after he married her, and there was no need of worrying. All we had to do, he said, was to give her to him; then he would take good care of her. Even though we did not ask him, he had a complete trousseau ready for her. Therefore, you were, in every way, the wife of his choice."

Oseki's mother continued. "Your father and I don't call on you too frequently; but it's not because we are scared of Isamu-san's status. After all, we didn't give you away as his mistress, or anything of the sort. We are the parents of his legal bride—the bride he had eagerly sought by resorting to all sorts of means; therefore we could proudly call on you. Nevertheless, we are in such frugal circumstances while he is making a fine living, and we would resent, if people misunderstood and thought that through our daughter we were receiving aid from our son-in-law. It is not our intention to keep up a false front. However, we have at least fulfilled our social obligations by paying him our respects, though refraining from seeing our dear daughter often. How ridiculous it is considering all this! He seems to think that he has picked up an orphan or someone. How arrogant he is! Why should he fuss over whether you are accomplished or not? If you keep silent, the situation is sure to become infinitely aggravated. His abuse will grow into a habit. In the first place, your dignity as the lady of the house will be hurt in the eyes of your maids, and in the end they will not listen to you. In bringing up Tarō, too, what would you do, if he should begin to look down upon you? You must say all you have the right to say. Should he rebuke you on account of it, it would be a good idea to run away from him, telling him that you have a home of your own. What awful nonsense! How in the world could you have kept all this to yourself till today? You've probably been too meek, and caused him to become more selfwilled than ever because of it. It makes me provoked to hear these things. Hereafter, you needn't be so timid. What is there in social standing? You have your mother and father and your brother Inosuke, although he is still young. There is no sense in your keeping on in the midst of such turmoil. What do you think, Father? Don't you think it might be a good idea to see Isamu-san once and thrash this all out with him?" She was so furious she could not even think of the consequences.

For some time, Oseki's father listened with his eyes closed and arms folded. Then he interrupted his wife, "Now, Mother, you shouldn't say such unreasonable things. Hearing this for the first time, I don't know what to do. Considering how Oseki is, I am sure she would not have said all this unless this situation was extreme. She must have run away because things have become unbearable." Oseki's father calmly asked her, "Does your husband happen to be out tonight? Has something serious come up recently? Has he definitely spoken to you about a divorce?"

"He hasn't come home since day before yesterday. It is not unusual for him to be away from home for five or six days. I never think much about it. Before leaving home he became indignant with me, saying that I did not arrange his kimono in the proper way. I apologized over and over, but he wouldn't listen. He threw onto the floor the kimono he had begun to put on, and he himself took out a suit and put it on. Then he left the house saying, 'Ah! there is nobody as unfortunate as I, having a wife like you.' What could have been the matter? For the three hundred and sixty-five days of the year, we have nothing to say to each other, but if he speaks at all, he flings such cruel remarks at me. In spite of all this do I still wish to be called the wife of Harada? Do I still wish to claim myself as the mother of Tarō, while I secretly wipe away tears? I myself don't understand why I have to put up with all this. I must completely forget that I have ever had a husband and a child. When I think back on my maiden days, I have nothing to regret. Since I have made up my mind to leave Tarō behind while looking at his innocent sleeping face, I can never return to live with Isamu. They say that a child grows without his parents. Perhaps it might be better for Tarō to be brought up by a stepmother, or a mistress, whoever suits Isamu's fancy, rather than to be in the hands of such an ill-fated mother as I. Then his father might begin to treat him with affection. But I will never return to Isamu after tonight." She spoke clearly, but her voice trembled; for how could she cut herself off from her beloved child!

With a sigh her father spoke again. "You may well say that. It must be hard for you to stay there. It is a distressing relationship!"

For a while he kept his eyes on Oseki's face and thought to himself, "How natural she looks now in her black silk crape wrap and with her hair fastened with a gold circlet and done up in the fashion of a young matron. In anybody's eyes she appears as a perfectly poised lady, in spite of her being my daughter. How could I bear to see her scrubbing and washing in a cotton-silk house jacket, her sleeves tucked up, and with her hair in a plain coil? Besides, there is the child, Tarō. In a moment of anger she might lose a hundred years of good fortune only to become an object of ridicule. Once she had reinstated herself as the daughter of Kazue Saito, no amount of smiles or tears could reinstate her as the mother of Tarō Harada. She might not feel any regret over her husband, but her affection toward her son could not be severed so easily. Should she once separate herself from them, her anxiety would grow greater and greater, until she might even begin to long for her present hardship. It is her misfortune to have been born so fair. What suffering she has to undergo in such an ill-matched marriage!"

Feeling all the more sorrowful, he said, "If I say this to you, you may think I am merciless and not able to enter into your feelings; but I don't intend to scold you. When there is a difference in social standing, the ways of thinking also differ. Even when you are eager to serve with your whole heart, depending upon how he takes them, your actions may not always please him. Clever and learned as he is, Isamu knows what is right and what is not. I don't think he means to be unreasonably cruel to you. Men who are capable enough to be an object of praise are prone to be extremely dreadful egoists. He may manage his outside affairs with skill and ease, but he may bring home grievances from his office to work off there. It must be terribly hard on you to take all that, but it is the duty of the wife of such an able man. His social position is different, for example, from that of the man who starts the kitchen fire and who commutes to a ward office with his lunch box tied to his waistband. Therefore, although he may be exacting and hard to please, it is the duty of his wife to act adroitly at all times, so as to please him. I have no way of knowing, but I don't think every one of the so-called distinguished wives is blessed with a happy relationship with her husband. If you think you are the only one suffering, you may become resentful. After all, it is part of your duty in society. Especially when there is such a difference in your social status, it's natural that you go through more suffering than others. Even though your mother is talking big, wasn't it through Mr. Harada's recommendation that Ino recently found a salaried position? We should never even for a moment deny the great favor he has done us. It may be hard to take, but what you go through is for the sake of your parents and your brother. Moreover, think of your son Tarō. If you have been able to endure up till now, you can perhaps do the same hereafter. Now, do you still prefer to obtain the divorce and leave Harada? If you do, Tarō will belong to Harada, and you will again become the daughter of Saitō. Once your relationship is severed, you will never be able to see your child's face again. If you have to cry over your misfortune, cry yourself out as the wife of Harada. Isn't that right, Oseki? If you can understand this, keep everything to yourself and return tonight pretending that nothing has happened. I want you to live your life with discretion, as you have done in the past. Even if you had told us nothing, we would understand and so would your brother. We will all share your tears and cry with you." Thus, having persuaded his daughter to bow to what appeared inevitable, he too wiped his tears.

Oseki cried out and said, "I realize now that it was my selfishness that made me speak of divorce. Really, if I should be parted from Tarō and no longer see him, what would be the use of living. What good would it do to try to escape from the agony I face? If I could persuade myself that I am dead, perfect harmony will reign on all sides, and I could see to it that my son Tarō would be brought up by his own parents. In spite of all this, I have indulged in a stupid thought and made you listen to disagreeable things. If I can but think of myself as perishing tonight, leaving only my soul behind in this world to safeguard Tarō, I can per- haps endure my husband's cruelty even for as long as a hundred years.

I thoroughly understand what you have said. I won't make you listen to things like this again. Don't worry about me anymore." She wiped her eyes, only to let more tears flow.

"What an unfortunate girl you are!" said her mother as she burst out crying.

The cloudless moon seemed melancholy. There in a tall vase were arranged some stalks of wild pampas grass, which Inosuke had picked on the river bank behind the house. Even their plumes stirred tonight in a sad gesture of pity.

Oseki's parental home was situated at the foot of the Shinzaka slope in Ueno, on a road leading to Surugadai, in a rather lonely neighborhood thickly shaded by trees, but tonight the moon was so bright that out in the Hirokōji main thoroughfare, it was like broad daylight. Naturally, Oseki's parents had no ricksha station which they regularly patronized, and to send Oseki home, they called out from their window and stopped a ricksha, which happened to be passing by.

"If you understand what I have said, return to your husband. You have left home in his absence without his permission. You'd have no word of apology to offer, should he reprimand you about this. It is getting late, but it will be only a short distance by ricksha. We'll come over to hear more about this. For tonight, I want you to return to your husband."

They took her by her hands and almost dragged her out of their house. This was because of their parental pity; for they did not wish to see the matter aggravated.

Realizing there was nothing else to be done, Oseki made her resolution and said, "Father! Mother! I'll forget all that has happened tonight. I have made up my mind to return to my husband: therefore I shall remain as the wife of Harada. There was no excuse for speaking ill of him, so I'll say nothing more. As long as you are happy and contented over the fact that I am being helpful to my brother because of my husband, I am satisfied. I'll never, never yield to a mistaken notion of taking my own life, so please don't worry about that. After tonight I'll think of myself as completely belonging to Isamu and I'll let him do whatever he wants to. There, I'm leaving now! When Ino comes home, please say 'hello' to him for me. Good-bye then, Father and Mother! The next time I come, I'll come with a smile." She stood up reluctantly.

Her mother went out holding her purse, which contained what little she had, and called to the ricksha-man, "What do you charge to Surugadai?"

"Oh, Mother," exclaimed Oseki as she bowed gently to her, "I'll pay him myself. Thank you very much!" Then she stooped through the lattice doors and hiding her tears in the sleeve of her kimono she stepped into the ricksha. What a pity it was!

Inside the house her father cleared his throat, and his coughs sounded tearful, too.

II

The moon was bright and the soft breeze was barely audible. Out in Ueno the faint chirping of insects sounded rather plaintive. When the ricksha-man had gone hardly a hundred yards after coming into Ueno, for some unknown reason he suddenly lowered the shafts and said, "I'm very sorry, but I'd like to be excused. Please get off, and I won't ask you for the fare."

It was so utterly unexpected that Oseki was astounded and she said, "What? How can you say such a thing to me? I am in a hurry and I will pay you extra; do make an effort. In a lonely place like this, I wouldn't be able to find another ricksha. You are doing this only to work a hardship on me. Do stop being difficult and go on!" She spoke in a pleading tone, with a slight tremble in her voice.

"I'm not asking for extra. I beg you; please get off. I've grown tired of pulling," he repeated.

"Then are you sick or something? What's the matter?" she protested, raising her voice. "It would hardly do to say that you are tired of pulling, after having brought me this far."

"I beg your pardon, lady. Anyway, I'm tired of doing this and I can't help it." With his paper lantern in his hand, suddenly he stepped aside from the shafts.

"What a selfish ricksha-man you are! Then I will not ask you to go where I first told you, but take me where I can find another ricksha. I'll pay you; so please take me somewhere out there, at least to Hirokoji." She spoke to him gently in a coaxing voice.

"You are right. Being young as you are, you wouldn't know what to do if left alone in a lonely place like this. It is bad of me. Certainly, I'll be glad to give you a ride. I'm afraid I've shocked you." As he said this he shifted the lantern from one hand to the other. There was not a trace of toughness in him.

Oseki drew a long breath of relief, and reassured, she looked at the ricksha-man's face. He was about twenty-five or six. He was small, and slight in build and his complexion was rather dark.

"Ah! That face, turned away from the moon, is that of someone I know! He looks like someone I know!" The name of the person came to the tip of her tongue. Involuntarily she spoke to him, "By any chance, are you . . . ?"

"What?" In surprise he looked up at her.

"You, you are that . . . ! Of all persons! you haven't forgotten me, have you?" She slipped down from the ricksha and gazed intently at him.

"You are Miss Oseki Saitō, aren't you?" he exclaimed. "I'm ashamed of my appearance. How could I tell it was you, without eyes in the back of my head? I should have recognized you from your voice; I must have grown awfully stupid!" He lowered his head, feeling humbled.

Scrutinizing him from the top of his head to the tip of his toes, Oseki cried, "No, no! I wouldn't have recognized you even if I had come across you on the street. Till a moment ago I had thought you were just another ricksha-man. It's natural that you didn't recognize me. I've made unpardonable remarks, but I wish you'd forgive me, as I didn't know it was you. How long have you been in this occupation? Isn't it rather strenuous for one of your build? I heard incidentally that your aunt has retired to the countryside, closing up her shop on Ogawa-machi. I am no longer the same Oseki you used to know, and I must be cautious of what I do now. I haven't been able even to write you, to say nothing of calling at your home. Where do you live now? Is your wife well? Do you have any children? I occasionally go down even now to Ogawa-machi to take a look at the stores there; and whenever I'm there, I usually look into the tobacco shop, which is now called Noto-ya. The shop looks exactly the way it used to when your folks owned it. I always recall your childhood, saying to myself, 'Oh, yes, when Kōsaka's Roku-san was little, I used to stop in at his shop on my way to and from school, and how proudly I used to puff away on the butts of cigarettes which were given to me.' I've often wondered where and how you've been. I've been anxious to know how anyone as easygoing as you has been making a living these hard times. Whenever I visit my folks I ask them about you, thinking they might know. It's been five years since I moved away from Sarugaku-chō, so I haven't had any occasion to hear about you. How I've missed you all these years!" Even forgetting her own status, she poured out these inquiries.

He wiped the streaming perspiration from his face with his towel and said, "I've fallen into such a shameful lot, and I don't even have a house to my name." He lowered his head as he continued, "I have a place to sleep in a cheap inn run by a man named Murata on Asakusa-machi. I spend my days idly upstairs of the inn. When the whim is on me, I work till late, like tonight, and when I'm not in the mood to work, I loaf all day as spiritless as smoke. You certainly look beautiful as usual! Ever since the time I heard about your marriage, I've held on to a faint hope of seeing you once again even from a distance to adore you, or to exchange words with you. Until today I've thought of myself as being useless and treated myself like a total loss; but because I have lived to this day I have been able to see you. It is good of you to have remembered me as Rokunosuke Kōsaka."

"And now," Oseki continued, "Tell me about your wife."

"You probably know her," Rokunosuke replied. "She is the daughter of the Sugitas, who were diagonally opposite our place. She is the girl who was highly praised by everybody. She was known for her fair skin and figure. When I became terribly dissolute and stopped going home, a relative of mine—an obstinate one—mistook my loose conduct as being because I had no wife although I was old enough to be married. At the same time my mother took special note of this girl and insisted upon my agreeing to marry her immediately. Mother was so persistent and made such a fuss that finally I gave up in desperation. That was about the time when I heard that you were pregnant. A year afterwards, at our place, too, we were congratulated over our child. We began to have a display of papier-mâché dogs and windmills and what not. But all these events were not enough to pull me out of my wildness. People must have figured that I might change when I took a nice looking wife and became a father. I concluded, however, that my habits were incurable, even if Komachi and Hsi Shi came hand in hand and even if Sotōri-hime danced before me.[1] How could I be converted just by seeing the baby's face that smelled of milk. I indulged myself to my heart's content and drank to the dregs. I neglected my home and business, until by year before last I didn't even have a chopstick to my name. My mother went to live with my married older sister in the country, and I sent my wife to her former home with her child. Ever since then, I haven't heard a word from them. The child being a girl, I don't particularly miss her; but according to reports, she died of typhoid fever toward the end of last year. Girls tend to be precocious. She must have longed for me and called for me in her last moments. If she had lived, she would have been five this year. Such uninteresting affairs of mine—not even worth talking about!"

With a faint smile on his cheerless face, he continued, "Not knowing it was you, I've committed a terribly selfish blunder. Please get into the ricksha; I'll take you home. No doubt, you must have been terrified. I am a ricksha-man only in name. I hold the shafts, but there is nothing I can look forward to! I work like an ox or a horse, but I have no hope! Am I glad when I get money? Am I happy when I can drink? The more

I think, the more disgusted I get. Whether I am giving a ride to a passenger or not, when I grow tired, I simply can't do anything about it. I am a downright selfish fellow. Who wouldn't get sick of a man like me? Now, please get in; I'll take you."

Being thus persuaded she replied, "While I was unaware of your being the ricksha-man, it couldn't be helped: but after knowing it, how can I get into your ricksha? But I am afraid to walk alone in such a lonely place, so please accompany me to Hirokōji. We can talk on our way."

Oseki lifted the hem of her kimono slightly as she walked. The patter of her lacquered clogs sounded desolate in the night air.

Of all her old acquaintances, Rokunosuke was the one for whom she had an unforgettable attachment. He was the only son of Mr. Kōsaka, who owned a neat tobacco shop on Ogawamachi. Now he looked unsightly and darker, but in his better days he had appeared smart in his silk outfit. He used to be affable and friendly. People used to compliment him by saying that although he was young, his shop was more thriving than in his father's time. He seemed to be such an intelligent man! How he had changed!

About the time when the rumor of her own marriage began to spread, she heard people speak of his reckless fun and roistering. They said that he was no longer like his former self, and they wondered if perhaps he was possessed by an evil spirit, or was suffering from some sort of curse. At any rate, it was beyond the ordinary. As she saw him on this night, he certainly looked shabby. It was unthinkable that he should have fallen so low as to find shelter in a cheap inn.

"He had been in love with me," Oseki recollected, "and as I used to see him mornings and evenings during the years when I was twelve to seventeen, I used to imagine myself being seated in his shop reading papers or waiting on customers. Suddenly my own marriage with someone unexpected was being arranged. How could I have objected to that marriage, since it was a matter decided by my parents? In my naive childish mind I used to long to become Roku-san's wife. Neither he nor his parents had ever mentioned anything of the sort, and naturally my people did not say a word about it. If it was love, it was as vague as a dream. I told myself to forget about him and I was determined to keep him completely out of my mind. Finally the time came for me to become the bride of Harada, but till the last moment my tears flowed for Roku-san whom I was unable to forget. He must have thought of me as much as I did of him. I may have been the cause of his ruin. I must be a bitter sight to him here with my formal coiffure as if to show off my position. But really I am not so happy as I might look."

As Oseki turned back to look at Rokunosuke, she noticed a blank look on his face. What could he have been thinking? He did not seem to be rejoiced over seeing her on this rare occasion.

They were now out in Hirokōji where Oseki could catch a ricksha. She took some paper money out of her purse and gracefully wrapped it in a piece of soft paper.

Handing it to Rokunosuke, Oseki said, "Roku-san, please pardon my rudeness, but I wish you'd buy some paper handkerchiefs or something with this. Seeing you after such a long silence, somehow I feel there are many things I would like to say to you, but I can't begin to tell you all. I hope you'll understand. I must say good-bye now. Please take good care of yourself, and do your best to set your mother's mind at rest. I wish the best for you, too. I want you to be the same Rokusan that I used to know, and please let me see you open up your shop once again. Good-bye!"

Politely accepting the paper-wrapped money, Rokunosuke replied, "I really should refuse this offer, but since it is something you've given me personally, I am going to keep it as a remembrance. Although I don't feel like parting from you, if this reunion of ours is to be but a fleeting dream, what can we do? Now, please get started; I'm going home, too. Late as it is, you must find it lonely to walk alone."

Rokunosuke started on his way holding the shafts of the empty ricksha. After going a little way, he turned around to see Oseki—his way was to the east and hers to the south. The drooping willows on the main thoroughfare were waving softly in the moonlight. The faint patter of Oseki's lacquered clogs echoed her pensive mood.

The one who lived on the second floor at Murata's and the other who was the wife of Harada—each bore a share of the manifold sorrows of this world.

Note

1. Komachi was a Japanese poetess who lived during the ninth century and Hsi Shi (Xi Shi) lived during the Zhou dynasty in China. Sotōri-hime was a consort to the Emperor Ingyō (376–453). All three of them were known for their beauty.

26

Stories

Natsume Sōseki

Natsume Soseki (born Natsume Kinnosuke, 1867–1916) grew up in Tokyo and studied Chinese literature, then architecture, and finally turned to Western literature. From 1895 to 1896 he taught at a rural middle school, like the protagonist of *Botchan*, and after two years of studying in London (1900–1902) he became a university professor of English literature. In 1907 he quit teaching to write full-time. To this day he is considered the most eminent of modern Japanese writers. His most respected work is *Kokoro* (1914), which explores the sense of isolation of a man struggling to adapt as Japan modernizes and grappling with feelings of guilt for having betrayed a friend in his youth. *Botchan* (1906), Soseki's most beloved novel, is a humorous account of a self-righteous yet humble young man from Tokyo trying to settle into his first teaching job in a school where the students are unruly and school officials are manipulative and self-serving.

Botchan Questions

1. Do you think Botchan is naive?
2. What is admirable about him?
3. Identify the humorous moments in this chapter.

Ten Nights' Dreams Questions

1. What is the concept of art implicit in the sixth night's dream?

2. What might be the meaning of the final line, that Unkei is still alive?
3. What lessons seem implicit in the seventh night's dream?

Natsume Soseki

> *Botchan* excerpt adapted from Natsume Kinnosuke,
> *Botchan* (*Master Darling*), translated by Morri Yasotaro
> and revised by J.R. Kennedy, 1919, Chapter 8.
> "The Sixth Night" and "The Seventh Night" from
> Natsume Soseki, *Ten Nights' Dreams*, translated by
> Takumi Kashima and Loretta R. Lorenz
> (London: Soseki Museum, 2000), pp. 23–30.

Botchan (1906) by Natsume Soseki

The narrator, Botchan (a term referring to a young man from a well-to-do family and implying naïveté), has been reassessing his colleagues, to whom he has assigned various nicknames. Early on, Porcupine had treated Botchan to a dish of shaved ice, at the trifling cost of 1.5 sen [less than a penny in the early twentieth century]. Botchan, alienated from Porcupine due to lies by Red Shirt, tried to pay it back, but Porcupine was insulted and refused to accept the money, so it lies untouched on Porcupine's desk. More recently, Porcupine is the only teacher at the teachers' meeting who supports punishing the students who taunted Botchan during his first turn at night duty at the boarding school. In this chapter, Botchan finds out that Squash is being forced to transfer and Red Shirt is essentially trying to bribe Botchan into becoming an ally.

Characters

Red Shirt: the assistant principal
Porcupine: head of the math section
The old lady: Botchan's landlady, who lives in Squash's neighborhood
Squash: an English teacher
The Madonna: the English teacher's fiancée who is wooed away from him by Red Shirt
Kiyo: Botchan's former nanny in Tokyo

Chapter 8

Since returning from the afternoon of fishing to which Red Shirt had invited me, I began to suspect Porcupine, but when I heard from the old lady about Porcupine confronting the Principal for the sake of Squash to stop Red Shirt from meddling with the Madonna, I clapped my hands and hoorayed for him. Judging by these facts, I began to wonder if Porcupine was in fact a good man, and Red Shirt a rascal. At this juncture I had seen Red Shirt taking a walk with the Madonna on the levee of the Nozeri River, and I decided that Red Shirt might be a scoundrel. I am not sure of his being really scoundrel at heart, but at any rate he is not a good fellow. He is a fellow with a double face. A man deserves no confidence unless he is as straight as the bamboo. One may fight a straight fellow, and feel satisfied. Red Shirt, who seems kind, gentle, refined, and takes pride in his pipe, is someone to be watched closely, and I could not be too careful in getting into a scrap with a fellow of this type. I may fight, but I would not get a fair match as at the sumo matches in the Wrestling Amphitheatre in Tokyo. Come to think of it, Porcupine who turned against me and startled the whole teachers' room over the amount of one sen and a half is far more like a man. When he stared at me with owlish eyes at the teachers' meeting, I branded him as a spiteful guy, but as I consider the matter now, he is better than the feline voice of Red Shirt. To tell the truth, I tried to reconcile with Porcupine, and after the meeting, spoke a word or two to him, but he shut up like a clam and kept glaring at me. So I got sore, and let it go at that.

Porcupine has not spoken to me since. The one sen and a half which I paid him back upon the desk is still there, well covered with dust. I could not touch it, nor would Porcupine take it. This one sen and a half has become a barrier between us two. We two were cursed with this one sen and a half. Later indeed I got so sick of its sight that I hated to see it.

While Porcupine and I were thus estranged, Red Shirt and I continued friendly relations and associated together. On the day following my accidental meeting with him near the Nozeri River, for instance, Red Shirt came to my desk as soon as he came to the school, and asked me how I liked the new boarding house. He said we would go fishing together again, and talked of many things. I felt a bit piqued, and said, "I saw you twice last night," and he answered, "Yes, at the station. Do

you go there at that time every day? Isn't it late?" I startled him with
the remark, "I met you on the levee of the Nozeri River too, didn't I?"
and he replied, "No, I didn't go in that direction. I returned right after
my bath."

What is the use of trying to keep secrets. Didn't we meet actually face
to face? He tells too many lies. If one can hold the job of an assistant
principal and act in this fashion, I should be able to run the position of
Chancellor of a university. From this time on, my confidence in Red
Shirt shrank further. I talk with Red Shirt whom I do not trust, and I
keep silent with Porcupine whom I respect. Funny things do happen in
this world.

One day Red Shirt asked me to come over to his house as he had
something to tell me, and much as I would miss my daily trip to the hot
springs, I started for his house at about 4 o'clock. Red Shirt is single,
but in keeping with the dignity of an assistant principal, he gave up the
boarding house life long ago, and lives in a fine house. The house rent, I
understood, was nine yen and fifty sen. The front entrance was so attractive that I thought if one can live in such a splendid house at nine yen and
a half in the country, it would be a good game to call Kiyo from Tokyo
and make her heart glad. The younger brother of Red Shirt answered my
bell. This brother gets his lessons on algebra and mathematics from me
at the school. He is a weak student and, being an outsider, he is a worse
rascal than the native boys.

I met Red Shirt. Smoking the same old unsavory amber pipe, he said
something to the following effect:

"Since you've been with us, our work has been more satisfactory than
it was under your predecessor, and the principal is very glad to have got
the right person in the right place. I wish you to work as hard as you can,
for the school is depending upon you."

"Well, is that so. I don't think I can work any harder than
now. . . ."

"What you're doing now is enough. Only don't forget what I told you
the other day."

"Meaning that one who helps me find a boarding house is dangerous?"

"If you state it so baldly, there is no meaning to it. . . . But that's
all right. . . . I believe you understand the spirit of my advice. And
if you keep on in the way you're going today. . . . We have not been
blind . . . we might offer you a better treatment later on if we can
manage it."

"In salary? I don't care about the salary, though the more the better."

"And fortunately there is going to be one teacher transferred . . . however, I can't guarantee, of course, until I talk it over with the principal . . . and we might give you something out of his salary."

"Thank you. Who is going to be transferred?"

"I think I may tell you now; 'tis going to be announced soon. Koga is the man."

"But isn't Mr. Koga a native of this town?"

"Yes, he is. But there are some circumstances . . . and it is partly by his own preference."

"Where is he going?"

"To Nobeoka in Hyuga province. As the place is so far away, he is going there with his salary raised a grade higher."

"Is someone coming to take his place?"

"His successor is almost decided upon."

"Well, that's fine, though I'm not very anxious to have my salary raised."

"I'm going to talk to the principal about that anyway. And, we may have to ask you to work more sometime later . . . and the principal appears to be of the same opinion. . . . I want you to go ahead with that in your mind."

"Going to increase my working hours?"

"No. The working hours may be reduced. . . ."

"The working hours shortened and yet work more? Sounds funny."

"It does sound funny . . . I can't say definitely just yet . . . it means that we may have to ask you to assume more responsibility."

I could not make out what he meant. To assume more responsibility might mean my appointment to the senior instructor of mathematics, but Porcupine is the senior instructor and there is no danger of his resigning. Besides, he is so very popular among the students that his transfer or discharge would be inadvisable. Red Shirt always misses the point. And though he did not get to the point, the object of my visit was ended. We talked a while on sundry matters, Red Shirt proposing a farewell dinner party for Squash, asking me if I drink liquor and praising Squash as an amiable gentleman, etc. Finally he changed the topic and asked me if I take an interest in haiku. Here is where I beat it, I thought, and, saying "No, I don't, goodbye," hastily left the house. The "haiku" should be a diversion of Bashō or the boss of a barbershop. It would not do for the teacher of mathematics to rave over the old wooden bucket and the morning glory.[1]

I returned home and thought it over. Here is a man whose mental process defies a layman's understanding. He is going to court hardships in a strange part of the country in preference of his home and the school where he is working—both of which should satisfy most anybody—because he is tired of them. That may be all right if the strange place happens to be a lively metropolis where electric cars run—but of all places, why Nobeoka in Hyuga province? This town here has a good steamship connection, yet I became sick of it and longed for home before one month had passed. Nobeoka is situated in the heart of a most mountainous country. According to Red Shirt, one has to make an all-day ride in a wagon to Miyazaki, and from Miyazaki another all-day ride in a rickshaw to Nobeoka. Its name alone does not commend itself as civilized. It sounds like a town inhabited by men and monkeys in equal numbers. However sage-like Squash might be I thought he would not become a friend of monkeys of his own choice. What a curious slant!

"Monkey" (1940) by Hashimoto Kansetsu (1883–1945), color on silk. Monkeys in Japan were often associated with being unenlightened in the Buddhist sense, namely, not being able to distinguish the true meaning of life from illusion. *(Wikimedia Commons, Adachi Art Museum)*

Just then the old lady brought in my supper—"Sweet potatoes again?" I asked, and she said, "No, Sir, it is tofu tonight." They are about the same thing.

"Say, I understand Mr. Koga is going to Nobeoka."

"Isn't it too bad?"

"Too bad? But it can't be helped if he goes there by his own preference."

"Going there by his own preference? Who, Sir?"

"Who? Why, he! Isn't Professor Koga going there by his own choice?"

"That's not the case at all, Sir."

"But Red Shirt told me so just now. If that's wrong, then Red Shirt is lying."

"The assistant principal may have said what he said, but the fact is Mr. Koga does not wish to go."

"Our old lady is impartial, and that is good. But how do you explain it?"

"Mr. Koga's mother was here this morning, and told me all the circumstances."

"Told you what circumstances?"

"Since Mr. Koga's father died, they have not been quite well off as we might have supposed, and the mother asked the principal if his salary could not be raised a little as Mr. Koga has been in service for four years. See?"

"Well?"

"The principal said that he would consider the matter, and she felt satisfied and expected the announcement of the increase before long. She hoped for its coming this month or next. Then the principal called Mr. Koga to his office one day and said that he was sorry but the school was short of money and could not raise his salary. But he said there is an opening in Nobeoka which would give him five yen extra a month and he thought that would suit his purpose, and the principal had made all arrangements and told Mr. Koga he had better go . . ."

"That wasn't a consultation but a command. Wasn't it?"

"Yes, Sir, Mr. Koga told the principal that he would rather stay here at the old salary than go elsewhere on an increased salary, because he has his own house and is living with his mother. But the matter has all been settled, and his successor already appointed and it couldn't be helped, said the principal."

"Hum, that's a jolly good trick, I should say. Then Mr. Koga has no interest in going there? No wonder I thought it strange. We would have to go a long way to find any blockhead to do a job in such a mountain village and get acquainted with monkeys for five yen extra."

"What is a blockhead, Sir?"

"Never mind. It was all the scheme of Red Shirt. A decidedly under-handed scheme, I should say. It was a stab in the back. And he means to raise my salary that way; that's not right. I won't take that raise. Let's see him try to give me a raise!"

"Is your salary going to be raised, Sir?"

"Yes, they said they would raise it, but I'm thinking of refusing it."

"Why will you refuse?"

"Why or no why, it's going to be refused. Say, Red Shirt is a fool; he is a coward."

"He may be a coward, but if he raises your salary, it would be best for you to make no fuss, but accept it. One is apt to get grouchy when young, but will always repent when he is grown up and thinks that it was pity he hadn't been a little more patient. Take an old woman's advice for once, and if Red Shirt-san says he will raise your salary, just take it with thanks."

"Don't meddle, old lady. It's none of your business."

The old lady withdrew in silence. The old man was chanting Noh passages in an off-key voice. Chanting Noh, I think, is a stunt that pur-posely makes a performance incomprehensible when one could easily understand it by reading it. I cannot fathom what is in the mind of the old man who spends every night at it. But I'm not in a position to be wondering about that. Red Shirt said he would have my salary raised, and though I did not care much about a raise, I accepted it because there was no use of leaving the money lying around. But I cannot stoop so low as accept a slice of the salary of a fellow teacher who is being transferred against his will. What in thunder do they mean by sending him away so far as Nobeoka when the fellow prefers to remain in his old position? Even Sugawara no Michizane did not have to go farther than Hakata; even Matagorō Kawai[2] stopped at Sagara. I shall not feel satisfied unless I see Red Shirt and tell him I refuse the raise.

I dressed again and went to his house. The same younger brother of Red Shirt again answered the bell, and looked at me with eyes which plainly said, "You here again?" I will come twice or thrice or as many times as I want to if there is business. I might even rouse them out of their beds at midnight. Don't mistake me for one coming to curry favor with an assistant principal. I was here to give back my salary. The younger brother said that there was a visitor just then, so I told him a brief word at the front door will do; won't take more than a minute, and he went in.

After a while Red Shirt appeared at the door with a lamp in his hand, and said, "Come in."

"This is good enough," I said, "it won't take long." I looked at his face, which was the color of a boiled lobster. He seemed to have been drinking.

"You told me that you would raise my salary, but I've changed my mind, and have come here to decline the offer."

Red Shirt, thrusting out the lamp forward, staring at me, at a loss for words. He seemed dazed. Did he think it strange that here was a fellow, the only one in the world, who does not want his salary raised, or was he taken aback that I should come back so soon even if I wished to decline it, or was it both combined. In any case he stood there silent with his mouth in a queer shape.

"I accepted your offer because I understood that Mr. Koga was being transferred by his own preference. . . ."

"Mr. Koga really is going to be transferred by his own preference."

"No, Sir. He would like to stay here. He doesn't mind his present salary if he can stay."

"Have you heard it from Mr. Koga himself?"

"No, not from him."

"Then, from who?"

"The old lady in my boarding house told me what she heard from Mr. Koga's mother."

"Then the old woman in your boarding house told you so?"

"Well, that's about the size of it."

"Excuse me, but I think you are wrong. According to what you say, it seems as if you believe what the old woman in the boarding house tells you, and choose not to believe what your assistant principal tells you. Have I got that right?"

I was stuck. A college graduate is confoundedly good in oratorical combat. He gets hold of an unexpected point, and pushes the other backward. My father used to tell me that I am too careless and no good, and now indeed I look that way. I ran out of the house on a moment's impulse when I heard the story from the old lady, and in fact I had not heard it from either Squash or his mother. In consequence, when I was challenged in this debate squad fashion, it was a bit difficult to defend myself. I could not deflect his frontal attack, but I had already declared in my mind a lack of confidence in Red Shirt. The old lady in the boarding house might be tight-fisted, but she is no liar. She is not double faced like Red Shirt. I was helpless, so I answered.

"What you say might be right. Nevertheless, I decline the raise."

"That's still funnier. I thought your coming here now was because you had found a certain reason for which you could not accept the raise. Then it is hard to understand to see you still insisting on declining the raise in spite of the reason having been eradicated by my explanation."

"It may be hard to understand, but anyway I don't want it."

"If you don't like it so much, I wouldn't force it on you. But if you change your mind within two or three hours for no particular reason, it will affect your credibility in the future."

"I don't care if it does."

"That can't be. Nothing is more important than credibility. Supposing the landlord of the boarding house . . ."

"Not the landlord, but the old lady."

"Makes no difference, suppose what the old woman in the boarding house told you was true, your salary increase is not coming from the reduction in Mr. Koga's income, is it? Mr. Koga is going to Nobeoka; his successor is coming here. Mr. Koga's successor's salary is a little less than Mr. Koga's, and we propose to give the difference to you. You need not be uncomfortable. Mr. Koga will be promoted; the successor is to start on less pay, and you get a raise, I think everything is satisfactory for all concerned. If you don't like it, that's all right, but suppose you think it over once more at home?"

My brain is not of the best stuff, and if another fellow flourishes his eloquence like this, I usually think, "Well, perhaps I was wrong," and consider myself defeated, but not tonight. From the time I came to this town I felt suspicious of Red Shirt. Once I had thought of him in a different light, taking him for a kind-hearted and somewhat feminine fellow. His kindness, however, began to look like anything but kindness, and as a result, I have been getting sick of him. So no matter how he might glory himself in logical grandiloquence, or how he might attempt to out-talk me in a head-teacher-style, I didn't care a snap. One who shines in argument is not necessarily a good guy, while the other who is out-talked is not necessarily a bad guy, either. Red Shirt is very, very reasonable as far as his reasoning goes, but however good he sounded, he could not win my respect. If money, authority or reasoning can command admiration, loan sharks, police officers and college professors should be liked best by all. I would not be moved in the least by the logic of so insignificant a fellow as the assistant principle of a middle school. Man works by feelings, not by logic.

"What you say is right, but I have begun to dislike the raise, so I decline. It will be the same if I think it over. Goodbye."

As I left the house of Red Shirt I noticed the Milky Way high in the sky.

Ten Nights' Dreams (1908) by Natsume Soseki

These ten pieces were published separately in newspapers in the summer of 1908. It is not known whether they were really records of dreams or just presented in that format. Unkei (ca. 1150–1223) was a sculptor whose style was more realistic and whose figures were more muscular than previously made.

The Sixth Night

I had heard that the great Unkei was carving the figures of the two Temple Guardians, the ancient Nio, at the main gate of Gokoku Temple, so I walked out to see it. There were many people already there before me all talking about the project.

Before the main gate stood a red pine tree five or six *ken* high (about ten meters), spreading its branches out against the blue sky far above, at an angle that partially screened its roof. The green of the pine tree and the vermilion of the lacquered gate reflected each other in beautiful harmony. The tree was well placed so that one heavy branch extended obliquely to avoid blocking the left side of the gate. It seemed somehow old-fashioned to let the branch stick out over the roof that way. It could have been the Kamakura Period.

However, the people looking at it, including me, were of the Meiji era. Most of them were rickshaw drivers. They must have been standing there because they were tired of waiting for passengers.

One said, "That's what I call big!"

"That must be harder than it is to make a man," said another.

Still another said, "Do they still carve the Nio nowadays? I thought that was all way back when."

"It looks plenty strong all right. They say there was never anyone as strong as the Nio. They say they were even stronger than Yamato-takeru-no-mikoto, that ancestor-god of the emperor himself." This speaker with his kimono tucked in was not wearing a hat. He seemed somewhat uncultured.

Unkei was working with his chisel and hammer, unconcerned about his reputation among the onlookers. He never turned to look at them. Perched on his high place, he went on carving the first Nio.

"Kongorikishi (Ni-o)" (early fourteenth century), wood. Pairs of these fierce-looking beings are often placed at the main entrance to Buddhist temples since their job is to protect the Buddha and, by extension, his believers against evil. *(Wikimedia Commons, Freer Gallery of Art, Washington, DC)*

Unkei was wearing the strange headgear of a bygone era and had his sleeves tied across his back. Anyway, his whole aspect was that of another age. He seemed to be ill-matched with his noisy audience. It was strange to be watching him there. I wondered why he was still alive in this modern period.

Unkei, however, was carving away as if everything were absolutely normal. A young man who was looking up at him turned to me and began extolling his work, saying, "He is great. We are beneath his notice. He seems to be telling us that he and the Nio are the world's only heroes. I think he is splendid."

I thought that his words were interesting. I glanced at him and he said at once, "Look how he uses the chisel and hammer. That's exquisite mastery."

He was now carving the Nio's eyebrow a *sun* (3.03 cm) sideways, and in the precise instant that he turned over the blade of the chisel, he brought the hammer down. He planed the hard wood and thick shavings flew with the sound of the hammer as the side of an angry nose emerged. He seemed to have an unconcerned way of working, yet his hand was perfectly sure.

"He uses the chisel in such an offhand manner. How can he make the eyebrows and nose the way he wants?" I was so impressed that I began talking to myself. "No," the young man at my side observed. "He doesn't do it with his chisel. All he does is just dig out the eyebrows and nose already buried in the wood. It's like digging stones out of the ground. He cannot make a mistake."

What a discovery. So this is what sculpture is! It occurred to me that if that is all there is to it, anybody can do it. I suddenly longed to make a statue of the Nio for myself, so I went off home there and then.

I got the chisel and hammer out of my toolbox. In the backyard there was a large stack of oak wood, already sawed up for firewood after a recent storm had scattered tree branches about.

I chose the biggest one and began to carve it vigorously, but unfortunately I couldn't seem to find the Nio. I couldn't find one in the next piece, either. Nor was it in the third. I carved into the stacked wood piece after piece, but in none was hidden the Nio. At last I had to accept the fact that the Nio does not reside in the wood of the Meiji period. I also learned the reason why Unkei is alive today.

The Seventh Night

I find myself on board an extraordinarily big ship.

The ship steams against the waves emitting black smoke continuously day and night and making a deafening noise. The trouble is, I have no idea where the ship is heading. The sun, reflected like burning tongs, seems to come from beneath the waves. I see the sun motionless above the tall mast for a time, but in the next moment it passes the big ship and finally disappears again into the depths, sputtering on the water as though the burning tongs had been suddenly dropped there. Each time this happens, blue waves turn blackish-red far beyond and the ship makes a terrible noise in a vain chase after the sun's traces.

Once I got hold of a crewman on deck. "Is this ship heading west?" The man glared at me for a moment. "Why?" he finally asked.

"Because the ship seems to be running after the setting sun," I replied.

The man gave a loud, amused laugh and went off. I heard the strains of a sea shanty:

"Is the Sun heading East? It may be, Ho!
Is its home in the West? Don't ask me, Ho!
It's a sailor I am and belong to the waves;
My ship is my home and ever I roam,
Sail on, sail on, sail on, Ho!"

I came to the forecastle deck and found a crowd of sailors hauling the big jib rope.

I felt completely lost, abandoned. I had no idea when I would be able to get off this ship. I didn't even know where it was heading. I was only sure the ship was steaming ahead against the waves, emitting its black smoke. The waves were fairly high and looked infinitely blue. The water sometimes turned purple, but white foam was always being blown back in the ship's wake. I felt completely lost. I thought of jumping into the sea to my death rather than staying on this ship.

There was a lot of company on board. Most people looked foreign, with very different types of features. As the ship pitched in the heavy, cloudy weather, I found a woman leaning against the rail, crying unceasingly. The handkerchief she used to wipe her tears looked white, I saw, but she wore printed Western clothes, probably cotton. When I looked at her, I realized that I was not the only one who was sad.

One night when I was alone on deck watching the stars, a foreigner came up and asked me if I knew any astronomy. Here I was almost ready to kill myself as a non-entity. What did I need to know about astronomy? But I kept silent. The foreign man began to tell me about the seven stars over Taurus. He said that the stars and the sea were something God had created. Finally he asked me if I believed in God. I just kept silent, looking up at the sky.

Going into the saloon one time, I saw a young woman dressed in flashy clothes. She had her back to me and was playing the piano. Beside her was a tall, fine gentleman singing a song. His mouth looked enormous.

Anyway, the man and woman appeared to be entirely indifferent to everyone but each other. They even seemed to have forgotten that they were on a ship.

I found myself getting more and more unhappy. In the end, I decided I would kill myself. One night when there was no one about, I ventured to throw myself into the sea, but just as my feet left the deck and my tie with the ship was severed, I wished from the bottom of my heart that I had not done this thing, but it was too late. I had to enter the sea whether I liked it or not. The ship was so tall that although I was physically parted from it, my feet would not touch the water that quickly, but with nothing to hold on to, it was getting closer and closer. However tightly I curled my legs under me, it was useless. The water was black.

The ship passed me, trailing its perpetual black smoke. I realized that it would have been better for me to stay on board even without knowing where the ship was bound, but I was unable to put this new wisdom to any practical use. I fell deep into the black waves quietly, with infinite regret and fear.

Notes

1. There is a well-known seventeen-syllable poem describing the scene of morning glories entwining around a wooden bucket.

2. Sugawara no Michizane (845–903) was slandered and exiled to Kyushu in 901; Matagorō Kawai was a notorious murderer in the early seventeenth century who was later killed in an authorized vendetta.

27

A Sudden Flash of Light

Nakazawa Keiji

Nakazawa Keiji (1939–2012) was a minor manga artist when he published the first installment of *Barefoot Gen* in 1973. He concluded the series in 1985 when it had reached ten volumes. His first work was as a sign painter; he became an assistant to a professional manga artist in Tokyo in 1961. For a time he reacted to the discrimination atomic bomb victims faced by hiding his personal experience. When his mother died in 1966 and he saw that even her bones were consumed in the cremation fire, he realized that this was an effect of exposure to radiation. It felt like a final insult and led him to the idea of avenging the deaths of his family members by fighting against war and nuclear weapons in his manga. He immediately wrote his first story with an atomic bomb victim as protagonist (*Pelted by Black Rain*). Major manga magazines did not dare to publish this controversial story, but a minor publisher was willing to take a risk. When the story was well received, Nakazawa went on to write many more manga about the atomic bombing. For relief from the intensity of that work he continued to write conventional stories, but in October 1972 an editor encouraged Nakazawa to write a short autobiographical manga and then to write a more extensive version. Nakazawa was ambivalent, self-conscious, and concerned about negative reactions, but also he wanted to expose the fascism of prewar Japan and express his deep hatred of war. *Barefoot Gen*, a somewhat fictionalized account of his own experiences, hit a chord with the public and sold extremely well. Nakazawa worked on *Barefoot Gen* off and on for fourteen years. The book version has been translated into several languages and sold millions of copies. Nakazawa continued to be active in the antiwar and antinuclear weapons movement until his death. Included here is a passage from his real autobiography (published in Japanese in 1987).

This passage describes the morning of August 6, 1945, and the immediate aftermath of the bombing. It goes on to describe the oily, black rain that soon fell briefly and how Nakazawa later learned that his father (an artist), sister, and brother were trapped in their house when it collapsed and they burned to death, while their mother, having finished hanging the laundry out to dry, was saved by being precisely under the eaves but not inside the house. His baby sister died four months later.

Questions

1. Examine your reactions to this account, as a human being and/or as an American.
2. What is the effect of combining a description of the horrifying effects of the atomic blast with objective, scientific facts about them?

Hiroshima: The Autobiography of Barefoot Gen

"A Sudden Flash of Light" from Nakazawa Keiji, translated and edited by Richard H. Minear, *Hiroshima: The Autobiography of Barefoot Gen* (Lanham, MD: Rowman & Littlefield, 2010), pp. 31–40. Used with permission of the publisher.

Chapter 2: A Sudden Flash of Light

The Day of the Flash and Boom

August 6, 1945, Monday. B-29s had flown over Hiroshima twice the night before, and air raid sirens had sounded constantly. I awoke unhappy that I hadn't gotten enough sleep. The weather the morning of August 6 swept that unhappiness away. The sky was cloudless and absolutely clear, bright sunlight pierced our eyes, and houses and trees stood out as if painted in primary colors. My eyes felt as if they'd been washed clean, and my unhappiness over lack of sleep vanished, too.

Suddenly, at about 7:20, soon after the whole family, gathered about the round table, had finished breakfast, the sirens sounded. I was surprised. Strange: I didn't remember sirens sounding that early in the morning. Dad muttered, "Mr. Enemy is coming really early. Unusual." Urged on by Mom, who said we'd be in danger if bombs fell, we made our preparations and headed for the neighborhood air raid trench. Mom's due date was approaching, and clutching her swollen belly, she huffed and puffed as she ran. In the trench, I said, "At worst, it's another observation plane. No need to worry," and played with Susumu. Sure enough, the megaphone voice came, "All clear!" and we returned home, kidding ourselves for getting all flustered over the alert—"An observation plane, after all."

Looking up into the clear blue sky, I could still see the contrail of the B-29, a white strip; in the distance it had already fanned out. Dad said to Mom, burdened by her big belly, "Today will be hot." The B-29 that flew in that morning was a reconnaissance plane to check the weather conditions over Hiroshima and to photograph the target before the bombing. Had the atomic bomb been dropped then, many would have survived because they'd run to the trenches.

The "all clear" came, and reassured, the four hundred thousand residents of Hiroshima all began the day's activities. City trolleys went busily on their rounds, car after car disgorging its passengers; a continual flow of people headed for businesses and factories. People began their activities. Children headed to school. Housewives cleared away breakfast things and set about cleaning or doing the wash. Soldiers started drilling. Mobilized for labor service, women and students collected the detritus from collapsed houses and carted the stuff off.

At that time the elementary school we were going to had no summer vacation; we had to go to school to study to become strong "little patriots." With my air raid hood hanging off one shoulder and my satchel on my back, I went out onto the clothes-drying porch off the second floor and said to Mom, who was hanging laundry out to dry, "I'm off." In her apron, wiping off sweat, Mom went on hanging out the clothes.

On the drying porch, flowers and plants in pots were lined up, models for Dad to paint. A strange thing had happened with these potted plants. There was fruit on the loquat. The whole family stared: "Fruit on a *potted* tree?" Dad told us, sharply, "When it's ripe, I'm going to paint it, so hands off!" With a sinister premonition, Mom worried, "Something must be out of kilter meteorologically." I'm not a fatalist, but Mom's sinister premonition turned out to be accurate.

With one eye on the loquat, I went downstairs. Eiko was sitting in the nine-by-twelve-foot room leading to the entryway. On the round table she'd lined up textbook and notes and was sharpening a pencil. I called to Eiko, "C'mon." For once Eiko said, "I have to look something up; you go on ahead." Beside the entryway was a nine-by-nine-foot room, and Dad, clad in kimono, was setting to work. I said to Dad, "I'm off," and he nodded and straightened his kimono. In the entryway my younger brother Susumu (age four) was plumped down, holding a model warship, pretending that it was making headway through waves. He was singing in a loud voice, "Tater, tater, white potato, sweet potato."[1] Seeing me, Susumu urged, "Hurry home after school. We'll go to the river and sail this ship."

I never dreamed that this would be the last time I saw Dad, Eiko, and Susumu. With Susumu's song at my back, I joined the neighborhood kids, and we went to Kanzaki Elementary School, less than half a mile from our house. Kanzaki Elementary School faced the trolley street linking Eba and Yokogawa. It was surrounded by a concrete wall. The gate on the trolley street was the back gate. In the center of the schoolyard towered a huge willow tree, spreading its branches wide. Behind it was the two-story wooden school building, L-shaped. Those of us in the lower grades would enter the school singing, led by students in the upper grades:

> We owe it to the soldiers
> That today, too, we can go to school
> Shoulder to shoulder with our classmates.
> Thank you, you soldiers
> Who fought for country, for country.

Singing at the top of our lungs this totally militaristic anthem, we'd advance up the trolley street and go through the gate.

A person's fate—life or death—truly is a matter of sheerest chance. Had I entered the gate that day as I always did, I would have been wiped off the face of the earth. Standing in the broad schoolyard with absolutely no cover, I would have been bathed—my whole body—in the rays the atomic bomb radiated, more than 9,000 degrees Fahrenheit, hot enough to melt iron. Burned pitch-black, I would have died.

That day, a moment before entering the gate, I was stopped by a classmate's mother. She asked me, "The air raid alert sounded a bit ago.

Are today's classes at the school or at the temple?" At that time, those in the lower grades alternated between the school and a local temple as place of instruction because of the danger that we wouldn't be able to flee if bombs fell. The concrete wall on either side of the gate was a foot thick. Moving close to it, I replied to her, "We won't know till we ask Teacher," and I happened to look up.

In the sky, the vapor trail of a B-29 stretched along the mountains of the Chugoku range, seemingly headed for the center of Hiroshima. The sun reflected off the nose of the plane's glittering duralumin body. Pointing at the B-29 approaching steadily, I called, "Ma'am, it's a B. . . ." She too looked up and said, "You're right: a B-29. Strange that the air raid alert hasn't sounded," and the two of us looked up at the approaching B-29.

Had the sirens sounded at this point, as they had earlier that morning with the reconnaissance plane, many people would have fled to air raid trenches and survived. I think it was truly a clever psychological tactic on the part of the U.S. military. To make the residents short of sleep from having the air raid alarm go off twice the previous night and to foster the mind-set "Hiroshima is safe": that's what enabled the *Enola Gay*, carrying the atomic bomb, to fly over majestically on the attack. That way, even if a B-29 flew over, we'd think, "It's only a reconnaissance plane," and let our guard down.

"Why didn't the air raid alert sound?" That thought has stayed in my heart forever, a gap in the Hiroshima story. After the war, I checked the documents and found that NHK Hiroshima began to broadcast an air raid alert at 8:15. It was at 8:15 that the bomb was dropped and exploded. If only the alert had sounded earlier!

The *Enola Gay* cut its engines, penetrated quietly to the heart of Hiroshima, and dropped the atomic bomb, raising the curtain on hell. Even today, if I close my eyes, the colors of the atomic bomb the moment it exploded come floating right up. A pale light like the flash of a flashbulb camera, white at the center, engulfed me, a great ball of light with yellow and red mixed at its outer edges. Once that violent flash burned itself onto my retinas, all memory stopped.

Pictures of Hell

How long was it? When consciousness returned and I opened my eyes, it was pitch dark. I was confused: "Huh? A moment ago it was broad daylight, and suddenly it's night?" When I rolled over and tried to stand, pain shot through my right cheek. "What happened?" I focused and looked about and saw that a six-inch nail sticking out of a board had pierced me. Raising my head had torn my cheek. Blood was flowing. The weird atmosphere frightened me. I realized I was sweating.

I tried to stand up, but my body didn't move. Turning my head, I saw that bricks, stones, tree branches, scraps of lumber lay on top of me. The concrete wall, too, had fallen over and was covering me.

Frantically I pushed at the stones and wood on top of me and scrambled my way out. Instinctively, I looked about for the satchel that had been on my back and the air raid hood that had been hanging from my shoulder. But I didn't find them—perhaps they'd been sent flying, torn off in the blast? Turning to look at the trolley street, I gasped.

Until just a moment ago, the mother of my classmate had been standing right in front of me and, like me, looking up at the B-29. Her entire body had been burned pitch-black. Her hair was in tatters. The workpants and jacket she'd been wearing, charred and looking like seaweed, hung about her neck and waist. And she'd been blown across to the other sidewalk and was lying on her back. Her white eyes, wide open in her blackened and sooty face, glared across at me.

Confused, not knowing what had happened, I stood in the middle of the trolley street. This familiar street had been transformed shockingly; I stood in amazement. The trolley wires had been cut from the poles lining either side of the street and were coiled like spiderwebs on the pavement; thick telephone line sagged from telephone poles like a great snake sleeping on a tree branch. It sagged into the distance. The rows of two-story houses on each side had been crushed, and the lower stories had collapsed utterly like popped paper balloons, flat. Atop them, the second stories lay piled, undulating off into the distance. Drop India ink into water, and it thins and spreads. Smoke just like pale ink covered the sky and wafted all about. The sky was like an ink painting; boards and sheets of metal danced helter-skelter into the sky, quite like birds. Every now and then, out of the collapsed rows of houses a dragon's tongue of bright red flames crawled, disappeared, moved. Aghast, I burned that scene onto my retinas.

I learned that when people are thrust suddenly into extremity, they are without emotion. They act only by instinct. Returning instinctively to the nest, my feet moved on their own in the direction of home. There's an expression, "Spinning your wheels," and that's precisely the way it was. I felt I was running and running, yet getting nowhere. Up ahead, the pale-ink smoke drifted, as if bubbling up. When people materialized out of it, I was shocked and raced up to them, wanting to know what on earth had happened to them.

First I met five or six women. Hiroshima's summers are very hot, so they'd probably been wearing only simple chemises as they tidied their kitchens or cleaned house. One after another, the women I saw had chemises on. As I got near them, I was amazed. They had countless slivers of glass sticking in their flesh: in the front of some of the women, on the right sides of others, on the left or on the backs of still others.

People who'd been in rooms with windows to their right had been pierced only on the right sides of their bodies as the bomb blast pulverized the windowpanes. They were like pincushions, with blood flowing. People who'd been in rooms with windows straight ahead of them had their fronts covered with glass splinters. The glass splinters had pierced even their eyeballs, so they couldn't open their eyes. They felt their way along, like blind people. How they'd been standing in relation to the windows determined where on their bodies the glass splinters stuck, and one person differed from the next.

I noticed one woman. Her hair was dusty and swirling in disarray, the shoulder strap of her chemise was cut and her breasts exposed, and her breasts were blue, as if tattooed. As I was able to understand later, the glass splinters looked blue, and she had so many piercing her, mainly her breasts, and countless splinters buried in her that the glass splinters seemed like a tattoo dyeing her breasts blue.

The women pierced by glass splinters were bleeding. They walked silently. Countless pieces of glass were embedded in their bodies, so that each time they took a step, the glass splinters jingle-jangled. Aghast, I watched these women go by, then raced for home.

On the sidewalk on the left side of the trolley street, naked people burned so black that I couldn't tell male from female sat with both legs outstretched, eyes wide and fixed on a point in the sky, cowering, as if simpleminded. Pumps for firefighting had been installed earlier at set intervals along the sidewalk on the right side of the trolley street. Uninjured people hurried to those pumps, twisted the cocks, and scooped up water. People clustered suddenly about the pumps. The women with innumerable glass splinters in them took the pump's water with both hands and poured it all over themselves. Washing their blackened bodies covered with blood and dust, they exposed the glass fragments that stuck into their bodies and silently pulled them out.

On the opposite pavement, too, were people with not a stitch on, dazed and burned so black I couldn't tell male from female. Seeing water flowing from the pumps, they crawled sluggishly along the ground and approached the pumps, each of them sticking their hands into the flow of water, scooping up water and lifting it trancelike to their mouths. Around the pump women gathered, absorbed in washing off the blood and picking out glass splinters, and people burned black were drinking water blindly. The same scene occurred at each pump. They were acting simply on instinct. The glass was sticking into them, and it hurt, so they pulled it out. They'd been burned all over by the rays, and they were thirsty, so they drank. Neither words nor poses showed conscious intent.

In scenes of carnage—fire or calamity—in movies or plays, voices cry, "Ouch!" "Horrible!" "Help!" People suffer and writhe. But those scenes are unreal. When people are thrown suddenly into the carnage of an extreme situation, they utter not a single emotion-laden word but act silently on instinct. Just as if watching a silent movie, I, too, looked on at the quiet scene, not saying a word. From time to time gasoline drums exploded, the sound carrying in all directions.

Coming to myself, I took the street leading to our house. But at the beginning of the lane to our home, fires were spreading along the row of structures on either side. Flames crept along the ground. The two fires stretched forward from either side, as if joining hands, and in an instant the road became a sea of fire. The roadway functioned as a chimney, and a hot wind gusted through. The road ahead became a wall of fire, and flames completely blocked the way.

Sensing instinctively that I'd burn to death if I went farther, I reversed course, as if in a daze. I followed the trolley street, and suddenly, for the first time, like an electric current running through my body, wild terror ruled. Loneliness—my family's abandoned me!—and terror—I'm all alone!—seized my mind. I ran back and forth on the trolley street, searching desperately, crying "Daddy!" "Mommy!"

The trolley street from Funairi Naka-chō as far as Saiwai-chō was a human exhibition, inhuman forms utterly transformed. Naked bodies moving sluggishly, burned by rays and trailing blackened bits of clothing like seaweed. Moving forward, glass splinters from the explosion sticking into all parts of their bodies, spurting blood. People whose eyeballs hung down their cheeks and trembled; they'd been blown out by the sudden pressure of the blast. People whose bellies had been ripped open, trailing a yard of intestines, crawling along on all fours. Shrikes impale fish and frogs on dead tree branches, storing them to eat later; people, too, had been sent flying and hung from branches, impaled. I ran among these horrific humans, threading my way, crying out, searching for family.

Black smoke eddied violently, covering the area. Flames danced crazily, wildly. The trolley street, too, became dangerous. The terror I felt then sank into my heart; I will have it with me as long as I live.

Black Rain

Luckily, a neighbor found me as I was running about and crying. She too wore a chemise, and bits of glass pierced her entire body. She was dousing herself with pump water to wash off the blood. Her white chemise was dyed bright red. It was as if it had been red to begin with.

"Aren't you Nakazawa Kei?" she asked. "Your mother's on this road at the Funairi Kawaguchi-chō trolley stop. Quick, go!" In a trance, I headed for the Funairi Kawaguchi-chō trolley stop. The crowd fleeing in the same direction proceeded, naked bodies blackened, each holding both hands chest-high, leaning forward, just like the specters depicted in paintings.

In this sluggish procession, I noticed a strange thing. The parts of a person wearing white clothing—white shirt, white pants—were completely uninjured. White shirt, white pants alone caught my eye, bright, as if dancing in space, flickering. When the instant rays, hotter than 9,000 degrees, shone on people on the ground below, their white clothing acted as a mirror, reflecting the rays. By contrast, people wearing black were consumed instantly, clothing and body, by the radiant light. During the war, clothing that stood out and was easy for enemy planes to spot was outlawed, so most people wore dark clothes. Hence the number of those suffering from burns over their entire body increased several times over.

Struck by 9,000 degree rays, your skin immediately developed countless blisters, one connected with the next; scattered over your whole body, they grew to eight inches in diameter. When you walked, the fluid inside the large blisters sloshed with the vibration, and finally the fragile blisters burst, the liquid poured out, and the skin peeled off.

I wouldn't have thought human skin would peel so easily. The skin of the chest peeled off, from the shoulders down; the backs of the hands peeled; the skin of the arms peeled off, down to the five fingernails, and dangled. From the fingertips of both hands, yard-long skin hung and trembled. The skin of the back peeled from both shoulders, stopped at the waist, and hung like a droopy loincloth. The skin of the legs peeled to the anklebone and dragged, a yard long, on the ground. People couldn't help looking like apparitions. If they walked with arms down, the skin hanging off their fingertips dragged painfully on the ground, so they raised their arms and held them at shoulder level, which was less painful. Even if they wanted to run, the skin of their legs was dragging along on the ground, impeding their steps. Shuffling one step at a time, they proceeded, a procession of ghosts.

In this procession of ghosts, I made my way to the Funairi Kawaguchi-chō trolley stop. On both sides of the trolley street in Kawaguchi-chō were sweet potato and vegetable fields. The farmhouses scattered in the fields were leaning from the blast. Wide-eyed, I looked about the trolley street. There, on the sidewalk on the left, sat Mom. She had spread a blanket on the sidewalk, set some pots beside it, and was sitting in her apron, face sooty, a vacant expression on her face. I stood in front of her. We looked each other in the face, silent, exhausted, and I sank to the ground beside her. I was overcome with joy and relief that I had finally found family. Soon I noticed that Mom was holding carefully to her chest something wrapped in a dirty blanket. I peeked inside the blanket and saw a baby, newborn, face red and wrinkled. It was a mystery: "Huh? Suddenly a baby. . . ." I looked again at Mom's tummy, and it had shrunk.

The shock had sent Mom into labor, and in the carnage of atomic hell she had given birth on the pavement to a baby girl. As she writhed in pain on the pavement, several passersby had gathered and helped with the birth.

Note

1. This ditty was a take-off on the "Battleship March," which had the syllable *mo* twice in its opening line: *Imo* is the Japanese word for "potato."

Part III

Korea

As part of the Asian mainland, Korea was influenced by China earlier, more directly, and for a longer period of time than Japan. China controlled part of the northern Korean peninsula for 400 years beginning in 108 BCE and introduced technology such as iron making and writing with characters. After the Korean kingdom of Koguryŏ (37 BCE–668 CE) expelled the Chinese In 313 CE, Korea was divided between three native states, Koguryŏ, Paekche, and Silla; however, many Chinese cultural institutions were embraced, especially those that helped rulers secure or extend their power. For example, in the late fourth century, Koguryŏ established a Chinese-style bureaucracy and a Confucian academy and accepted Buddhism. Silla, in the southeast, unified Korea by first allying with China against its rival Korean states and then turning against China, but it too retained a Chinese style of government. Silla's power eventually disintegrated in the late ninth century and Silla was replaced by the state of Koryŏ (918–1392). Koryŏ also ruled through a government modeled on that of China, including, after 958, an examination system to select government officials. The curriculum was the same as in China: the Four Books and Five Classics. However, only members of the Korean aristocracy were permitted to take the tests, so social mobility was not possible as it was in China.

While the social elite primarily wrote in classical Chinese, songs and oral narratives in the Korean language also flourished during the Koryŏ period. *Sijo*, a three-line lyric poem, emerged in the thirteenth century. The musicality and brevity of *sijo* made it conducive to oral transmission and it came to be enjoyed by people at all levels of society. Korea's famed celadon stoneware and the world's first movable type made of metal also date from this period.

In the mid-thirteenth century, Koryŏ was repeatedly attacked by Mongols. The *Tripitaka Koreana*, a complete set of the Buddhist scriptures carved onto more than 80,000 wooden blocks, were created at this time as an offering to accompany prayers for divine assistance in resisting the Mongol invasions, but the Mongols were victorious. Koryŏ kings were allowed to retain their titles, but Mongol officials wielded all political power. While the myth of Tan'gun purports to recount the founding of the first Korean state, the earliest extant text of this myth dates from the thirteenth century and may be a reflection of the development of a distinctly Korean identity rather than a truly ancient myth. In 1368 the Chinese overthrew their Mongol rulers, and Korea was torn between allying itself with the new Ming dynasty in China or remaining affiliated with the Mongols. Instead, General Yi Songgye rebelled and founded the Chosŏn dynasty in 1392.

Early Chosŏn kings eliminated their rivals, redistributed land, and reformed the government, improving both the stability of their regime and living conditions for the general populace. They suppressed Buddhism but continued to embrace Confucianism, although with somewhat different results than in China. For example, the idea of official censors, whose duty was to criticize the king and government policies, is based on traditional Confucian principles, but in Korea it allowed the aristocracy to limit the power of kings to an extent never seen in China. (The hero in *Song of a Faithful Wife, Ch'un-hyang* is a censor.) King Sejong (1418–1450) commissioned the invention of a phonetic script (*hangul*), thus making literacy possible for ordinary people: The *hangul* alphabet can be memorized in just a few hours. Chinese remained the language of governance and the elite while the majority of Koreans remained illiterate, but *hangul* was adopted by women and for popular fiction, such as *The Tale of Hong Kiltong*. In the 1890s *hangul* was used in elementary schools and in some newspapers, but Koreans were required to use only Japanese in 1938 during the Japanese occupation of Korea. *Hangul* finally became the standard writing system in 1946.

After King Sejong's reign, factionalism became an enduring problem that weakened the central Korean government. Ming China came to Korea's aid when Japan invaded in 1592 and the Japanese withdrew in 1598, but Korea had suffered massive destruction as a result of the widespread fighting. In 1637, long before the country had recovered, Korea was forced to pledge allegiance to the Manchus, who conquered China shortly thereafter (1644). Some positive results of this development were that Korea enjoyed two centuries of peace and officials were briefly inspired to institute a variety of reforms that benefited both the government and the people. However, the central government remained fundamentally too weak to manage the economy effectively. Taxes on those with the least resources were heavy, periodic famines caused high death rates, and civil unrest broke out frequently.

Although Confucian ideology remained a touchstone and Chinese models were the most respected in painting and literature throughout the Chosŏn dynasty, new, indigenous trends developed. In the seventeenth century, artists such as Chŏng Sŏn (1676–1759) increasingly painted in indigenous styles. *P'ansori*, a new form of oral narrative, emerged among commoners and eventually gained favor with the elite as well. The *Song of a Faithful Wife, Ch'un-hyang*, the best known *p'ansori* and one of the few that are still performed today, celebrates the Confucian virtues of feminine chastity and loyalty. Chinese vernacular fiction, including *Journey to the West* and *Outlaws of the Marsh*, was imported, grew popular, and stimulated the development of Korean vernacular fiction written in *hangul*. Since such fiction was disreputable, its history is obscure, but *The Tale of Hong Kiltong* is considered to be the earliest example. In the highly conservative, rigidly stratified Confucian society of Chosŏn Korea, large audiences enjoyed stories featuring heroes like Hong, who confronts unexpected danger, defeats evildoers, and challenges the discrimination he faces as the son of a concubine. Furthermore, literacy expanded due to the emergence of a money economy that facilitated innovations like lending libraries and woodblock-printed books. Finally, a new consciousness of the injustice of hereditary status, be it aristocratic or slave, and resentment of heavy tax burdens and corrupt government also inspired new content in art. The difference in status between the nobility and the peasants is starkly depicted in paintings by Kim Tŭksin (1754–1822).

In the nineteenth century, Korea tended toward a foreign policy of isolationism, but the Chosŏn government was not strong enough to resist international pressure to open its ports to trade. This dilemma inspired a reform movement in the 1880s and 1890s, but when a religious minority rebelled in 1894 and the king asked for Chinese troops to suppress it, Japan intervened, declared war on China, and tried to establish a puppet government in Korea. International pressure forced Japan to abandon its efforts to control Korea at that point, but the Japanese were able to make Korea a protectorate in 1905 as a result of their war with Russia. Japan made Korea a colony in 1910.

Japanese colonialism was brutal in enforcing a ban on all political activity by Koreans, including the sudden, massive, and peaceful demonstrations of March 1, 1919. After 1937, Japan drafted Korean men as soldiers and laborers and coerced Korean women to serve as prostitutes for the military. Japan also implemented a policy of cultural assimilation that forbade the use of the Korean language and required Koreans to worship the Japanese emperor. Japan even pressured Koreans to take Japanese surnames, which had the effect of cutting people off from their ancestors. On the other hand, Japanese colonialism brought industrialization, urbanization, expanded educational opportunities, social mobility, and some rights for women.

Modern Korean literature is said to have begun in 1917 with the publication of Yi Kwangsu's novel *Heartlessness* (Mujong). Its prose, written entirely in *hangul*, was close to the speech of contemporary spoken Korean, and its focus upon the interior consciousness of the individual self, liberated from the confines of traditional Confucian norms, replaced the "traditional pattern of conflict between a virtuous character and hostile external forces."[1] Much of the new experimental literature between 1910 and 1930—poetry, short fiction, and essays, written by authors who had studied in Japan—was heavily influenced by Western literary trends and was published in small literary journals, as was the pattern in Japan at the time. Novels for the less educated reader were serialized in newspapers. Many writers used fables

and satire to address contemporary social and political concerns. Trends toward realism and naturalism led to a focus on
the struggles of ordinary people. Class consciousness was sharp-
ened in Korea, as it was throughout the world, in the wake of
the Russian Revolution of 1917 and the First World War, and fiction
depicting class divisions appeared, along with stories set in an
urban environment and written in a modernist vein.

The end of World War II and the liberation of Korea were followed by a three-year civil war (1950–1953) between the South
Koreans, backed by the United States, and the North Koreans,
supported by the Soviet Union (now Russia). Much of the literature
published in the following decades addressed the suffering
caused by the civil war and the trauma of the postwar division
of Korea into North and South, which tore apart many families.
Hwang Sunwŏn (1915–2000) exposed the artificial social divisions
produced by political ideologies in his story "Cranes." In "The
Bird of Passage" by O Youngsu (1914–1979), traditional values
such as the respect and loyalty due to a teacher are contrasted
with the social and economic chaos of postwar Korea. In more
recent years, as the South Korean economy has become one
of the most vibrant in the world, there has been a notable expansion of literary voices, styles, and themes, including a growing
number of women novelists and poets. Literature in North Korea,
where life is rigidly guided by the ideology of *juche* (self-reliance
and autonomy), is apparently extremely didactic. Art in the North
also serves to celebrate the accomplishments of its leaders and
remind the populace of its duty to be loyal. Typical of this genre
are the large images of Kim Il Sung (1912–1994), Eternal President
of North Korea, in the capital P'yongyang and throughout the
country.

Note

1. Joshua S. Mostow, *The Columbia Companion to Modern East Asian Literature* (New York: Columbia University Press, 2003), p. 649.

28

Tan'gun

Although Chinese influence on Korean culture was profound and extensive, Korea has a distinct culture. One example is the foundation myth recounting the supernatural ancestry of Tan'gun, the legendary founder of Korea. Tan'gun is said to have established Ko Chosŏn ("Old Chosŏn"), the forerunner of the Korean state, in 2333 BCE, a date that would make the founding of Korea as old as the first Chinese dynasty, the Xia. Actually, it was not until the first century BCE that the kingdom of Koguryŏ was established in northern Korea and the chiefs of statelets, which consisted of a small number of walled-town communities, formed larger confederacies known as Mahan, Chinhan, and Pyŏnhan in southern Korea.

The account of the god Hwan'in sending his son Hwan'ung to earth is reminiscent of the Japanese foundation myth in which the divine beings Izanami and Izanagi, sister and brother, descend to earth from heaven and create the Japanese islands. Bears have long been worshipped in North Asia as a totemic animal. The mugwort and garlic suggest the predominance of shamanic rituals in prehistoric Korea.

Questions

1. What might be the symbolism of the offspring of an interspecies marriage becoming the founder of Korea?
2. Why might a bear be a fitting ancestor for the ruler of a nation?

Tan'gun

The *Wei shu* tells us that 2,000 years ago, when the wise Emperor Yao ruled China, Tan'gun Wanggŏm chose Asadal as his capital and founded the country of Chosŏn.

The *Old Record* notes that in olden times Hwan'in's stepson, Hwan'ung, wished to descend from heaven and live in the world of man. Guessing his son's desire, Hwan'in surveyed the three highest mountains and found Mount T'aebaek the most suitable place for his son to settle to help mankind. Therefore he gave Hwan'ung three heavenly seals and allowed him to rule over the people. Hwan'ung descended with 3,000 followers to a spot under a sandalwood tree atop Mount T'aebaek, and he called this place the City of God. He was the Heavenly King Hwan'ung. Leading the Earl of Wind, the Master of Rain, and the Master of Clouds, he took charge of some 360 areas of responsibility, including agriculture, allotted lifespans, illness, punishment, and good and evil, and he brought culture to his people.

At that time a bear and a tiger who were living in the same cave prayed to Hwan'ung to transform them into human beings. The king gave them a bundle of sacred mugwort and twenty cloves of garlic and said, "If you eat these and shun the sunlight for 100 days, you will assume human forms."

Both animals ate the herbs and avoided the sun. After twenty-one days the bear became a woman, but the tiger, unable to observe the taboo [for more than twenty days], remained a tiger. Unable to find a husband, the bear-woman prayed under the sandalwood tree for a child. Hwan'ung metamorphosed himself, lay with her, and begot a son called Tan'gun Wanggŏm.

In the fiftieth year of the reign of Emperor Yao, Tan'gun made P'yongyang the capital of his country, called Chosŏn, or Bright Morning, and then moved to Asadal on Mount Paegak, where he ruled for 1,500 years. When King Wu of Chou enfeoffed Ch'i Tzu to Chosŏn, Tan'gun moved to Changdanggyŏng, then back to Asadal, where he became a mountain god at the age of 1,908.

"Tiger, Magpies and Pine" (nineteenth century), hanging scroll, ink and color on paper. Motifs in East Asian art often have symbolic meanings. The pine, an ever-green, signifies integrity and longevity, while the tiger and magpie bring good luck and repel the bad. (*Los Angeles County Museum of Art*)

29

The Tale of Hong Kiltong

Hŏ Kyun

The author of *The Tale of Hong Kiltong*, Hŏ Kyun (1569–1618), was no stranger to how birth order and politics entwine in ancient Korea. As the third son of Minister Hŏ Yŏp, Hŏ Kyun attained a high position at court, but he later was executed due to his involvement in a coup attempted by a group of dissatisfied illegitimate sons.

Hŏ Kyun's story was inspired by *Outlaws of the Marsh*, the late fourteenth-century Chinese novel which is excerpted in this textbook. Like Sung Chiang and his band of outlaws, Hong Kiltong wants to rectify discrimination, but only for himself. He tries to correct social problems but does not repudiate the nobility and Confucian social stratification in general. He hopes instead to be accepted as a legitimate member of the literati class despite his mother's status. Because this goal is denied him, he can act as a full-fledged member of the Hong family and conduct Confucian rituals for his parents only on a far-away island. This story can be said therefore to be somewhat autobiographical, even though not written in the first person.

Questions

1. In what aspects is this story similar to Chinese popular fiction such as *Monkey* and *Outlaws of the Marsh*?
2. The primary theme here is the injustice of discrimination, but compassion is also an issue. Discuss points in the story where compassion or its lack influences plot developments.

3. Kiltong pursues justice but uses deceit and magic to succeed. Does this contribute to his image as a hero or detract from it?

The Tale of Hong Kiltong

Excerpt from Hŏ Kyun, *Anthology of Korean Literature: From Early Times to the Nineteenth Century*, compiled and edited by Peter H. Lee (Honolulu: University Press of Hawaii, 1981), pp. 119–131. Copyright © 1981 by University Press of Hawaii, Honolulu. Used with permission of University Press of Hawaii.

The Tale of Hong Kiltong, by Hŏ Kyun

During the reign of King Sejong in Chosŏn there was a minister whose name was Hong. Scion of a long-established and illustrious family, he passed the civil examinations at an early age and went on to attain the post of Minister of Personnel. He enjoyed a good reputation both in and out of government circles and his name resounded throughout the country as a man in whom loyalty and filial piety were combined.

Early in life he had two sons. The first son, named In-hyŏng, was born to his official wife, who was of the Yu clan, and the other son, Kiltong, was the child of his maid-servant Ch'unsŏm. Minister Hong once dreamed of Kiltong's birth: sudden thunderbolts resounded and a green dragon with flailing whiskers leaped at him; he woke frightened, only to find it was but a passing spring dream. In his heart he was overjoyed; he thought: "Surely this dream must herald the birth of a lovely son!" And with this thought he rushed to the inner room where his wife rose to meet him.

In joy he took her jade hands to draw her near to him and press his love upon her, but she stiffened and said, "Here, you, a minister of state, forget your dignified position and take to the vulgar antics of a giddy youth! I will not submit to it."

So saying she drew her hands away and left the room. The minister, disconcerted and unable to endure his exasperation, returned to the outer room where he deplored his lady's lack of understanding, when the maidservant Ch'unsŏm came to serve him tea. Quietly, he drew the girl to him and led her to a room, where he made love to her. Ch'unsŏm at this time was eighteen. Having once given her body to the minister, she never left his gates again and had no thoughts of accepting another lover. The minister, delighted with her, made her his concubine. Indeed, from that month she began to show the signs of pregnancy and in the ninth month gave birth to a child of jade-fair beauty whose frame and vigor were like no other and whose mien and spirit betold a brilliant hero. The minister was happy, but still saddened that the child had not been born to his proper wife.

Kiltong grew steadily and when he was eight years old he could already grasp a hundred things from hearing only one. The minister was more devoted to this son but, owing to the boy's ignoble birth, felt compelled to rebuke him promptly whenever the child called him *father*, or his brother *brother*. Even after Kiltong had reached the age of ten he could not presume to address his father and brother as such. Moreover, he was scorned even by the servants. This grieved him deeply and he could not still the turmoil within himself.

Once, at the full moon of the ninth month, a time when the bright clarity of the moon and the brisk coolness of the wind conspire to engage a man's passions, Kiltong in his study set aside his reading and, pushing the table away, lamented, "When one born to a man's role cannot model himself after Confucius and Mencius then he had best learn the martial arts. With a general's insignia tucked into his waistband he should chastize the east and subjugate the west, render meritorious service to the state, and illuminate the generations with his name. That's the glory of manhood. But why have I been left disconsolate, why my heart rent that I may not name my own father and brother? Have I not cause for grief?" Kiltong stepped down into the garden and set about practicing his swordsmanship. The minister, also out enjoying the moonlight, caught sight of his son pacing the garden and called him over to ask the reason.

"What's gotten into you—not asleep so late at night?"

Kiltong answered respectfully, "I have always enjoyed the moonlight, but there is something else tonight. While Heaven created all things with the idea that mankind is the most precious, how can I be called a man when such value does not extend to me?"

The minister knew what he meant, but scolded, "What are you talking about?"

Kiltong bowed twice and explained. "Though I grow to manhood by the vigor your excellency has passed to me and realize the profound debt I owe for your gift of life and mother's upbringing, my life still bears one great sorrow: how can I regard myself as a man when I can address

"Portrait of a Scholar-Official in a Black Robe" (nineteenth century), hanging scroll, ink and color on silk. Images such as these were often hung during special ceremonies honoring the family's ancestors. (*Wikimedia Commons, Los Angeles County Museum of Art*)

neither my father as *father* not my brother as *brother*?" He wiped off his flowing tears with the sleeve of his jacket.

The minister heard him out and though he felt compassion for his son, he could only rebuke him severely for fear an expression of sympathy might give him license. "You're not the only child born to a maidservant in the home of a minister. How dare you show such willful arrogance? If ever I hear such talk as this again, I will not allow you in my presence!"

Kiltong dared not utter a word but could only sink to the ground in tears. The minister ordered him away and Kiltong returned to his quarters where he was overcome with sorrow. He was by nature uncommonly gifted and was a boy given to thoughtfulness and generosity. So it was that he could not quiet his heart or manage to sleep at night.

One day Kiltong went to his mother's room and in tears said, "We are in this world as mother and son out of the deep ties we had in a former life. My debt to you is immense. But in my wretched fortune I was born ignoble and the regret I harbor is bottomless. When a man makes his way in the world he cannot submit to the scorn of others. I cannot suppress this spirit innate in me and have chosen to leave your side, Mother. But I beg you not to worry about me and to take care of yourself."

Astonished, his mother replied, "You are not the only boy born humbly in a minister's home. How can you be so selfish? Why do you tear at your mother's heart so?"

Kiltong replied, "Long ago, Chi-shan, the illegitimate son of Chang Chung, left his mother when he was thirteen. In the Yŭn-feng Mountains he perfected the Way and left a glorious name to posterity. Since I have decided to follow his example and leave the vulgar world, I pray you wait in peace for another day. From the recent behavior of the Koksan woman, it appears she has taken us for enemies out of fear that she might lose the minister's favor. I'm afraid she plots misfortune for me. Please don't let my departure worry you so."

But his mother was saddened.

The Koksan woman, originally a *kisaeng* [female professional entertainer] from Koksan named Ch'onan, had become the minister's favorite concubine. Since she was extremely arrogant and quick to carry false tales to the minister about anyone who displeased her, she was at the center of countless difficulties in the household. Ch'onan had no son of her own and, having seen the affection shown Ch'unsŏm by the minister after Kiltong's birth, she plotted with all her spite to eliminate the boy.

Then one day, her scheme conceived, she called in a shaman and said, "I must have this Kiltong out of the way to find any peace in life. If you can carry out my wishes, I shall reward you handsomely."

The shaman listened and replied with pleasure. "I know of an excellent physiognomist living outside Hŭngin Gate who with only one look at a person's face can divine the good and evil of both past and future. What we should do is call the woman in, explain your desires to her, and then recommend her to the minister. When she tells him about events of the past and future just as if she had seen them herself, he is sure to fall under her influence and could be made to get rid of the child. Then if we only wait for the opportune moment and do thus-and-so, how could we fail?"

Ch'onan was very pleased. Straightaway she gave the shaman fifty *yang* in silver and then sent her off to call in the physiognomist. The shaman bowed low and left.

The next day when the minister was in the women's quarters talking about Kiltong with his wife, praising the boy's uncommon virtues and regretting his low birth, a woman suddenly appeared in the courtyard below and bowed to him. Thinking it strange, the minister questioned her.

"Who are you? What do you want here?"

"I practice physiognomy for my living and just happened to be passing by Your Excellency's gate."

This reminded the minister of Kiltong, for he wanted to know the boy's future. He called the boy immediately and showed him to the woman. She looked him over for some time and in her astonishment almost blurted out, "I see in your son's face a hero, unchallenged by history and peerless in his own age! Only his lineage would be a drawback—there should be no other cause for concern!" But instead she only faltered and stopped.

The minister and his wife were puzzled and asked, "Whatever it is, we want you to speak directly with us."

The woman, feeling compelled, asked that the others retire. "From what I see, the boy cherishes elaborate and untamed dreams. The lustrous ether of the hills and streams radiates from between his eyebrows—a royal countenance. Your Excellency had best watch him carefully, for your household will surely be visited with ruinous misfortune when he grows up."

After a moment of stunned silence, the minister finally gathered himself and said, "Though I know man cannot escape his fate, I still forbid you to reveal this to anyone." With this command he gave the woman a little silver and sent her away. Not long after, the minister moved Kiltong into a cabin in the mountains where he could keep careful watch over his movements.

Unable to overcome the even greater sadness he felt at this turn of events and seeing no way out, Kiltong occupied himself with studying the military arts, astronomy, and geography. The minister was disturbed when he learned of this. "If the boy uses his native talent to further ideas that go beyond his station, the physiognomist will have been proven right. What am I to do?"

In the meantime, Ch'onan maintained her secret contacts with the shaman and physiognomist and through them managed to keep the minister stirred up. Intent on getting rid of Kiltong, she secured at great expense an assassin named T'ŭkchae and explained the circumstances to him. She then approached the minister. "It was uncanny that day the way the physiognomist could perceive events. What do you think? What are you going to do now about Kiltong's future? Even I was surprised and frightened. Doesn't it seem the only choice is to have him put out of the way?"

The minister worked his brows as he listened. "The matter is in my hands and I want you to refrain from involving yourself in it." He dismissed her but was left troubled and confused. Finding it impossible to sleep at night, he soon grew ill. His wife and son In-hyŏng—the latter now an assistant section chief in a ministry—were greatly worried and at a loss for what to do.

Ch'onan, who had been attending the minister, one day remarked, "The minister's critical condition is brought about by the presence of Kiltong. Now this is the way I see it. If we just do away with the boy, not only will the minister completely recover, but the whole household too will be assured of security. How is it you haven't considered this?"

"You may be right, but who could possibly do such a thing that violates the most solemn strictures of moral law?" the wife asked.

"I have heard there is an assassin called T'ŭkchae who claims he can kill a man as easily as picking something out of his pocket. Give him a thousand *yang* and then let him sneak in at night to do the job. By the time the minister finds out, there will be nothing he can do about it. I suggest, my lady, you give this serious thought."

The wife and her son broke into tears as they replied. "Painful as it may be, such a move would not only serve the good of the country, but help the minister and indeed protect the Hong family. Yes, do as you have planned!"

Highly pleased, Ch'onan called T'ŭkchae in again and explained in detail what she had been told. Ordered to do his work with dispatch that very night, T'ŭkchae agreed and waited for dark to come.

The story goes on: When Kiltong considered the sorrow and pain of his present situation he had no wish to remain any longer, but his father's strict commands left him with no choice. He passed the nights without sleep. On this night, he had lit the candle and to steady his wits had turned to the *Book of Changes*, when suddenly he heard a raven cry three times as it passed. Kiltong thought this ominous and said to himself: "This bird usually avoids the night. Crying out in passing like this must surely bode ill." He spread out the eight trigrams and studied them and was alarmed at what they portended. He pushed his desk aside and, employing his knowledge of magic, made himself invisible and watched and waited.

It was during the fourth watch that a man carrying a dagger stealthily opened the door and entered his room. Kiltong, making sure he was unseen, chanted a mantra. A cold wind suddenly filled the room and in a moment the house had vanished—in its place was only the fresh beauty of a vaulted mountain recess. Terrified by Kiltong's marvelous powers, T'ŭkchae concealed his dagger and sought to escape. But the road ahead was suddenly cut off when a lofty, bouldered cliff rose to block his way. Trapped, he groped frantically about him. Just then he heard the sound of an eight-holed flute and, pulling himself together, looked up to see a young boy approaching astride a donkey.

The boy stopped playing the flute and began to rebuke T'ŭkchae. "Why would you want to kill me? Do you think you can harm a guiltless man for no good reason and still avoid the retribution of Heaven?"

He chanted one more mantra, a black cloud formed, and sand and stones flew through the air. When T'ŭkchae managed to gather his wits and look about he discovered Kiltong before him. "Even with his marvelous powers, how could this child be any match for me?" thought T'ŭkchae and flew at him.

"Though this is your death, bear me no malice! It was Ch'onan who swayed the minister through a shaman and a physiognomist to have you killed. Don't hold it against me," he cried as he leaped, dagger in hand.

Kiltong could not control his rage. Blinding T'ŭkchae with magic, he snatched the dagger away and denounced the would-be killer under the blade of his own knife.

"If your greed allows you to murder so easily, then I can kill your brutish sort without a second thought," Kiltong said and sent T'ŭkchae's head flying across the room with a single sweep of the blade. Still overcome by anger, Kiltong went that same night and seized the physiognomist and pushed her into the room with the dead T'ŭkchae. "What have you against me, to plot my murder with Ch'onan?" He chastized her, then slit her throat.

Was it not a terrible thing?

Kiltong had killed them. Now he looked up into the night sky where the Milky Way trailed to the west. Moved by the clarity of the moon's thin light, Kiltong, in his rage, thought to kill Ch'onan. But the thought of the minister's love for her dissuaded him; he threw away the dagger and resolved to seek an exile's life. He went directly to the minister's room to take formal leave of him.

Startled to hear the footfalls outside, the minister opened his window and discovered Kiltong there. He called him in and asked, "What are you doing up and about so late at night?"

Kiltong prostrated himself and answered, "I have always intended to pay back the life's debt I owe you and my mother, if only one ten-thousandth part. But someone of evil design in the household has deceived your Excellency and attempted to kill me. Though I have escaped with my life, I know I cannot remain here and serve your Excellency any longer. So I have come now to bid you farewell."

The startled minister asked, "What calamity could have occurred that would force you to leave your childhood home? Where do you intend to go?"

Kiltong answered, "By the time day breaks you will have learned the circumstances as a matter of course. And, as for me, why worry about the whereabouts of this cast-off child? It's my lot to wander aimlessly as a cloud." In twin streams his tears poured forth; his words faltered. The minister was moved to pity at the sight and began to offer counsel.

"I can appreciate the grief you must be suffering. I am going to give you my permission to address me and your brother as *Father* and *Brother* from this day on."

Kiltong bowed twice and said, "Now that my father has cleared away this one small sadness of mine, I know I could die without regret. I sincerely wish you a long, untroubled life, my father." Again he bowed twice to take his leave, and the minister, unable to stay his son, could only ask him to take care.

Kiltong then went to his mother's chambers to inform her of his departure. "Though I am leaving your side now, there will be a day when I can come back to serve you. I pray take care of your health while I am away."

As she listened, it crossed her mind there might have been some ca-lamity but, seeing him bow now in departure, she grasped his hands and cried, "Where will you go? Even in the same house it has always seemed difficult to accept the small distance that has separated our quarters. But now how am I to endure, having sent you off to an unknown place? I only pray you will return soon so we can be together again." Kiltong bowed twice in taking his leave and, passing through the gate of his home, headed aimlessly toward the shrouded mountain recesses.

Is this not a pitiful thing?

The story goes on: Extremely apprehensive at receiving no word from T'ŭkchae, Ch'onan inquired into what had happened. She learned that Kiltong had disappeared without a trace and that the bodies of T'ŭkchae and the woman had been found in the room. Stricken with terror, she flew to inform the minister's wife of what she had found out. The lady, equally alarmed, called in her son, the assistant section chief, to tell him what she had heard.

When all this was finally reported to the minister, he went white with shock and said, "Kiltong came to me last night and with heavy heart bade me farewell. I thought it very strange at the time—but now, this!"

In-hyŏng dared withhold no longer what he knew of Ch'onan's involvement in the affair. Greatly angered, the minister had Ch'onan driven out of the house and the bodies quietly removed. He then called in the servants and ordered them never to speak of the matter.

The story continues: After leaving his parents and going out through the gates of his home, Kiltong wandered aimlessly until one day he happened upon a place where the scenery surpassed anything he had ever seen. He ventured further, looking for a house, and discovered a closed stone portal at the base of a huge boulder. Opening the door with care, he stepped through it and saw hundreds of houses set out neatly across a wide and level plain. A great number of men were gathered before him, enjoying themselves at a feast; this valley was a bandit's lair. Suddenly they caught sight of Kiltong and were pleased to see from his appearance that he was a man of no mean quality.

"Who are you?" they questioned him. "Why have you sought out this place? The braves you see gathered here have not yet been able to settle upon a leader. Now, if you think you have courage and vigor enough to join our ranks, see if you can lift that rock over there."

Sensing good fortune in what he heard, Kiltong bowed and said, "I am Hong Kiltong from Seoul, the son of Minister Hong by his concubine. But when I could no longer endure the scorn I suffered there, I left and have since been roaming the four seas and eight directions until I chanced upon this place. I am overwhelmed with gratitude that you speak of my becoming your comrade. But what trouble should it be for a man to lift a rock like that?" With this, he hoisted the rock, which weighed one thousand catties [about 1,300 pounds], and walked some ten paces.

The assembled braves praised him with a voice. "Here is a real man among men! Not one man in all our thousands could lift that rock, but beneficent Heaven has today given us a general!" They seated him at the place of honor and each in turn pressed wine upon him. Swearing oaths of fealty in the blood of a white horse, the assemblage raised its unanimous approval and celebrated the day long.

Kiltong and his men practiced the martial arts until, after several months, they had quite refined their tactics.

Then one day some of the men approached Kiltong. "For some time now, we have wanted to raid the Haein temple at Hapch'ŏn and strip it of its treasures, but we have been unable to carry out our plan for lack of a clever strategy. Now, as our general, what do you think of the idea?"

Kiltong was pleased and answered, "I shall send out an expedition soon and you should be ready to follow my commands."

In black-belted blue ceremonial robes, Kiltong mounted a donkey and prepared to leave camp with several followers in attendance. As he started out, he said, "I am going to that temple now and shall return after looking over the situation." He looked every inch the scion of a high minister's family.

When he arrived at the temple, he first called the abbot to him. "I am the son of Minister Hong of Seoul. I have come to this temple to pursue my literary studies and shall have twenty bushels of white rice shipped in for you tomorrow. If you are tidy about preparing the food, I will be glad to join you and your people for a meal at that time." Kiltong looked over the temple and left its precincts, having made promises for another day with the overjoyed monks.

As soon as he got back, Kiltong sent off some twenty bushels of white rice and called his men together. "Now, on a certain day I wish to go to the temple and do such-and-such." When the appointed day arrived, Kiltong took some tens of his followers and went ahead to the Haein temple. He was received by the monks, who all came out to meet his party.

He called an elder to him and asked, "With the rice I sent, were you able to make enough food?"

"Enough, sir? We have been overwhelmed!"

Kiltong took his seat in the place of honor and bade the monks share his company, each having been given a tray of wine and savories. He then led the drinking and pressed each monk in turn to join him. All were filled with gratitude.

Kiltong received his own tray and, while eating, suddenly bit with a loud crack on some sand he had secretly slipped into his mouth. The monks, startled at the sound, begged his forgiveness, but Kiltong feigned a great rage and rebuked them, saying, "How could you be so careless in preparing my food? This is indeed an insufferable insult and humiliation!" So saying, he ordered his followers to bind the monks together with a single rope and sit them on the floor. The monks were in a state of shock, no one knew what to do. In no time, several hundred fearsome bandits came swooping into the temple and set about carrying off all its treasures. The helpless monks could only look on, screaming their laments.

Soon after, a temple scullion, on his way back from an errand, saw what had happened and hurried off to notify the local government office. When he heard about this, the magistrate of Hapch'ŏn called out his militia and charged them to capture the bandits.

The several hundred troops who dashed off in pursuit soon came upon a figure in black robes and a nun's pine-bark cap who called to them from a promontory: "The bandits took the back road to the north. Hurry and catch them!" Believing this to be a helpful member of the temple, the soldiers flew like the wind and rain down the northerly back road, only to return empty-handed at nightfall.

It was Kiltong who, after sending his men along the main road to the south, had remained behind to deceive the troops in this clerical disguise. Safely back in the bandit lair, he found the men had all returned and were already sizing up the treasures. They rushed out to meet him and shower rewards upon him but Kiltong laughed and said, "If a man hadn't even this little talent, how could he become your leader?"

Kiltong later named his band the "Save-the-Poor" and led them through the eight provinces of Korea, stopping in each township to confiscate the wealth unjustly gained by magistrates and to succor the poor and helpless. But they never preyed upon the common people nor ever once touched the rightful property of the state.

So it was that the bandits submitted to Kiltong's will.

One day Kiltong gathered his men around him to discuss their plans. "I am told the governor of Hamgyŏng province with his rapacious officials has been squeezing the citizenry to a point where the people can no longer endure it. We cannot just stand by and do nothing. Now, I want you to follow my instructions exactly."

Thus the braves slipped one by one into the Hamgyŏng area and, on an agreed night, built a fire outside the South Gate of the provincial capital. When the governor, in a state of alarm, called for the fire to be extinguished, the *yamen* (government offices) clerks and the city's populace all rushed forth to put it out. Meantime, several hundred of Kiltong's bandits poured into the heart of the city and opened the warehouse to uncover the stores of grain, money, and weapons, which they carried out the North Gate, leaving the city to churn in chaos. These unexpected events left the governor helpless. When at dawn he discovered the warehouses stripped of their grain, money, and weapons, he paled in consternation and bent all efforts toward the capture of the bandits. The notice he forthwith posted on the North Gate named Hong Kiltong as leader of the Save-the-Poor Party and responsible for looting the city stores. Troops were dispatched to bring in the outlaws.

While Kiltong, with his band, had made a good haul of the grain and such, he was still concerned lest they be apprehended on the road by some misadventure. Thus he exercised his occult knowledge and ability to shrink distances, bringing them back apace to the lair where they ended the day.

Another day, Kiltong again gathered his men around him to discuss plans. "Now that we have looted the Haein temple at Hapch'ŏn of its treasures and robbed the governor of Hamgyŏng of his grain and money, not only have rumors about us spread across the country but my name has been posted at the provincial offices for all to see. If I don't take steps I am likely to be caught before long. Now, just watch this trick!"

Whereupon, Kiltong made seven straw men and, chanting mantras, invested them with such spirit that seven Kiltongs all at once sprouted arms, cried aloud, and fell into animated chatter with one another. From appearances alone, no one could tell which was the real Kiltong. They separated, each going to a province and taking several hundred men under his command. And now no one knew where the real Kiltong had gone.

Synopsis of the remainder of the tale

Kiltong then leads raids all over Korea until the king demands he be subdued. Yi Hŭp, a bold captain, volunteers for the mission but is tricked, captured, humbled, and released. Finally the king summons Kiltong's half-brother In-hyŏng and orders him to apprehend Kiltong. After In-hyŏng posts notices all over Korea asking Kiltong to respect the traditional values of loyalty and filial piety and surrender, all eight Kiltongs surrender just long enough to defend their actions as having brought justice to the people by confiscating the ill-gotten gains of corrupt officials. Eventually Kiltong demands that he be appointed Minister of War. The king fulfills that request in hopes of capturing Kiltong, but then Kiltong magically appears, announces that receiving the appointment has erased his long harbored resentment and declares

THE TALE OF HONG KILTONG 295

his intention to leave Korea. The king therefore pardons Kiltong. Kiltong finds a far-away island, brings his men there and colonizes it. Subsequently Kiltong rescues two young women from some monsters and marries them both. Later, anticipating his father's impending death, Kiltong prepares a gravesite, then fetches his natal family and conducts impressive burial rites for his father. Next Kiltong attacks and quickly subdues a neighboring country. He rules wisely and brings peace. Notably, he does not discriminate between his children by different wives. The tale ends with his death and burial and the comment that his legacy was many generations of peaceful rule by his descendants.

30

Korean Poetry

There is a long tradition of both vernacular and Chinese poetry and song in Korea. We have chosen poems from the genre known as *sijo*, as they are the most popular form of poetry in Korea and their charm survives translation quite well. Loyalty was one prominent theme, but poems about the difficulties of love and the beauty of nature are even more numerous. In the eighteenth century, the melody for singing *sijo* was standardized. We can read a *sijo* in a few seconds, but when sung they last about two minutes.

Korean Poetry

Poems 1, 8, 9, 10, 11 translated by Seyool Oh, Ji-Yeon Lee, Emily Guerin, and Margaret Helen Childs from Yi Kwang-sik, *Uri yet sijo yŏhaeng: yet sijo ro ttŏnanŭn Chosŏn sidae yŏhaeng* (Seoul, Korea: Karam Kihoek, 2004), pp. 218–227. Poems 2, 3, 4, 5, 6, 7 translated by Chung Chong-wha from *Love in Mid-Winter Night: Korean Sijo Poetry* (London: KPI Limited, 1985), pp. 45, 46, 49, 53, 56, 74. Used with permission of the publisher. Poem 12 translated by Seyool Oh, Ji-Yeon Lee, Emily Guerin, and Margaret Helen Childs from Yi Sang-bo, *Han'guk ŭi yet sijo* (Kyŏnggi-do P'aju: Pŏmusa, 2004), pp. 195–196.

1. Chŏng Mongju (1337–1392)

This poem is probably the most famous of all *sijo*. In it Chŏng Mongju proclaims his loyalty to the last king of the Koryŏ dynasty (918–1392) after being asked to join a rebellion against the court. Chŏng was assassinated after leaving the banquet where he composed this poem.

> I may die and die, die a hundred times over.
> My bones may turn to dust; my soul may burst.
> Still my single heart for my Lord will not waver.

2. Kim Sangyong (1561–1637)

> Love is false, that he loves me is a lie.
> That he saw me in a dream is a worse lie.
> If you are sleepless as I, in which dream would you see me?

3. Anonymous

> On such a bright moonlit night why do grasshoppers so loudly
>   weep?
> If my love was not coming, at least he should have sent me
>   sleep.
> My heart grieves sadly, for I even have to wait for sleep.

4. Anonymous

> Your farewell has set a fire and burns my heart.
> The rain of my tears could damp down the blaze.
> Alas! The wind of my sighs keeps the fire ablaze.

5. Anonymous

> May my sighs become the wind and tears the rain;
> To blow and shower on the window where my love sleeps.
> I'd like to wake him up from the deep sleep in which he's
>   forgotten me.

"After Rain at Mount Inwang" (1751) by Jeong Seon (1676–1759), ink on paper. Empty space in East Asian painting is a treasured artistic convention. Often read as mist, water, or air, it serves to demarcate foreground, midground, and background. *(Wikimedia Commons, Ho-Am Art Museum)*

6. Anonymous

Wind, don't blow; rainy wind, don't come.
Complaining of the wet road, my fickle love may not come.
But shower down a nine-year flood after he comes to my home.

7. Chu Ŭisik (1675–1720)

I've counted life; it is nothing but a dream.
Our tears and laughter are all dreams within dreams.
Let it be. What else is there but to enjoy this dream of life?

8. Hwang Chin'i (ca. 1506–1544)

Hwang Chin'i was a famously beautiful and talented *kisaeng* [female professional entertainer] poet. The first of her poems given below (#8–11) is considered one of the best *sijo*.

I will carve out the back of a long, long night in December,
And put it under the blanket of a spring wind.
Then, I will lay it out on the night when my love comes.

9.

The blue mountain is my longing, green water, my lover's
   affection.
The green water flows away, but the blue mountain is changeless.
The green water cannot forget the blue mountain; it weeps
   as it goes.

"Geumgang Mountain" by Jeong Seon (1676–1759), who exemplifies mid-Chosŏn
dynasty artists who moved away from idealized Chinese-style landscapes to depict
particular Korean locations and subjects. *(Wikimedia Commons)*

10.

Blue Stream[1] in green valley, don't boast about how fast you
  can go.
Once you arrive at the sea, it's not easy to return.
Why not rest with me here while the bright moon fills the
  empty mountains?

11.

Mountains are eternal, but water is not.
How could water be permanent? It runs day and night.
The great ones are like water: they leave and never come back.

"Scholar Overlooking the Water" by Kang Hŭi-an (1395–1459), ink on paper. Kang Hŭi-an was a scholar-official who passed the Korean civil service exam during the reign of King Sejong. His knowledge and skill as a painter shine through the Chinese Song dynasty elements in this work. *(Wikimedia Commons)*

12. Yun Sŏndo (1587–1671)

Yun is considered the best *sijo* poet of all. He was a scholar who held various government positions, such as tutor to the crown prince, but spent fourteen years of his life in exile for criticizing more powerful officials. His "Song of Five Friends" is a set of six *sijo*.

> When I count my friends, they are water, boulders, pine and
> bamboo.
> And the moon that rises over eastern hills is a sight I'm glad
> to see.
> They are enough. I need no more than these five.

> The color of clouds is clean, but clouds often turn black.
> The sound of wind is clear, but the wind often stops.
> It is only water that is both clean and unceasing.

> Why do flowers wilt so soon after they bloom?
> How is it that green grass quickly yellows?
> It is perhaps only boulders that do not change.

> Flowers bloom when the world warms, and leaves fall when
> it grows cold.
> Pine trees, you are oblivious to snow and frost,
> Because your roots reach deep down into the earth.

> You are neither a tree nor a grass.
> Who made you grow so straight? And why are you empty inside?
> Yet throughout the year you are always green.
> That's why I like you, bamboo.

> You are small but rise high and shine over the entire world.
> What else can shine as brightly at night as you?
> You see me, but we need not speak.
> That's why you, moon, are my friend.

Note

1. Blue Stream is a pun that refers to a man who was said to have bragged that he was immune to Hwang's beauty.

31

Song of a Faithful Wife, Ch'un-hyang

Song of a Faithful Wife originally circulated as an oral narrative; written versions date from at least 1754, when it appeared as a long poem in Chinese. It has been told and retold in every format imaginable, but is best known as a *p'ansori*, or popular Korean opera. Below are excerpts from a translation of the oldest and longest extant version, which dates from the late nineteenth century. It is the tale of the love between Ch'un-hyang, daughter of a *kisaeng* (female professional entertainer), and Mong-nyong, the son of an upright governor in the town of Namwŏn. Thanks to an auspicious dream of Ch'un-hyang's mother, she endorses the match and the two young people secretly marry. After one happy year of marriage, Mong-nyong leaves when his father is transferred to Seoul. Ch'un-hyang hopes to follow him, but he is concerned about propriety and insists that she wait for him to pass the civil service exam and establish himself in the world. The new governor of Namwŏn is infuriated when Ch'un-hyang refuses his demand that she become his consort and has her tortured and imprisoned. Mong-nyong passes the civil service exam with the highest grade and is appointed to the post of royal inspector. As such, he travels incognito to ensure good government in the provinces, and his first stop is Namwŏn where he rescues Ch'un-hyang.

Questions

1. Compare this love story to Shakespeare's Romeo and Juliet. What obstacle does each couple face? What support does each couple receive?
2. Why is this story entitled just "Ch'un-hyang" and not "Ch'un-hyang and Mong-nyong"? What motivates Ch'un-hyang besides her love for Mong-nyong?
3. According to Rachel E. Chang, this tale presents "social criticism only thinly veiled by the humor."[1] What aspects of the tale suggest social criticism?

Song of a Faithful Wife, Ch'un-hyang

Song of a Faithful Wife, Ch'un-hyang from Richard Rutt,
Kim Chong-un, and Man-jung Kim, *Virtuous Women:
Three Classic Korean Novels* (Seoul: Royal Asiatic Society,
Korea Branch, 1979), pp. 250–253, 260–261, 270–271,
285–286, 292–293, 300–302, 305–306, 332–333.
Used with permission of RASKB.

When King Sukchong[2] first ascended the throne, virtue flowed out from him over all the land; the king had sons and grandsons, so the succession was assured; the times were secure and seasons harmonious as in the days of Yao and Shun; administration and culture were as efficient and flourishing as in the days of Yü and T'ang. The ministers of the crown were strong pillars of the state and the generals and marshals were faithful warriors. The good influence of the court reached the remotest countryside, peace and security reigned within the four seas. There were faithful subjects in the palace and filial sons and virtuous wives in the homes of the people. It was a wonderful time! The weather was favorable, the people were well-fed and happy, and everywhere could be heard the happy songs of the farmers at work.

At this time, in Chŏlla province[3] in the city of Namwŏn, there lived a *kisaeng* named Wŏl-mae. She was famous throughout the three southern provinces, but she had retired early and was living with a gentleman named Song. Time passed, and she was over forty years of age, but she had no children. She worried so much about this that she became ill. Then one day she suddenly remembered some stories of people of former times, and asked to see her husband. She spoke to him very respectfully, like this:

'I think I must have committed some very serious sin in a former existence. In this life I have given up singing and entertaining, become a married woman, observed all the rites and worked hard to do all that a woman should; nevertheless, I must have some great guilt, because I have not had any children. When I am dead, who will burn incense or offer sacrifices in my memory and who will look after my funeral? But if I go to pray at some famous shrine and am able to bear at least one child, the greatest sorrow of my life will be at an end.

'Will you let me go?'

Song replied: 'It is true: you are very unfortunate. But if children could be had by praying, would there be any childless women?'

Wŏl-mae answered: 'Confucius was the greatest sage in the world, and he went to pray at the mountain of Ni-ch'iu; Cheng Tzu-ch'an of the kingdom of Cheng prayed at the mountain of Yu-ching; and both were answered. Have we no famous mountains here in Korea? When Chu T'ien-i of Ungch'ŏn, in Kyŏngsang Province, was old but had no children, he went to pray at the highest peak there and as a result a son was born who became the first Ming emperor. If such things can happen for the imperial house, let us see what prayer can do for us. *Don't knock down your own pagoda or trample on your own saplings.*'

From that day onward she began to purify herself with baths and fasting, and made pilgrimages to holy mountain places.

Synopsis: Wŏl-mae dreams that a fairy woman entered her body and subsequently gives birth to her daughter, Ch'un-hyang, who grows into a bright and virtuous child.

At this time there was a gentleman in Seoul, a civil official named Yi, who lived in Samch'ŏng-dong. He was descended from a famous family, and many of his ancestors had been loyal subjects. One day when the king was reviewing the list of meritorious subjects for new appointments, he promoted Yi from his post at Kwach'ŏn, near Seoul, to be prefect of Kŭnsan in Chŏlla province. Soon afterward he transferred him to higher office as governor of the city of Namwŏn. Yi presented himself before the king to offer thanks for his new appointment and take his leave, and set out for Namwŏn to take up his new post. He governed his district wisely and well. There were no disturbances or complaints, and everywhere the people rejoiced that at last they had a just governor. Life was like a fairy-tale: there was peace and plenty, the people did their duty; it was like the days of Yao and Shun all over again.

What time of year was it? It was springtime, the cheerful season. The swifts and swallows and all the other birds had found their mates and flew hither and thither in pairs, twittering. Spring was in the air. Flowers covered the south mountain, and the north mountain too was pink with flowers; the golden orioles called to each other among the myriad fronds of the weeping willows. All the trees were in full leaf and the cuckoos were calling; it was the loveliest time of the year.

The governor's son, young master Yi, was now fifteen years old. He was as handsome as Tu Mu, he was as generous as the ocean is wide, and wonderfully clever: a Li Po for composing verses and a Wang Hsi-chih for calligraphy. One day he called his valet and said: 'Where are the local beauty-spots? Poetry and spring-time go together; tell me where the most beautiful places are.'

The valet replied: 'The young master is supposed to be studying, not going out to look at beauty-spots.'

The boy said: 'That just shows how ignorant you are. From ancient times great writers have always gone to beautiful places for inspiration. They are the basis of lyric poetry. The fairy spirits also travel round from place to place. How dare you say going out is wrong? Szu-ma Chiang, when he was traveling southward by boat on the Yangtze and Hui Rivers, was sailing against the stream; a cold wind was howling, and from this experience he wrote about the continual changing of all created things, always surprising, sometimes delightful, sometimes gentle, always material for poetry. Li Po was the greatest genius among poets, and went for pleasure outings on the Ts'ai-shih River; Su Tung-p'o delighted in moonlit nights at the Red Cliff; Po Chü-i sang of the moon shining at night on the Hsin-yang River; King Sejo liked to visit Munjang-dae in Songni-san, near Poŭn.'

Synopsis: The governor's son gets permission from his father to go to a nearby scenic spot, the Kwanghal pavilion, and there catches a glimpse of Ch'un-hyang. The boy sends his valet to fetch the girl but she considers such a request impertinent and refuses. The valet reports back to his master, who dispatches his valet again. This time the valet finds Ch'un-hyang at home. When he repeats his request more respectfully, Ch'un-hyang's mother reveals that she has had an auspicious dream and encourages her daughter to comply. At this point the boy's name is revealed to be Mong-nyong or 'dream of a dragon.'

Ch'un-hyang, pretending to be reluctant, rose and went out to the Kwanghal-lu. She walked like a swallow on a roof-beam in the Tae-myŏng-jŏn[4] like a hen picking up grain in a sunny yard, like a golden turtle walking on the white sands; lovely as a flower in the moonlight, her slow swimming gait was like Hsi-shih walking to T'u-ch'eng. As she came over to the pavilion the boy stood half leaning on the balustrade, eagerly looking out for her. When she drew close and he could see her clearly, he was delighted. She was fresh and pretty. There was no one to compare with her for loveliness. Her complexion was clear, like a crane white as snow, playing in the moonlight on a clear stream. Her rosy lips were parted to show her white teeth, like stars, like jade. She was beautifully dressed, with a purple gauze skirt enveloping her like twilight mist, a kingfisher-green underskirt glimmering underneath, its pattern rippling like the waves of the Milky Way. Gracefully and sedately she went up into the pavilion and stood there waiting shyly till he said to one of the servants: 'Tell her to sit down.'

Now he could take in the whole of her beauty. He noticed her modest expression and the dignified way in which she sat, like a white pebble in a green stream, a pebble newly washed by the rain; like a roosting swallow surprised by the sight of a man. Although she was not richly dressed, she had outstanding natural beauty. Now that he sat facing her, her face was like the bright moon seen between the clouds, her half-opened pink lips like a lotus flower amid the waters.

'I have never seen a fairy, but surely a fairy from Ying-chou has been exiled to Namwŏn, or else the fairies of the moon have lost one of their companions. Your face and your grace do not belong to this world.'

At the same time Ch'un-hyang lifted her eyelids for a moment and looked at the boy. He was a handsome lad, remarkably good-looking. His high forehead showed promise of early success; the fine bones of his face showed that he would become a distinguished statesman. She was filled with admiration, but she lowered her eyebrows and remained kneeling before him. The boy said: 'The sages have said that one should not marry someone with the same surname. Tell me what your surname is and how old you are.'

'My name is Sŏng, and I am fifteen years old.'

See what the boy does:

'That's good news. You were born in the same year as me; we are both fifteen, and now I know your surname I am sure this is heaven's destiny for us. Marriage is called *yi-sŏng-ji-hap*, the union of two surnames, a pun on Yi and Sŏng. This is a good omen that we shall be happy for the rest of our lives. Are your parents still alive?'

'I live with my widowed mother.'

'How many brothers do you have?'

'My mother is sixty years old; she has no sons, and I am her only daughter.'

'So you are a precious child. We two have met by a special decree of heaven. We shall be happy forever.'

See what Ch'un-hyang does: she knits her eyebrows, half-opens her lips, and gently murmurs: 'A loyal subject cannot serve two kings, and a faithful wife cannot honor two husbands. I have read this in an old book. You are from a noble family, but I am a woman of the people. After we have plighted our troth, if you put me away because of my low birth, I shall nevertheless be bound to remain faithful to you, and have to spend the rest of my life grieving in a lonely room, and there will be no one to help me. Do not make me do this.'

Synopsis: Mong-nyong promises to visit Ch'un-hyang at her house that night. Mong-nyong tries to study his texts, such as The Doctrine of the Mean and the Analects, but he is constantly interrupted by thoughts of Ch'un-hyang. At midnight Mong-nyong sneaks out to go to Ch'un-hyang's house to ask Ch'un-hyang's mother to allow him to marry Ch'un-hyang.

When Ch'un-hyang's mother heard this, she said: 'It says in an old book, *No one knows a subject better than his king; no one knows a son better than his father.* Who should know a daughter better than her mother? I know the sort of girl my daughter is. From the time she was a child she has been strong-willed, and she has worried lest she should do anything in the least improper. She is determined to be faithful to her husband, and her iron will is as unchanging as the pine, bamboo and fir, which stay green through the four seasons. Even though the world were turned upside down and the mulberry orchards became oceans, she would never change her mind. If gold and silver, jade and silks from Wu and Shu were piled up like mountains, they would not move her. Her heart is as clear as the finest jade, and as pure as the clear breeze. Her sole desire is to live according to the ancient ideals. Your lordship has been tempted by desire to form a tie with her, and if without the knowledge of your parents you fall deeply in love, but later decide to give her up because of gossip, my poor daughter will be cast off like a broken trinket of finely mottled tortoiseshell or pretty pearl. She will be like a mandarin duck that has lost the drake she played with so happily in sunnier days. If your intentions are really sincere, think very carefully before you act.'

Mong-nyong felt more frustrated than ever: 'Please stop worrying about that at once. My mind is completely made up and my heart is firm. Even though we have different social obligations, when she and I are betrothed, whether or not we go through the full formalities—the presentation of the goose and the red and blue silks—my love for her is as deep as the sea.'

He was more in earnest saying this than he would have been if he had gone through the ceremonies of the red and blue cords and the rest of the six rites of a wedding: 'I will treat her as my first wife, so do not worry that I shall put her into a subordinate position. Don't worry about the formalities of the wedding; would a gentleman such as I treat her shabbily? Please give your consent.'

Synopsis: Ch'un-hyang's mother believes the match is a matter of destiny and gives her approval. They all eat and drink wine as a kind of wedding banquet and then Mong-nyong and Ch'un-hyang consummate their marriage. Their second night together, when they become playful and share jokes, is described in considerable detail. Months pass, then suddenly Mong-nyong's father is transferred to Seoul and Mong-nyong must leave the next day. Mong-nyong is distraught but Ch'un-hyang assumes she will follow him and live separately until Mong-nyong has risen in the world and can recognize her as a secondary wife. Fearful of the repercussions if word of his scandalous relationship with Ch'un-hyang gets out, Mong-nyong rejects her plan and insists that she stay behind.

When Ch'un-hyang heard this, her face suddenly lost its color. She looked around this way and that, she frowned with flashing eyes, she contracted her brows, her nostrils flared, she ground her teeth, her whole body curled up like a broom-corn leaf. She came down like a hawk pouncing on a pheasant: 'What do you mean by that?'

She stamped, tore her skirt, threw the pieces about, pulled her hair out in handfuls and threw it at him: 'Why has all this happened? All these things are useless!' She picked up the big mirror and her coral hairpin and threw them out of the door, still stamping her feet, and pounding her hands together, till she turned round and collapsed on the floor. How she wailed in her distress!

Ch'un-hyang without a husband!
What need has she of household things?
Who will be pleased if she makes herself pretty?
This is a criminal's destiny!
At the tender age of fifteen
How can I bear to be parted?
I count for nothing: lying words
Have laid up for me a life of grief.
Oh, oh, the pity of it!

Then she turned round and said calmly: 'Now look here: is it true what you've just said? Or are you joking? When we two first met and married each other, did your father and mother approve of it? Why are you trying to make excuses? We saw one another for a little while at the Kwanghal-lu, then you came here to look for me, late at night when no one was about. You sat there and I sat here, and you told me that you would never break your promise. Last year at Tano,[5] it was. You held my wrist and we went outside, and as we stood in the court you pointed to the shimmering sky and repeated your promise ten thousand times. I believed you entirely. Parting when we grow old would be natural, but how can a girl of my age live without a husband? How can I bear the long autumn nights alone in an empty room? Oh, the pity of it, the pity of it! It's cruel, cruel! It's evil, you Seoul men are evil! You are hateful! High-born and humble can never be matched! The love of husband and wife lets the man be the master everywhere in the world, but where in the world is there such a cruel man as you? Oh, oh, it's all my fault! Don't think that you can throw me off and be done with me because I'm humbly born. Unhappy Ch'un-hyang will not be able to eat or sleep: how long do you think she'll stay alive? I shall soon pine away, wretched creature that I am, and die. My wretched ghost will linger here and haunt you. Think what that will do to you! You can't treat me like this—how can you even think of doing it? I want to die, I want to die! Oh, what misery!'

"Nobleman (*Yangban*) and Peasants" by Kim Tŭksin (1754–1822), a royal court artist known for his genre paintings depicting the Confucian themes of elite aristocrats and content commoners. *(Wikimedia Commons)*

Synopsis: Ch'un-hyang's mother is also furious at the news, but eventually Ch'un-hyang realizes it would be folly to accompany Mong-nyong to Seoul and agrees to wait for him until he passes the civil service examinations. After an emotional parting, Ch'un-hyang is left with her thoughts:

'Mankind is born for partings, but how can I bear this empty room? Who can understand how desperately I want to see him again? I am so distraught and bewildered that whether I lie down to sleep, or wake and try to eat, I feel choked by my longings. I yearn to see his handsome face and hear his voice ringing in my ears. Oh, I want to see him again! I want to see him! I want to hear him again! I want to hear him!

'What enemy from a former life arranged that we should be born like this, to love one another, to vow that we should never forget one another but live together till death, a vow more precious than gold or jewels—why should the world come between us? A spring should grow into a stream: how could I know that our love, piled high like mountains upon mountains, would crumble like this? Some evil spirit has harmed us, or creation envies us. When shall I see again the husband I parted from this morning? I have plumbed the depths of a thousand griefs and ten thousand sorrows.

'My face and hair will grow old and useless, and the sun and moon will give me no joy. On autumn nights the moon will shine through the paulownia branches and make me sad. The sunshine on the summer leaves will only make me miserable. Even if he knows how much I love him, and he loves me too, I shall still be lying alone in this empty room with no company save my sighs and tears wrung from my tortured heart. I will collect my tears to make a sea, and my sighs to make a breeze, and sail a little boat to Seoul to seek my love. In the sadness of the moonlit nights I will pray for him with tears—and he will shine in my dreams.

'The cuckoo crying in the moonlight may reach the ears of my beloved, but only I shall know my sorrows. In the gloom of the night, the fireflies gleam outside the windows; I sit up at midnight wondering whether he shall come. Even though I lie down, shall I be able to sleep? Neither sleep nor my lover shall come. What can I do? Fate is cruel.

'*After joy comes sorrow; after the bitter, the sweet,*' is an old saying, but there seems no end to waiting, and who can unravel the sorrows of my heart except my own beloved?

'High heaven, look down kindly and let me see him soon. Let us meet again to complete our love, and never part till the white hairs of old age fall in death. Green waters and blue hills, I beg of you! I was suddenly deprived of my love, and no news comes; he must be made of wood or stone. Oh dear, the pity of it!'

She passed her time praying and grieving. Meanwhile the boy, as he stopped for the night on his way to Seoul, could not sleep: 'I want to see her, I want to see my love. Day and night the thought of her never leaves me. She is longing for me, let me see her soon and satisfy her.'

So the day and months passed, and he looked forward to his name appearing in the list of examination successes.

After some months a new governor was appointed to Namwŏn, Pyŏn Hak-to, of Chaha-dong, in Seoul. He was a famous author and a fine figure of a man, well-versed in music and widely respected, but he had one fault: he sometimes behaved irresponsibly, forgot his morals and made errors of judgment. So it was commonly said of him that he was unusually stubborn.

Synopsis: Despite having been told that she is not a kisaeng and that she is in a relationship with the former governor's son, the new governor sends for Ch'un-hyang and demands that she enter his service. She replies:

'Your commands must be respected, but since I am married I cannot do as you say.'

The governor laughed: 'A pretty girl, a pretty girl! And a virtuous woman too! Your chastity is wonderful. You are quite right to reply like that. But young Yi is the eldest son of a famous family in Seoul, and do you think he regards you as anything more than a flower he plucked in passing? You are a faithful child and while you keep faith the bloom will fade from your face, your hair will grow white and lose its lustre. As you bewail the vain passing of the years, who will there be to blame but yourself? However faithful you remain, who will recognize it? Forget all that. Is it better to belong to your governor or to be tied to a child? Let me hear what you have to say.'

Ch'un-hyang replied: '*A subject cannot serve two kings, and a wife cannot belong to two husbands;* that is my principle. I would rather die than do as you say, however many times you ask me. Please allow me to hold to my ideal: I cannot have more than one husband.'

The treasurer spoke to her then: 'Look here, now; that lad is fickle. Life is no more than a mayfly, and men are all the same. Why should you take so much trouble? His Excellency proposes to lift you up in the world. What do you singing girls know about faithfulness and chastity? The old governor has gone and the new governor has arrived: it's proper for you to obey him. Stop talking strangely. What have loyalty and faithfulness to do with people of your sort?'

Ch'un-hyang was amazed. She relaxed her posture and said: 'A woman's virtue is the same for high ranks and low. If you listen I will explain. Let's speak of *kisaeng*. There are no virtuous ones, you say; but I will tell them to you one by one: Nong-sŏn of Haesŏ died at Tongsŏn Pass; there was a child *kisaeng* of Sŏnch'ŏn who learned all about the Seven Reasons for divorce; Non-gae is so famous as a patriot that a memorial was erected to her and sacrifices are offered there; Hwa-wŏl of Ch'ŏngju had a three-storied pavilion raised in her memory; Wŏl-sŏn of P'yŏng'yang has a memorial; Il-chi-hong of Andong had a memorial erected in her lifetime, and was raised to the nobility; so do not belittle *kisaeng.*'

Then she turned to the governor again: 'Even a mighty man like Meng Pen could not wrest from me my determination to stay a faithful wife and keep the oath, high as the mountains and deep as the sea, that I made to young master Yi. The eloquence of Su Ch'in or Ch'ang Yi could not move my heart. Chu-ko Liang was so clever that he could restrain the southeast wind, but he could not change my heart. Hsü Yu would not bend his will to Yao; Po I and Shu Ch'i would not eat the grain of Chou. Were it not for *Hsü* Yu there would be no high-principled ministers; were it not for Po I and Shu Ch'i there would be many more criminals and robbers. I may be of humble birth, but I know these examples. If I forsook my husband and became a concubine, it would be treason as much as it is for a minister to betray his king. But the decision is yours.'

The governor was furious: 'Listen, girl: treason is a capital offence, and insulting royal officers is equally serious. Refusing to obey a governor meets the same punishment. Don't put yourself in danger of death.'

Ch'un-hyang burst out: 'If the rape of a married woman is not a crime, what is?'

The governor in his fury pounded the writing-desk with such force that his hat-band snapped and his top-knot came undone. His voice grew harsh: 'Take this girl away,' he shouted. The *yamen* [local government headquarters] guards and servants answered: 'Yes, sir,' and ran forward to catch Ch'un-hyang by the hair and drag her away.

'Slaves!'

'Yes, sir!'

'Take this girl away.'

Ch'un-hyang trembled: 'Let go of me!'

She had come halfway down the steps when the slaves rushed up: 'You stupid woman, if you talk to the officers like that, you'll never save your life.'

They pulled her down to the ground of the courtyard. The fearsome soldiers and *yamen* servants swarmed around her like bees and grabbed her hair, black as black seaweed, coiled like a kite-string on its reel in springtime, like a lantern on Buddha's birthday, coiled tightly. They threw her down on the ground. It was pitiful. Her white jade body was crumpled up like a figure six; she was surrounded by grim soldiers holding spears, clubs, paddles and red cudgels.

'Call the executioner.'

'Bow your heads, the executioner comes!'

The governor had recovered a little, but he was still trembling and panting: 'Executioner, there is no need for any interrogation of this girl. Bind her to the frame immediately. Break her shin-bones and prepare the writ of execution.'

See what the jailers do while he binds her to the frame: the noise they make as they pile the paddles and clubs in armfuls beside the frame makes Ch'un-hyang faint.

Watch the executioner: he tries the paddles one by one, tests them for strength and suppleness, chooses one that will break easily and raises it over his right shoulder waiting for the governor's order.

'Receive your orders: if you pretend to beat her harder than you do, because you pity her, you will be punished on the spot. Beat her hard.'

The executioner replied loudly: 'Your orders will be obeyed. Why should we pity her? Now, girl, don't move your legs; if you do, your bones will break.'

He yelled as he danced about her brandishing the paddle. Then he stood still and said to her quietly: 'Just stand a couple of blows. I can't avoid it, but thrash your legs about wildly, as though it were hurting more than it does.'

'Beat her hard.'

'Yes, sir, I'll beat her!'

At the first stroke the broken pieces of the paddle flew through the air and fell in front of the governor. Ch'un-hyang tried to bear the pain but ground her teeth and flung her head back, screaming: 'What have I done?'

During the practice strokes, the executioner stood alone, but from the time he took the paddle to give the legal punishment, a servant stood facing him. Like a pair of fighting-cocks, as one stooped to beat, the other stooped to mark the tally, in the same way that ignorant penniless fellows in the wine-shop mark on the wall the number of cups they have drunk. He drew a line for the first stroke. Ch'un-hyang cried unrestrainedly:

One heart undivided,
Faithful to one husband,
One punishment before one year is over,
But for one moment I will not change.

Synopsis: The executioner delivers twenty-five strokes but all the while Ch'un-hyang proclaims her loyalty to her beloved husband.

Ch'un-hyang cried in her bitterness: 'Do not treat a girl like this. Better kill me quickly, and when I am dead my soul will become a cuckoo like the bird of Ch'u, crying in the empty hills on moonlit nights and breaking the dreams of young master Yi after he has gone to sleep.'

She could not finish her words before she fainted. The officers and servants turned their heads and wiped their tears. The executioner who had beaten her also turned away, wiping his eyes: 'No son of man should do such things.'

All the onlookers and officials standing round also wiped their eyes and looked away, unable to bear the sight. 'We shall never see anyone who takes a beating like Ch'un-hyang. Oh, it's cruel, it's cruel! Her chastity is cruel; her virtue is from heaven.'

Men and women, young and old, all alike were weeping, and the governor was displeased: 'Now, girl, you have been beaten for insulting the governor. What good has it done you? Will you persist in your disobedience?'

Half dead and half alive, Ch'un-hyang answered proudly: 'Listen to me, governor; don't you understand an oath that binds till death? A faithless woman brings frost in summer weather. My soul will fly to the king and present its petitions. You will not escape; please let me die.'

The governor was exasperated: 'The girl is beyond reason. Put her in a cangue [large wooden collar worn as punishment by criminals] and send her to the prison.'

Synopsis: Ch'un-hyang languishes in prison but Mong-nyong passes the civil service examination as the top graduate and is given the post of Royal Inspector of Chŏlla province. He travels there incognito, learns about Ch'un-hyang's imprisonment from some farmers he meets along the way, and even intercepts a letter she has written to him. He visits his mother-in-law and Ch'un-hyang in prison but pretends his family has fallen on hard times and that he is penniless and unable to help Ch'un-hyang. Ch'un-hyang expects to die but does not waver in her loyalty to Mong-nyong. Mong-nyong continues his inspection for another day, then summons his soldiers and takes over the government. The chaos as the governor and other local officials flee is comically described. When order is restored, Mong-nyong summons Ch'un-hyang and tests her one last time:

The inspector said: 'Do you think that a person like you can create a disturbance in the *yamen* on the pretence of being faithful, and hope to live? You deserve to die. Will you refuse to enter my service?'

Ch'un-hyang was in despair: 'All you officers who come here are the same. I beg you to listen to me. Can the winds wear away the high rocks of a mountain cliff? Can the snow change the greenness of the pine and bamboo? Do not ask me to do such a thing. Have me killed quickly.'

Then she turned to [her maid] Hyang-dan: 'Hyang-dan, go and look for my husband. When he came to the jail last night he made me hope for deliverance. I wonder where he has gone; he cannot know that I am about to die.'

The inspector ordered her: 'Raise your eyes. Look at me.'

Ch'un-hyang lifted her head and looked up to the dais. There was no question that it was her husband, who had come as a beggar, sitting up there now as a judge.

Synopsis: Mong-nyong sends Ch'un-hyang, her mother and her maid to Seoul, files his reports, and receives praise and a promotion. The story concludes as follows:

Later on Mong-nyong passed through high office in the Boards of Civil Affairs and Revenue and through deputy ministries till he became Prime Minister, and after his retirement lived to a happy old age with his faithful wife. She bore him three sons and two daughters, who were more brilliant than their father and whose descendants were raised to the first rank of nobility for generation after generation.

Notes

1. Rachel E. Chang, "The Song of the Faithful Wife Ch'unhyang," in William Theodore De Bary, *Finding Wisdom in East Asian Classics* (New York: Columbia University Press, 2011) p. 368.
2. King Sukchong (1661–1720).
3. The southwest corner of the Korean peninsula.
4. A royal palace in Kaesŏng.
5. Tano is the fifth day of the fifth lunar month, which corresponds to early June.

32

Modern Korean Short Fiction

Cranes by Hwang Sunwŏn (1915-2000)

Hwang wrote seven novels and more than 100 short stories, making him the most prolific of modern Korean authors. Quite a few of these works are available in translation. He won awards such as the Asian Freedom Literature Prize in 1955 and the Korean Academy of Arts Prize in 1961.

Questions

1. The conclusion of this story does not disclose the fate of Sŏngsam and Tŏkchae. What do you think happens to them and why do you think so?
2. What is the main reason Tŏkchae stayed on his farm when he should have fled when the South invaded the North?
3. What are the several ways that Tŏkchae surprises Sŏngsam and what is the effect of each?

The Bird of Passage by O Yŏngsu (1914-1979)

O Yŏngsu was a founding member and later the chief editor of the prestigious literary journal *Hyŏndae Munhak* (Modern literature). He wrote more than 100 stories and received considerable recognition for his work, including the Asian Freedom Literature Prize in 1959 and the Republic of Korea's Order of Merit (1978).

"The Bird of Passage" was first published in *Hyŏndae Munhak* in February 1958.

Questions

1. What is the significance of the opening passage about the flocking behavior of migratory birds?
2. What does this story reveal about economic conditions in the late 1950s in Korea?
3. Discuss the relationship between Minu and Kuch'iri. Why does Minu take an interest in Kuch'iri? Why would the boy refuse to take money from Minu and then try to steal a pair of shoes for him?

Modern Korean Short Fiction

"Cranes" and "The Bird of Passage" from Peter H. Lee, *Flowers of Fire: Twentieth-Century Korean Stories*, revised edition (Honolulu: University of Hawaii Press, 1986), pp. 86–91, 189–204. Used with permission.

Cranes by Hwang Sunwŏn

The northern village lay snug beneath the high, bright autumn sky, near the border at the Thirty-eighth Parallel.

White gourds lay one against the other on the dirt floor of an empty farmhouse. Any village elders who passed by extinguished their bamboo pipes first, and the children, too, turned back some distance off. Their faces were marked with fear.

As a whole, the village showed little damage from the war, but it still did not seem like the same village Sŏngsam had known as a boy.

At the foot of a chestnut grove on the hill behind the village he stopped and climbed a chestnut tree. Somewhere far back in his mind he heard the old man with a wen shout, "You bad boy, climbing up my chestnut tree again!"

The old man must have passed away, for he was not among the few village elders Sŏngsam had met. Holding on to the trunk of the tree, Sŏngsam gazed up at the blue sky for a time. Some chestnuts fell to the ground as the dry clusters opened of their own accord.

A young man stood, his hands bound, before a farmhouse that had been converted into a Public Peace Police office. He seemed to be a stranger, so Sŏngsam went up for a closer look. He was stunned: this young man was none other than his boyhood playmate, Tŏkchae.

Sŏngsam asked the police officer who had come with him from Ch'ŏnt'ae for an explanation. The prisoner was the vice-chairman of the Farmers' Communist League and had just been flushed out of hiding in his own house, Sŏngsam learned.

Sŏngsam sat down on the dirt floor and lit a cigarette.

Tŏkchae was to be escorted to Ch'ŏngdan by one of the peace police. After a time, Sŏngsam lit a new cigarette from the first and stood up. "I'll take him with me."

Tŏkchae averted his face and refused to look at Sŏngsam. The two left the village.

Sŏngsam went on smoking, but the tobacco had no flavor. He just kept drawing the smoke in and blowing it out. Then suddenly he thought that Tŏkchae, too, must want a puff. He thought of the days when they had shared dried gourd leaves behind sheltering walls, hidden from the adults' view. But today, how could he offer a cigarette to a fellow like this?

Once, when they were small, he went with Tŏkchae to steal some chestnuts from the old man with the wen. It was Sŏngsam's turn to climb the tree. Suddenly the old man began shouting. Sŏngsam slipped and fell to the ground. He got chestnut burrs all over his bottom, but he kept on running. Only when the two had reached a safe place where the old man could not overtake them did Sŏngsam turn his bottom to Tŏkchae. The burrs hurt so much as they were plucked out that Sŏngsam could not keep tears from welling up in his eyes. Tŏkchae produced a fistful of chestnuts from his pocket and thrust them into Sŏngsam's. . . . Sŏngsam threw away the cigarette he had just lit, and then made up his mind not to light another while he was escorting Tŏkchae.

They reached the pass at the hill where he and Tŏkchae had cut fodder for the cows until Sŏngsam had to move to a spot near Ch'ŏnt'ae, south of the Thirty-eighth Parallel, two years before the liberation.

Sŏngsam felt a sudden surge of anger in spite of himself and shouted, "So how many have you killed?"

For the first time, Tŏkchae cast a quick glance at him and then looked away.

"You! How many have you killed?" he asked again.

Tŏkchae looked at him again and glared. The glare grew intense, and his mouth twitched.

"So you managed to kill quite a few, eh?" Sŏngsam felt his mind becoming clear of itself, as if some obstruction had been removed. "If you were vice-chairman of the Communist League, why didn't you run? You must have been lying low with a secret mission."

Tŏkchae did not reply.

"Speak up. What was your mission?"

Tŏkchae kept walking. Tŏkchae was hiding something, Sŏngsam thought. He wanted to take a good look at him, but Tŏkchae kept his face averted.

Fingering the revolver at his side, Sŏngsam went on: "There's no need to make excuses. You're going to be shot anyway. Why don't you tell the truth here and now?"

"I'm not going to make any excuses. They made me vice-chairman of the League because I was a hardworking farmer, and one of the poorest. If that's a capital offense, so be it. I'm still what I used to be—the only thing I'm good at is tilling the soil." After a short pause, he added, "My old man is bedridden at home. He's bccn ill almost half a year." Tŏkchae's father was a widower, a poor, hardworking farmer who lived only for his son. Seven years before his back had given out, and he had contracted a skin disease.

"Are you married?"

"Yes," Tŏkchae replied after a time.

"To whom?"

"Shorty."

"To Shorty?" How interesting! A woman so small and plump that she knew the earth's vastness, but not the sky's height. Such a cold fish! He and Tŏkchae had teased her and made her cry. And Tŏkchae had married her!

"How many kids?"

"The first is arriving this fall, she says."

Sŏngsam had difficulty swallowing a laugh that he was about to let burst forth in spite of himself. Although he had asked how many children Tŏkchae had, he could not help wanting to break out laughing at the thought of the wife sitting there with her huge stomach, one span around. But he realized that this was no time for joking.

"Anyway, it's strange you didn't run away."

"Victorious Fatherland Liberation War Museum Mural (detail)" (late twentieth century). This work presents North Korea's version of events of the Korean War. The
name of the museum and the mural suggests that North Korea, under the leadership
of the Great Leader, Kim Il Sung, won the Korean War. In fact, the war technically
has not ended. There is only a ceasefire agreement. *(Wikimedia Commons, Pyong-
yang, North Korea)*

"I tried to escape. They said that once the South invaded, not a man
would be spared. So all of us between seventeen and forty were taken to
the North. I thought of evacuating, even if I had to carry my father on my
back. But Father said no. How could we farmers leave the land behind
when the crops were ready for harvesting? He grew old on that farm
depending on me as the prop and the mainstay of the family. I wanted to
be with him in his last moments so I could close his eyes with my own
hand. Besides, where can farmers like us go, when all we know how to
do is live on the land?"

Sŏngsam had had to flee the previous June. At night he had broken
the news privately to his father. But his father had said the same thing:
Where could a farmer go, leaving all the chores behind? So Sŏngsam had
left alone. Roaming about the strange streets and villages in the South,
Sŏngsam had been haunted by thoughts of his old parents and the young
children, who had been left with all the chores. Fortunately, his family
had been safe then, as it was now.

They had crossed over a hill. This time Sŏngsam walked with his face averted. The autumn sun was hot on his forehead. This was an ideal day for the harvest, he thought.

When they reached the foot of the hill, Sŏngsam gradually came to a halt. In the middle of a field he espied a group of cranes that resembled men in white, all bent over. This had been the demilitarized zone along the Thirty-eighth Parallel. The cranes were still living here, as before, though the people were all gone.

Once, when Sŏngsam and Tikchae were about twelve, they had set a trap here, unbeknown to the adults, and caught a crane, a Tanjŏng crane. They had tied the crane up, even binding its wings, and paid it daily visits, patting its neck and riding on its back. Then one day they overheard the neighbors whispering: someone had come from Seoul with a permit from the governor-general's office to catch cranes as some kind of specimens. Then and there the two boys had dashed off to the field. That they would be found out and punished had no longer mattered; all they cared about was the fate of their crane. Without a moment's delay, still out of breath from running, they untied the crane's feet and wings, but the bird could hardly walk. It must have been weak from having been bound.

The two held the crane up. Then, suddenly, they heard a gunshot. The crane fluttered its wings once or twice and then sank back to the ground.

The boys thought their crane had been shot. But the next moment, as another crane from a nearby bush fluttered its wings, the boys' crane stretched its long neck, gave out a whoop, and disappeared into the sky. For a long while the two boys could not tear their eyes away from the blue sky up into which their crane had soared.

"Hey, why don't we stop here for a crane hunt?" Sŏngsam said suddenly.

Tŏkchae was dumbfounded.

"I'll make a trap with this rope; you flush a crane over here." Sŏngsam had untied Tŏkchae's hands and was already crawling through the weeds.

Tŏkchae's face whitened. "You're sure to be shot anyway"—these words flashed through his mind. Any instant a bullet would come flying from Sŏngsam's direction, Tŏkchae thought.

Some paces away, Sŏngsam quickly turned toward him.

"Hey, how come you're standing there like a dummy? Go flush a crane!"

Only then did Tŏkchae understand. He began crawling through the weeds.

A pair of Tanjŏng cranes soared high into the clear blue autumn sky, flapping their huge wings.

The Bird of Passage, by O Yŏngsu

They come with the warm weather and go away when it grows cold.
Or they come with the cold and leave when it grows warm.

They always go off in search of food in flocks, and then flock together
again when they return.

Such is the behavior of migratory birds. But there are some that follow
a different pattern.

It happened last autumn. The leaves of the city's trees were just beginning to fall. So it must have been mid-October.

Minu was walking down Ŭlchiro Sixth Avenue, heading for his quarters
outside the East Gate, when suddenly a shoeshine boy was blocking his
way and tugging at his sleeve. Minu was in a sour mood just then, and
the sight of that grimy hand grasping the sleeve of his new suit irritated

"Koryŏ Celadon Inlaid with Cranes" (twelfth century), National Treasure of South
Korea. The Korean inlay process, in which spaces in the body of the vessel are filled
with darker or lighter clays before glazing, is a traditional technique. *(Wikimedia
Commons, Gansong Art Museum)*

him. "No shine! Hands off!" he shouted. The boy, unabashed, kept tugging at Minu's sleeve.

"But . . . Teacher, don't you recognize me?" he asked.

Then Minu looked at the boy. Indeed it did seem that he had often seen
that face before, but for a moment he could not recall where.

"In Pusan. I used to shine your shoes all the time."

Then it came back to Minu clearly. "Oh, now I remember. You're
Kuch'iri, that's right. When did you come to Seoul?"

"Last spring."

"You did? You didn't do well in Pusan?"

At these words Kuch'iri released Minu's sleeve; his face fell, a tear
struck the tip of his shoe, as he lowered his gaze to the pavement. Though
he did not know what had happened, Minu, too, felt sad.

Kuch'iri's turtleneck pullover had tattered elbows and frayed cuffs.
His trousers were glossy with dirt. He looked like any other shoeshine
boy, except that the army boots he was wearing were absurdly blunt-toed
and each one was big enough alone to hold both feet. They were clumsy,
even comical.

Minu took out a cigarette. "Did you come alone?"

Instead of answering, Kuch'iri pulled Minu's sleeve: "Please come
over here." Minu followed him into a nearby alley. Kuch'iri put down
his plain wooden stool by the concrete outer wall of a house and asked
Minu to sit. He wanted to shine Minu's shoes before telling his story.

Minu placed one foot on the shoeshine box. "It's been a long time
since you shined my shoes. More than a year, isn't it?"

"Aren't these the same shoes you had then?"

The boy's home was in Ch'ungch'ŏng Province, but he could speak
the Pusan dialect fluently.

"Yes, they're the same shoes. But why'd you come to Seoul? Didn't
it go well at the school?"

Kuch'iri dislodged some dirt from the sole of Minu's shoe with a
metal scraper and said, "Please don't ask about the school. I got into
trouble."

"Trouble? What kind of trouble?"

"Just a while after you left for Seoul . . ."

"What happened?"

"Some money disappeared from the office. Seven thousand hwan[1]

"Really?"

"Yeah, and the Disciplinarian claimed I took it. He took me into the
storeroom and gave me an awful beating."

"You mean that Mr. Ch'oe?"

"Yes. And even though I told him I didn't take it . . ."

"But whose money was it?"

"They said it was the Patriots' Club dues."

"Then what did the Disciplinarian do?"

"He said if I didn't confess by the next day he'd tell the police."

"And then?"

"Please put your other foot up."

"And?"

"The next day he stuck a pencil between my fingers and twisted it hard. I thought I'd die . . ."

"He did what?"

"So I told him I took the money; he asked how come I didn't confess earlier. And he kept asking me what I'd done with the money."

"So what did you say?"

"I told him I only confessed because of the pain, that I really didn't take the money. He said I made a fool of him and took the leg of a chair and beat me so hard that I . . ."

"Hey, enough polishing. A quick shine is all I want. So what happened next?"

"I don't know. When I opened my eyes the old janitor was splashing water on my face."

"Hmmm. And then?"

"So the janitor took me home. I was sick for days."

"Just a quick shine, I said."

"But I'll have to get that dirt off. Anyway, I was sick in bed at home, and my friend came and told me Mr. Ch'oe was asking for me. My big sister took me to him. I went limping along."

"What did he say?"

"He said they'd caught the guy who took the money. He said he was sorry, and he gave me two hundred hwan and told me to buy some dog soup with it."

"Who did take the money?"

"He said it was that bastard of an office boy!"

"Did you get some dog soup, then?"

"I was crying so hard. All I did was cry. My big sister was crying, too."

"Really . . . ?"

"I said I didn't want any money, and we went back home. I kept thinking of you, Teacher."

"Is that why you left for Seoul?"

"Since I was sick I couldn't make any money, so my stepmother kept telling me to get out of the house. My father got drunk and gave me a beating. So I got in with a bunch of guys who were going to Seoul and I came up here with them."

"Hm."

"Look at this, Teacher."

The boy held out his hand. The flesh of the second and third fingers was discolored, and the joints were swollen. This, he said, was due to the cruel twisting of the pencil that day. Minu gently felt the injured fingers, then released them.

"Does it still hurt?"

Kuch'iri was silent.

"How are the shoes coming?"

"They're all done."

Minu knew the boy would not let him pay so he thought he would take him for something to eat. When he stood up Kuch'iri stood up, too, packed up his shoeshine box, and followed along as if by agreement. When they got to the Kyerim movie theater, Kuch'iri caught Minu's sleeve again and pointed to the billboard. "Teacher, have you seen that movie?" he asked.

Minu just shook his head.

"Teacher, please go see it. I'll treat you."

For a moment Minu merely gazed dumbfounded at Kuch'iri.

"Teacher! That guy with one eye closed, holding the pistol—see? He's great!"

"Okay, I'll take you in."

"No. I've seen it. You watch it. I can get us in for free. Come on, let's go."

"Kuch'iri, the next time a good movie comes along, I'll take you to see it. I'm pretty busy today."

Kuch'iri seemed to be on the verge of tears. "Please don't go. Come see the movie. Please come with me," he said, tugging harder on Minu's sleeve.

Kuch'iri was not going to give up until Minu agreed to watch the movie. It was an awkward fix, for Minu saw that an abrupt refusal would hurt the boy's feelings. He hesitated a moment and then said, "Okay. Let's go."

Kuch'iri set down his shoeshine box at the side of the theater and left Minu standing next to it. He went to the entrance and negotiated briefly. Soon he came hurrying back, waving one arm and mincing along in his

GI boots. He shouldered the shoeshine box and took the stool in one hand. With the other he led Minu along. "It's all settled," he said. "Come with me. Let's go in now."

Just as Kuch'iri had promised, he and Minu entered the theater unchallenged. When they got inside, Kuch'iri hurried up to the front, found a seat, and showed Minu to it. He whispered in his ear, "The show's continuous, you know. It'll start from the beginning again soon. You stay here and watch. I'll go shine those people's shoes over there and then I'll come back." With these words he was gone.

The film was a western. Minu's eyes were on the screen, but his own thoughts absorbed all his attention.

Minu had been teaching at W Middle School in Pusan, where he stayed until the recapture of Seoul. They called it a school, but it was a makeshift affair, just a group of tents with no fence or wall. All kinds of peddlers came there, but the shoeshine boys were the worst. Sometimes as many as seven or eight would come in one group. Over forty teachers sat back-to-back in the small office, and even a shoeshine would cause a stir. To Minu, whose responsibility it was to keep the campus in order, fell the futile task of ejecting the shoeshine boys, only to have them reappear once his back was turned. The boys swarmed to the school like flies to carrion, sometimes camping quietly beside the office and playing marbles or batting about a shuttlecock.

One day, Minu was on his way back from the washroom after having ejected that morning's crowd of shoeshine boys. One of the shoeshine boys, who had somehow managed to follow him, held out his stool and said, "Shine, sir?"

"But I just got rid of you guys!"

Minu, half smiling, half frowning, took a poke at the boy with his fist, but the boy pulled a tin out of his pocket and held it out, saying, "Teacher, this is the best American polish, you've heard of it, haven't you? I bought it yesterday. Please be my first customer." Minu had no class during the first hour, so he set his foot on the box. The boy threw himself into the job, spitting and shining the first shoe. Then, "Sir!"

"What?"

"There are too many shoeshine boys here, aren't there?"

"They're a headache!"

"I have an idea, Teacher. I'll shine all the teachers' shoes for just twenty hwan, and with the best polish, if you will make it so that I'm the only one allowed to shine shoes here."

"You're a greedy one!"

"Come on, let me, sir!"

It made sense. If he authorized just one boy to shine shoes, the others would not come.

Moreover, the teachers would welcome this new price of twenty hwan, instead of the usual thirty.

"I'll talk to the others about it."

"Please, sir!"

That afternoon in the general meeting Minu made the proposal. From the principal and the supervisor on down, all agreed. They decided the chosen boy should wear an armband. The next day Minu made an armband of yellow cloth with a W on it. He called the shoeshine boys together and made the announcement: "The boy wearing this armband is the only one who will be allowed to shine shoes here. There's no need for the rest of you to come anymore. You'd better go elsewhere."

However, the boys all protested, some of them pressing home their grievances: "Aren't we all refugees together here?" "That's unfair." "Choose one each day and we'll take turns." "Make it one a week . . ."

"Maybe you're right," Minu replied. "But it's been decided, so there's nothing I can do about it." Thus Minu managed to quiet the boys. Yet he could not help feeling moved when they said that they were all refugees together, for Minu himself was a refugee school teacher who had left his home in the North.

The boy who received the armband would arrive early each morning and bow smartly to each of the teachers. When the principal arrived, the boy would promptly bring his slippers, exchange them for his shoes, and begin polishing.

In a spare moment one day, Minu had his shoes shined. "How many pairs do you shine every day?"

"Including the students', it comes to about twenty pairs."

"Two times two is four. . . . Can you make a profit at four hundred hwan?"

"It's fine."

"Is it better than before?"

"BETTER? Before it was hard to take in even two hundred a day."

"Hmmm . . . What's your name?"

"Yi Kuch'ŏl."

Just then the P.E. teacher came by. He said, "No, it can't be Kuch'ŏl—since you shine shoes you'd better change it to Kuch'iri[2]." And so Kuch'ŏl came to be known as Kuch'iri.

His home was in Ch'ungch'ŏng Province, and his father worked down on the docks.

Lunch hour was the busiest time for Kuch'iri. Some of the teachers had their shoes shined while they ate. Working in the small teachers' office, Kuch'iri was sometimes kicked in the seat of his pants or struck on the head with a roll-book. When they were busy, the teachers would ask him to get them lunch or have him do other small tasks in place of the errand boy.

When a new principal was appointed, Minu left the school and went to Seoul. He completely forgot about Kuch'iri.

Ch'oe's misunderstanding and mistreatment of the boy may have been increased by his dislike of Minu. Kuch'iri firmly refused to accept money from Minu, and this was all the more irritating. Once, when Kuch'iri said he had polished Ch'oe's shoes ten times, Ch'oe insisted that he had only done it six or seven times. At last Ch'oe derided Kuch'iri and soundly slapped his face. One day the teachers ordered lunch from the usual chophouse. Kuch'iri brought Minu's lunch first, and Ch'oe plainly showed his irritation. On one occasion Ch'oe and Minu nearly clashed openly.

When the teachers had a party, Ch'oe looked askance at Minu's gathering squid heads or leftover cooky bits and giving them to Kuch'iri; and when relief goods were distributed, Ch'oe was irritated by Minu's giving unwanted items to the boy. It was hard to know whether Ch'oe disliked Minu for taking sides with a boy he hated, or whether it was because he hated Minu that he could not stand Kuch'iri. In either case, Minu had no love for Ch'oe either.

Ch'oe could be quite cruel. For example, he would bring into the office two pupils accused of misbehaving in class. He would stand them face to face and order one to slap the other on the cheek. But eye to eye as they were, the two could only grin sheepishly. However, Ch'oe was standing there beside them, stick in hand. One pupil, seeing no escape, would lightly slap the other on the cheek. Then Ch'oe would tell the pupil who had been hit to return the blow. Helpless, the second pupil would slap back about as hard as the one he had been slapped. But the other boy, probably thinking this slap a bit harder than the first, would hit back still harder. And his comrade, thinking this slap much harder than the one he had delivered, would hit back hard indeed. By this time no threats from the teacher were necessary; the two would just go on slapping each other with all their strength until their ears and cheeks were red and swollen. Everyone would laugh at the spectacle.

As Minu sketched this portrait of Ch'oe in his mind's eye, he felt sure that Kuch'iri had been beaten all the harder on his account.

"Teacher, you see he's fallen off his horse. But it's a trick. He doesn't get killed. Watch him jump back and get away. He's really great!" Kuch'iri had come back and was sitting beside him explaining the movie.

Kuch'iri waited for Minu by the same corner every day, and each time he wanted to shine Minu's shoes. If Minu said he was busy, the boy would at least give the shoes a quick brushing. Sometimes, when Kuch'iri was busy shining someone else's shoes, Minu just went by in silence. When they met the next day, Kuch'iri would ask why Minu had not gone to work and where he had been, and he would say that he had waited for Minu until dark. One day when Minu was on his way home a little later than usual, he saw Kuch'iri, hands thrust into his pants pockets, whistling and marching along in time with the tune. It was a popular song that went " . . . though I miss my home . . ."

"What are you doing here so late?"

"I was waiting for you, Teacher;' he replied, shouldering his shoeshine box and walking along after Minu.

"What for?"

"Just because . . ."

When they got to the East Gate train station, Kuch'iri simply bowed to Minu and said, "Goodbye, Teacher."

Kuch'iri lived in the second-to-last shack in the row along the bank of the stream just outside the station. One time, thinking it odd that Kuch'iri went into the station every evening, Minu had asked him where he lived. Kuch'iri took his sleeve and drew him to the ticket gate, where he pointed out the shack just opposite. He said he lived there with an old lady who raised bean sprouts and sold them in the market.

Minu would leave work as early as possible, knowing that Kuch'iri was waiting for him. Somehow Kuch'iri had found a permanent place in his heart. This was Minu's weakness: if a neighbor's dog wagged its tail at him, he would feel fond of it. Or perhaps it was partly that Minu's youngest nephew was still in the North, where there was no way to get news of him, and whenever Minu saw Kuch'iri it was just like seeing the little nephew who had always tagged after him.

"How long are you going to go on shining shoes?"

"Why?"

"That's a job for little kids, you know."

Kuch'iri was silent.

"How old are you now?"

"On New Year's I'll turn fourteen."

"Wouldn't you like to get a job as a carpenter, or ironworker?" Such were Minu's hopes for the boy, and he had thoughts of sending him to night school.

"Well, what do you want to do?"

"I want to make some money so I can open a shoe store."

"Hm? A shoe store?"

"In Pusan, at the head of our alley."

"Why on earth there?"

"So I can show it to that kid."

"What kid?"

"My stepmother's kid."

"But still, he's your brother, isn't he?"

"Him? I can't stand that brat. Because of him I've been beaten enough. And my big sister, too. She's always getting a licking because of him. I really feel sorry for my big sister. If I open a shoe store, she can come live with me."

"It takes a lot of money to open a shoe store. Do you have any saved up?"

Kuch'iri looked up at Minu with a quick grin and rubbed harder with the polishing cloth. "I've saved six thousand hwan since I came to Seoul. Plus nine hundred I gave to the old woman to help her with her bean sprout business."

"How did you get to know her?"

"One time she asked me to open her bean sprout bucket for her. I could tell by her dialect that she was from Ch'ungch'ŏng, too."

"Does she have a family?"

"She says her husband died last year, and her son was killed in the war."

It was two days before Christmas.

Kuch'iri had been shining Minu's shoes once every two or three days but had refused to accept payment. Now Kuch'iri looked so cold that Minu handed him two thousand hwan and said, "Here, buy yourself a shirt. How can you go around in those clothes in the winter?"

Kuch'iri stared at the money and back at Minu, and deftly thrust the bills back into Minu's pocket. "I don't want it. I don't want your money."

Minu pulled the money back out and stuck it under Kuch'iri's nose. "Come on, take it," he said.

"I don't want it!"

"Hurry up and take it."

Kuch'iri did not move.

"Look, how can I accept your favors then?"

Minu dropped the money in front of Kuch'iri and turned away. But Kuch'iri, stumbling in his oversized boots, came from behind and stood in his path. "I don't want money. I don't want it." Wiping his eyes with his fist, he held the money out to Minu. Passersby turned to watch.

"What are you crying for?" Minu said.

"I don't want it. Money . . ."

This was a predicament. "Okay, then, bring your things and come with me."

Again Kuch'iri shoved the money back into Minu's overcoat pocket. He shouldered his stool and box and followed along. The two went into a restaurant and ordered two bowls of dumpling soup.

"Why do you wait for me every day?"

Kuch'iri lowered his gaze.

"Speak up!"

"Because I like you!"

"What do you mean, you like me?"

"I just do."

"Just do? What . . . ? Really!"

The waiter brought the soup.

"But look, Kuch'iri." Again Minu got out his money. "Look, you shine my shoes and then I'll buy you a shirt, okay? That's what people do at Christmas. So buy a shirt with this and start wearing it tomorrow, won't you?"

"But I don't want you to give me any money!"

"You're a stubborn little . . . Look, if you don't do what I tell you, I won't come by here and I won't let you shine my shoes anymore. How would you like that?"

Kuch'iri sniffed.

"Your nose is running into your soup."

Kuch'iri snuffled, and with a look of reproach for Minu he took the money.

They had left the restaurant and were walking side by side. Minu asked, "Do you want to see a movie? I'll treat you."

"No, thank you. I've got to go home now."

"What for?"

"The old woman can't see too well at night anymore."

"So what do you do?"

"I carry water and sort the bean sprouts for her."

They did not meet the next day, for it was Sunday.

When Kuch'iri saw Minu on Christmas morning, he was beaming as he held out his arms to show off the jacket he had gotten in a second-hand clothes shop. He also showed him a can of shoe polish he had bought with the change. Minu was pleased and said, "That's good. But you could use a haircut, too."

They say the peak season for shoeshine boys begins when the forsythia bloom, as people emerge into the fine weather wanting to look their best after a long winter indoors. For Kuch'iri work was plentiful, and he said that he could earn in one day now what during the winter had taken two days to earn.

While he was polishing Minu's shoes one day, Kuch'iri said, "Teacher, your shoes are all worn out."

"Yes, it's time to buy a new pair."

"Don't buy any. I'll get you some high-quality American ones from a guy I know." He measured Minu's foot with a cord.

A few days later Kuch'iri told him, "Teacher, I asked him to get the shoes. He says he'll get the best. It's okay if they're secondhand, isn't it?"

"What's the price?"

"Let's see . . . They'll sell them cheap to us, say about four or five thousand hwan."

"That low?"

"Yeah. On the black market a good pair of American shoes'll go for at least ten thousand hwan even if they're used."

After that, Kuch'iri worried about his offer each time he shined Minu's shoes. "I saw the guy yesterday and he says he'll get them soon," he would say, and then mutter something to himself.

One Saturday in early May, Minu left work somewhat earlier than usual. Kuch'iri was nowhere to be seen, though his box and stool lay abandoned on the ground. Thinking that Kuch'iri must have gone to the washroom, Minu sat down on the stool and took out a cigarette.

A clamor like that of quarrelling urchins came from a nearby alleyway. Minu smoked his cigarette and waited, but still Kuch'iri did not return. Thinking Kuch'iri might be watching the fight, Minu stepped into the alley. There from behind he saw a young man, apparently smartly dressed, surrounded by four or five shoeshine boys. The young man was striking somebody. He wore rubber slippers on his feet and held a pair of leather shoes in his hand. Minu moved closer, thinking that the boy being struck resembled Kuch'iri.

"Teacher, go away. Don't come in here. It's nothing." It was Kuch'iri. Blood dribbled from his nose and smeared his face.

"Kuch'iri! What's going on here?"

Kuch'iri, spitting blood and wiping the side of his mouth, yelled almost desperately, "Teacher, go away. It's nothing. Please go away!"

With that the young man turned and looked angrily at Minu. "Who are you?" he asked.

Minu had no ready answer, but hesitated a moment and then said, "It doesn't matter who I am, but what on earth . . ."

Kuch'iri took his chance to escape. He ran down the alley with all his might and was rounding the corner before the surprised young man uttered a curse and ran after him.

Minu thought to himself, "Whatever it's all about, I just hope Kuch'iri doesn't get caught." He asked the shoeshine boys standing there what had happened to Kuch'iri. But as if by agreement they did not say a word and slipped away. At that point, a boy came to pick up Kuch'iri's stool and box. The boy said that he was a friend of Kuch'iri, and that he would take care of Kuch'iri's things. Minu consented and had the boy shine his shoes, hoping to find out more. "Hey, what was that all about," he asked.

The boy glanced up at him and answered, "He was caught stealing shoes at the restaurant over there."

"Kuch'iri was?"

"Him and another kid, but the other one got away and Kuch'iri got caught."

Minu's head began to swim and his eyesight blurred. He shut his eyes for a moment to calm himself. "It was all because of that promise of his," he muttered. He was angered by this breach of faith, but he felt sorry for Kuch'iri. "If I see him, I'll really teach him a lesson, the little thief." Yet even as he said this, Minu really felt as if he would burst into tears if he met Kuch'iri now.

"Ha, if I'd only caught that bastard I'd have bashed his skull in like a chestnut!" It was the young man with the shoes, coming back out of breath.

"What happened?"

"He got away."

Minu was relieved.

"Look at this. It hasn't been a week since I bought these shoes." He took off the rubber slippers, put on the shoes, and headed off across the trolley line.

From that day on Kuch'iri was nowhere to be found.

On the fourth day Minu went to the shack outside the train station where the old lady who sold bean sprouts lived. The old lady did live there, he was told, but the door was latched; she must have been at the market.

Every day on his way to and from work, Minu stopped at Kuch'iri's old shoeshine spot. About ten days or so later, another boy took over the spot. Setting his foot on the box Minu asked, "Do you know Kuch'iri, who used to shine shoes here?"

"Yeah, I know him. He's gone to an American army base up near the DMZ."

"Alone?"

"No, he joined a group of guys who were going up there." The boy said that every summer groups of shoeshine boys went to the American army bases to make money. It would be autumn before they returned, the boy said in reply to Minu's query.

A wearisome August passed, and then September drew to a close. Autumn came late that year.

One day, as leaves were beginning to fall along the streets, Minu glanced up at the sky. A flock of geese flew by in a neat V, on their way from somewhere to somewhere else. Minu was deeply moved: "Kuch'iri, too, will be coming back soon," he thought.

Notes

1. The currency system in South Korea after the Korean War was very chaotic making exact calculations of equivalency difficult, but 7000 hwan was near to $300.

2. The boy's name Kuch'ŏl was changed to the similar-sounding name Kuch'iri, which means polish.

Bibliography

The editors wish to thank those who granted permission to reprint the selections in this book, listed below in order of appearance. Internet sources were accessed during May 2014.

Book of Songs based on James Legge, *The Chinese Classics with a Translation, Critical and Exegetical Notes, Prolegomena, and Copious Indexes*, vol. 4, *The She King* (Hong Kong: Lane, Crawford, 1871), pp. 1–4, 23 24, 26, 38–40, 167–168, 171–172, 586, 631–633.

Book of Documents based on James Legge, *The Chinese Classics with a Translation, Critical and Exegetical Notes, Prolegomena, and Copious Indexes*, vol. 3, part 1, *The Shoo King* (Hong Kong: James Legge, 1861), pp. 23–26. http://babel.hathitrust.org/cgi/pt?id=uc1.b3537002;view=1up;seq=5.

Book of Rites based on James Legge, *The Sacred Books of China*, vol. 4, *The Lî Kî (The Book of Rites)*, part 1 (Oxford: Clarendon Press, 1885). www.sacred-texts.com/cfu/liki/index.htm.

Analects based on James Legge, *The Four Books: Confucian Analects, the Great Learning, the Doctrine of the Mean, and the Works of Mencius* (Shanghai: Commercial Press, 1923), pp. 1–2, 5, 12–13, 16, 18–19, 21, 23, 26, 42–43, 45, 47, 87, 229. http://hdl.handle.net/2027/uc2.ark:/13960/t09w0b916.

Mencius based on James Legge, *The Four Books: Confucian Analects, the Great Learning, the Doctrine of the Mean, and the Works of Mencius* (Shanghai: Commercial Press, 1923), pp. 429–432, 444–446, 540–541, 548–552, 851–852, 947–948. http://hdl.handle.net/2027/uc2.ark:/13960/t09w0b916.

Great Learning based on James Legge, *The Four Books: Confucian Analects, the Great Learning, the Doctrine of the Mean, and the Works of Mencius* (Shanghai: Commercial Press, 1923), pp. 308–314, 323–324, 326–328. http://hdl.handle.net/2027/uc2.ark:/13960/t09w0b916.

Doctrine of the Mean based on James Legge, *The Four Books: Confucian Analects, the Great Learning, the Doctrine of the Mean, and the Works of Mencius* (Shanghi: Commercial Press, 1923), pp. 349–352, 367–368, 381–396. http://hdl.handle.net/2027/uc2.ark:/13960/t09w0b916.

Daoist Texts: Daodejing based on Lionel Giles, *The Sayings of Lao Tzŭ* (London: J. Murray, 1905), pp. 19, 22–24, 30–31, 37, 43–44, 47 (reorganized to reflect the order common in other translations). http://hdl.handle.net/2027/uc2. ark:/13960/t0xp74d74.

Daoist Texts: Zhuangzi based on James Legge, *The Sacred Books of China: The Text of Taoism* (London: Oxford University Press, 1891), part 1, pp. 172–175, 194, 197, 390, 391–392; part 2, pp. 4–5.

Chinese Poetry: 1, 2, 3, 6.1, 6.2, 6.3, 7 from Arthur Waley, *A Hundred and Seventy Chinese Poems* (London: Constable, 1918), pp. 64, 65, 76, 98, 150, 155, 157. http://hdl.handle.net/2027/uc1.32106001628343.

Chinese Poetry: 4.1 translated by Margaret Helen Childs from *Li Bai ji jiao zhu*, edited by Duiyuan Qu (Shanghai: Shanghai gu ji chu ban she: Xin hua shu dian Shanghai fa xing suo fa xing, 1980), p. 1340.

Chinese Poetry: 4.2, 4.3 from Arthur Waley, *The Poet Li Po A.D. 702–762* (London: East and West, 1919), pp. 23–24, 25–26. http://hdl.handle.net/2027/mdp.39015004960905.

Chinese Poetry: 5 from *Sunflower Splendor: Three Thousand Years of Chinese Poetry* edited by Wu-chi Liu and Irving Yucheng Lo (Bloomington: Indiana University Press, 1990), pp. 130–131. Copyright ©1990, Indiana University Press. Reprinted with permission of Indiana University Press.

The West Chamber excerpts from *The West Chamber: A Medieval Drama* by Wang Shifu, translated by Henry H. Hart (Stanford, CA: Stanford University Press, 1936), pp. 6, 10, 11, 32–33, 123–124, 138, 144–148. Copyright © 1936 by the Board of Trustees of the Leland Stanford Jr. University, renewed 1964. All rights reserved. Used with the permission of Stanford University Press, www.sup.org. See also Wang Shifu, edited and translated by Stephen H. West, and W.L. Idema, *The Moon and the Zither: The Story of the Western Wing [Xin Kan Qi Miao Quan Xiang Zhu Shi Xi Xiang Ji]* (Berkeley: University of California Press, 1991).

Journey to the West excerpts from Wu Cheng'en, translated by W.J.F. Jenner, *Journey to the West* (Beijing: Foreign Languages Press, 1982), pp. 4–5, 10–13, 36–37, 243, 264, 273–280. See also Wu Cheng'en, translated by Anthony C. Yu, *The Journey to the West* (Chicago: University of Chicago Press, 2012).

Outlaws of the Marsh excerpts from Shi Nai'an, Luo Guanzhong, translated by Sidney Shapiro, *Outlaws of the Marsh* (Beijing: Foreign Languages Press, 1980), pp. 271–273, 881–882, 886–893, 895–897, 937–938.

Short Stories: Kong Yiji and **A Small Incident** from Lu Xun, translated by Xianyi Yang and Gladys Yang, *Lu Xun: Selected Works* (Beijing: Foreign Languages Press, 2003), pp. 52–57, 76–78. See also Lu Xun translated by Julia Lovell, *The Real Story of Ah-Q and Other Tales of China: The Complete Fiction of Lu Xun* (London: Penguin Books, 2009).

Essays by Mao Zedong from *Selected Readings from the Works of Mao Tsetung* (Peking: Foreign Languages Press, 1971), pp. 23–39, 362–363.

The Old Gun from Mo Yan, translated by Duncan Hewitt, *Explosions and Other Stories* (Hong Kong: Research Centre for Translations, Chinese University of Hong Kong, 1991), pp. 59–75. First Published in Renditions paperback. Used with permission of the Research Centre for Translation, Chinese University of Hong Kong.

Japanese Poetry: Man'yōshū poems based on W.G. Aston, *A History of Japanese Literature* (New York: D. Appleton, 1899), pp. 36–38, 42.

Japanese Poetry: Kokinshū, Shūishū, Shinkokinshū, and haiku poems translated by Margaret Helen Childs from *Kokinwakashū, Shinkoten Nihon bungaku taikei* 5, edited by Noriyuki Kojima and Eizō Arai (Tokyo: Iwanami shoten, 1989); *Shūiwakashū, Shinkoten Nihon bungaku taikei* 7, edited by Teruhiko Komachi (Tokyo: Iwanami shoten, 1990); *Shinkokinwakashū, Shinkoten Nihon bungaku taikei 11*, edited by Yutaka Tanaka and Shingo Akase (Tokyo: Iwanami shoten, 1992); *Matsuo Bashōshū 1–2, Nihon Koten Bungaku Zenshū*, edited by Imoto Nōichi and Nobuo Hori (Tokyo: Shōgakukan 1995); *Ryōkan no haiku*, edited by Kawaguchi Seitei (Osaka: Yukawa shobo, 1977).

Japanese Poetry: Poems composed in the aftermath translated by Laurel R. Rodd, Amy V. Heinrich, and Joan E. Ericson from *The Sky Unchanged: Tears and Smiles [Kawaranai sora nakinagara, warainagara]* by 55 Japanese Affected by the Triple Disaster of March 2011 (Tokyo: Kōdansha, 2014), #5, 24, 36, 39, 71.

The Pillow Book selections translated by Margaret Helen Childs from Sei Shōnagon, *Makura no sōshi, Nihon koten bungaku taikei*, vol. 11 (Tokyo: Shōgakukan, 1974), 1, 25, 60, 74–75, 254. See also 1, 25, 44, 69, 148 in Sei Shōnagon and Meredith McKinney, *The Pillow Book* (London: Penguin, 2006), and 1, 14, 38, 45, 148 in Sei Shōnagon and Ivan I. Morris, *The Pillow Book of Sei Shōnagon* (Baltimore: Penguin, 1971).

The Tale of Genji excerpts from Murasaki Shikibu, *Genji and Heike: Selections from 'The Tale of Genji' and 'The Tale of the Heike'* translated with introductions by Helen Craig McCullough (Stanford, CA: Stanford University Press, 1994), pp. 113–123 (footnotes amended for clarity and simplicity). Copyright © 1994 by the Board of Trustees of the Leland Stanford Jr. University. All rights reserved. Used with the permission of Stanford University Press, www.sup.org.

Tales of Times Now Past excerpts from Marian Ury, *Tales of Times Now Past: Sixty-Two Stories from a Medieval Japanese Collection* (Berkeley: University of California Press, 1979), pp. 87–89, 143–145, 150–152. Used with permission.

The Tale of the Heike excerpts from Murasaki Shikibu, *Genji and Heike: Selections from the "The Tale of Genji" and "The Tale of the Heike,"* translated with introductions by Helen Craig McCullough (Stanford, CA: Stanford University Press, 1994), pp. 358–359, 378–381, 394–396 (footnotes amended for clarity and simplicity). Copyright © 1994 by the Board of Trustees of the Leland Stanford Jr. University, All rights reserved. Used with the permission of Stanford University Press, www.sup.org.

Essays in Idleness by Yoshida Kenkō based on G.B. Sansom, *The Tsuredzure Gusa of Yoshida no Kaneyoshi*, in *Transactions of the Asiatic Society of Japan* 39 (1911), pp. 13–14, 15–16, 17, 26–27, 32, 42, 85–86.

Nakamitsu translated by Margaret Helen Childs from Sanrai Kentarō, *Yōkyoku taikan*, vol. 4 (Tokyo: Meiji shoin, 1963), pp. 2307–2324. Also see Mae J. Smethurst in *Dramatic Representations of Filial Piety: Five Noh in Translation*, Cornell East Asia Series 97 (Ithaca, NY: Cornell University, East Asian Program, 1998).

Lord Kikui's Wife from *Rethinking Sorrow: Revelatory Tales of Late Medieval Japan* by Margaret Helen Childs, Michigan Monograph Series in Japanese Studies, No. 6 (Ann Arbor: Center for Japanese Studies, University of Michigan, 1991), pp. 114–119. © 1991 Regents of the University of Michigan. All rights reserved. Used with the permission of the publisher.

Short Stories: A Surprise Move—The Heir's Killer Replaces Him, Inspiration from a Gourd, and **The Mother Kept One Child and Abandoned the Other,** translated by Caryn A. Callahan, from Ihara Saikaku, *Tales of Samurai Honor: Buke Giri Monogatari* (Tokyo: Monumenta Nipponica, Sophia University, 1981), pp. 65–67, 71–74, 115–117. Used with permission.

Short Stories: Fireflies Also Work Their Asses Off at Night from *The Great Mirror of Male Love* by Ihara Saikaku, translated by Paul G. Schalow (Stanford, CA: Stanford University Press, 1990), pp. 247–253. Copyright © 1990 by the Board of Trustees of the Leland Stanford Jr. University. All rights reserved. Used with the permission of Sanford University Press, www.sup.org.

Jusan'ya. The Thirteenth Night excerpt from Higuchi Ichiyō, *Jusan'ya. The Thirteenth Night,* translated by Hisako Tanaka, in *Monumenta Nipponica* 16, no. 3/4 (October 1960–January 1961), pp. 377–394.

Botchan excerpt from Natsume Kinnosuke, translated by Yasotaro Morri and revised by J.R. Kennedy, *Botchan (Master Darling),* 1919, Chapter 8, www.gutenberg.org/cache/epub/8868/pg8868.html.

The Sixth Night and **The Seventh Night** from Natsume Soseki, *Ten Nights' Dreams* (London: Soseki Museum, 2000), pp. 23–30.

A Sudden Flash of Light from Nakazawa Keiji, translated and edited by Richard H. Minear, *Hiroshima: The Autobiography of Barefoot Gen* (Lanham, MD: Rowman & Littlefield, 2010), pp. 31–40. Used with permission of the publisher.

Tan'gun from *Anthology of Korean Literature: From Early Times to the Nineteenth Century,* compiled and edited by Peter H. Lee (Honolulu: University Press of Hawaii, 1981), p. 4. Copyright © 1981 by University Press of Hawaii, Honolulu. Used with permission of University Press of Hawaii.

The Tale of Hong Kiltong excerpt by Hŏ Kyun from *Anthology of Korean Literature: From Early Times to the Nineteenth Century,* compiled and edited by Peter H. Lee (Honolulu: University Press of Hawaii, 1981), pp. 119–131. Copyright © 1981 by University Press of Hawaii, Honolulu. Used with permission of University Press of Hawaii.

Korean Poetry: 1, 8, 9, 10, 11 translated by Seyool Oh, Ji-Yeon Lee, Emily Guerin, and Margaret Helen Childs from Yi Kwang-sik, *Uri yet sijo yŏhaeng: yet sijo ro ttŏnanŭn Chosŏn sidae yŏhaeng* (Seoul, Korea: Karam Kihoek, 2004), pp. 218–227.

Korean Poetry: 2, 3, 4, 5, 6, 7 translated by Chung Chong-wha from *Love in Mid-Winter Night: Korean Sijo Poetry* (London: KPI Limited, 1985), pp. 45, 46, 49, 53, 56, 74. Used with permission of the publisher.

Korean Poetry: 12 translated by Seyool Oh, Ji-Yeon Lee, Emily Guerin, and Margaret Helen Childs from Yi Sang-bo, *Han'guk ŭi yet sijo: Kyŏnggi-do P'aju* (Korea: Pŏmusa, 2004), pp. 195–196.

Song of a Faithful Wife, Ch'un-hyang from Richard Rutt, Kim Chong-un, and Man-jung Kim, *Virtuous Women: Three Classic Korean Novels* (Seoul: Royal Asiatic Society, Korea Branch, 1979), pp. 250–253, 260–261, 270–271, 285–286, 292–293, 300–302, 305–306, 332–333. Used with permission of Royal Asiatic Society, Korea Branch.

Modern Short Fiction: Cranes and **The Bird of Passage** from Peter H. Lee, *Flowers of Fire: Twentieth-Century Korean Stories,* revised edition (Honolulu: University of Hawaii Press, 1986), pp. 86–91, 189–204. Used with permission.

Thematic Index

Aesthetics: The Tale of Genji, 161; Essays in Idleness, 196; Tales of Times Now Past, How Minamoto no Hiromasa Ason Went to the Blind Man's House at Ōsaka, 180; The Sixth Night, 257.

Ancestor worship: Book of Songs, 17.

Atomic bomb: A Sudden Flash of Light, 262.

Banditry/rebellion: Outlaws of the Marsh, 81; The Tale of Hong Kiltong, 282,

Beauty of nature: Japanese Poetry, 145–147, 152–155; Korean Poetry, 301.

Buddhism: Journey to the West, 68; Japanese Poetry, 153; Tales of Times Now Past, How a Government Clerk of Higo Province Escaped a Rakshasa, 178; The Tale of the Heike, The Death of Atsumori, 193; Lord Kikui's Wife, 209.

Comedy: Journey to the West, 68; Pillow Book, 157; Saikaku, Fireflies Also Work Their Asses Off at Night, 224; Botchan, 248.

Confucianism: Book of Rites, 21; Book of Documents, 19; Analects, 25; Mencius, 29; Great Learning, 33; Doctrine of the Mean, 36; Song of a Faithful Wife, Ch'unghyang, 302.

Daoism: Daodejing, 43; Zhunagzi 45; Chinese Poetry, 50.

Education: Nakamitsu,202; Botchan, 248.

Friendship/loyalty: Chinese Poetry, 52–53, 57; Japanese Poetry, 148; The Tale of the Heike, The Death of Kiso, 189; Essays in Idleness, 196; Nakamitsu, 202; Korean Poetry, 297, 301; Cranes, 317; The Bird of Passage, 322.

Government: Book of Songs, 14; Book of Documents, 19; Analects, 25; Mencius, 29; Mao Zedong, Report on an Investigation of the Peasant Movement in Hunan, 105; Japanese Poetry, 143–144, 144; Tan'gun, 279.

About the Editors

Margaret Helen Childs earned an MA at Columbia University in 1978 and a PhD at the University of Pennsylvania in 1983. She is currently Associate Professor and Chair of the Department of East Asian Languages and Literatures at the University of Kansas. She also has taught Japanese literature and East Asian studies courses at Columbia University and the University of Michigan. Her research has focused on the classical narratives of romance, such as *The Tale of Genji*, and medieval didactic Buddhist tales in which monks and nuns explain their reasons for abandoning lay life, such as *The Seven Nuns*. Remembering her own awe as an undergraduate encountering East Asian traditions for the first time, she especially enjoys teaching introductory courses.

Nancy Francesca Hope is the associate director of the Kansas Consortium for Teaching about Asia and the associate director for special projects at the Confucius Institute at the University of Kansas. A specialist on East Asian art who has lived and traveled widely in Japan and China, she frequently teaches courses about East Asia, especially for schoolteachers and the public. Her master's degrees are from Boston University (1975), the University of Georgia (1990), and the University of Kansas (1992). She first was immersed in Asian culture when stationed in Japan as an officer in the United States Navy and later became a designer and dyer of kimono for a Japanese company in Kyoto.